A COUNTRY LAD LOOKS BACK

By Peter Wolfenden

First published in Great Britain in 2001
Peter Wolfenden, Barrowford, Lancashire
Re-printed in Paperback 2002

ISBN 0-9541644-1-5

Publisher
Hill Carr Books, 72 Carr Hall Road, Barrowford
Lancashire, BB9 6QG. Tel/Fax: 01282 617800

Produced by Rebecca Lord
Printed in Great Britain by CP Formstyle 01274 672000

Main Cover
Shire Horses by kind permission of J Mitson of Colne, Lancashire
Farmers Boy - Thomas Wolfenden of Laneshawbridge, Lancashire
Photography - Steve Krupa

Foreward
Harvey Smith

Bolton-by-Bowland Village Photos - R Buck & R Collinson

Sketches - R Bancroft of Skipton

Acknowledgments
Freda Reeves of Barroword, Lancashire
Margaret Trice Waters of Ulverston, Cumbria
Margaret Creesy of Long Preston, Yorkshire
Alwyne Plunkett of Barrowford, Lancashire
Lesley Horton of Keighley, Yorkshire
Lisette Davies of Colne, Lancashire

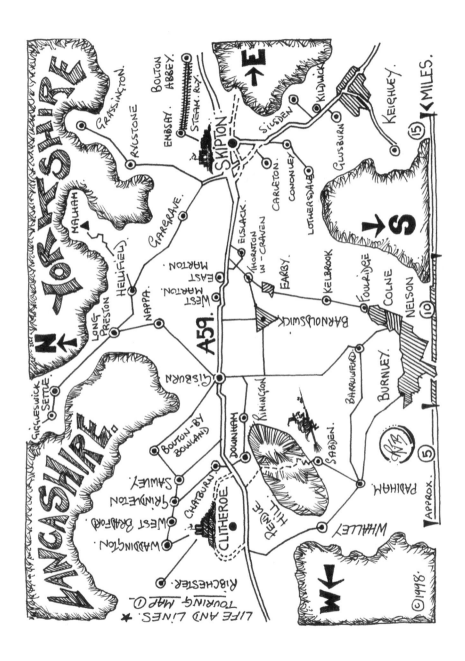

A Country Lad Looks Back

By Peter Wolfenden

Contents

Foreword
By Harvey Smith

After reading Peter's book I can say with confidence it brings back many memories enjoyed by myself as a young lad of that era when life on a farm was tough and not very rewarding for our parents.

From the first page to the final page I found every chapter very interesting, some educational and many quite hilarious.
Peter certainly had a great experience in his youth.

Introduction

This book is a true story of the life of a farmer's son born on a family farm in the mid nineteen thirties in a village in Ribblesdale, one of the most scenic areas of the British Isles.

The stories are all based on the experience of a young lads life among livestock during the early nineteen forties, also the everyday happenings on a family farm. The book also portrays the difficulties experienced through that period of life on a farm before mechanisation.

Portrayed in this book are details of the many country characters, and the annual community visitors over the years and seasons.

There are many details of the happenings in a country village; the wildlife in the countryside and the richness of a young lad living in the idyllic countryside even though there was little, or no, luxuries at that particular juncture of a country lad's life.

The book portrays annual events in the village which have been lost forever, also the misfortunes and tragic happenings on a family farm that leaves lasting memories.

The best things in life are free, especially in a English country village.

Characters and Places

Villages in the Ribble Valley vary in size according to their position. Some are built on the very fertile soil around the estuary, others in a remote, wooded valley, on a wind swept hilltop, or even near the river's source, on a rugged limestone plateau.

The settlements were built to accommodate the families and workers who followed a variety of occupations. On the hill farms, the work would be mainly sheep and lamb production, on the lowland farms, milk and livestock rearing, mainly cattle. On farms near the estuary, grain and vegetables such as potatoes, turnips, cabbage, etc. would be grown.

Most villages would be built of stone from the local quarry. In the Bowland area this was mainly limestone, which is a very hard, almost flint like rock, a drab grey in colour. This rock was very difficult to dress into standard size building blocks, which would have made construction easier. The Bowland farm houses and buildings, therefore, were built with random stone, i.e. stones of every shape and size.

The stones of these houses were not held together with sand or cement as with the more modern type buildings. They were always built with grey mortar, which was a simple mix of sand, burnt limestone and cinders. These would be mixed, not by hand, but with a large mortar-mixing machine. This machine consisted of two huge flat wheels that tracked round the base of a metal tub, and in doing so, crushed and mixed all in one operation.

Normally, the ashes would come from the cotton mills, which used large amounts of coal, to produce steam to drive the steam engines, that powered the many looms and textile machines.

The rock for the burnt limestone would have been quarried locally, then burnt in a simple limekiln, before being removed, basically, in the same size of cobs, as it was when placed into the kilns. The only difference was that it was snow white after the burning process. Once removed, it would be placed in a slaking tub. This was a large metal or wooden tub which would be half filled with burnt rock, then fresh clean water would be poured over it. Immediately the lime would begin to boil and bubble, leaving not a trace of the large blocks of burnt lime. It had all turned into a smooth white paste, ready for mixing into the mortar for building the cottages and houses.

The burnt and slacked lime was used extensively on the farm as whitewash for farmhouse and farm buildings, also to spread on the farm meadows and pastures, which, over the years, had become too acidic to grow a good crop of grass. The lime neutralises the excessive acid content of the land and promotes grass production, vital to all Bowland farmers.

On our farm in Bowland there was a lime-kiln and small quarry where the rock had been quarried and placed into the kiln some fifty yards from the quarry face.

Under the basin shaped kiln was a small stone cellar type building, where the fire would be lit to burn the limestone rock and also where the limestone would be removed from the kiln.

The small cellar during my time was never used as part of the limestone burning process, but was used as a donkey stable which we always called the donkey hall. The remains of the kiln can still be seen today.

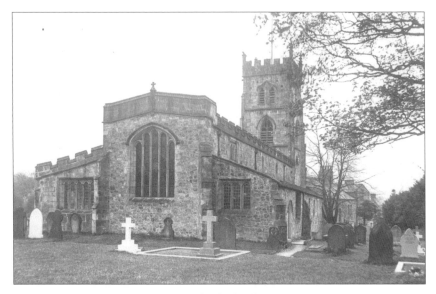

Bowland Church

Bowland, I believe, is one of the oldest villages in the Ribble Valley. It is richly endowed with buildings of historic interest. Bowland Church is many hundreds of years old, with battlements and bell tower. The design is fairly unique in the Ribble Valley. Inside the Church is a separate chapel, which, I understand, was used solely by the Pudsey family, and staff, of the now demolished Bolton Hall.

Inside the chapel

Inside the chapel is a tomb in memory of Sir Ralph Pudsey, his three wives and twenty-five children. Many villagers used to ask what Sir Ralph did in his spare time.

Bolton Hall

There is also the old courthouse, complete with cells. This is a very fine building, built at the top of Bowland village, facing the village green and the row of mature chestnut trees. I can remember the courthouse being used, probably for the last time, in the late 1940's. Usually, it was only minor crimes which came before Bowland magistrates, such as poaching, illegally taking fish from the river Ribble, stealing poultry for Christmas, or an over indulgence of alcohol.

There was always the persistent petty thief. One my father often talked about was called, 'Wack Pollard'. He believed in getting into jail for Christmas. His crime was usually stealing poultry. When Wack had taken the farmer's or villager's hens, he left a note, which read, 'You are rich and I am poor, when these are done, I'll come for more.' This was instantly recognised by the local bobby, who then apprehended Wack and locked him up for Christmas, which was just what Wack wanted, a warm, dry bed and fire, and reasonable food over the festive season.

Court House

Coach and Horses

The local public house, the Coach & Horses, was a large pub for a small village like Bowland. I was told that this was a pub where the long distance horse drawn carriages would stop for a night's rest, for the horses and the occupants of the coach. There were ample bedrooms for the travellers, coachmen and assistants, and always a good supply of beer.

Across the road from the Coach & Horses pub, was an old coach house, where the various coaches would be protected overnight from the inclement weather in Bowland. They were always safe when stored in this purpose-built building.

Next door to the coach house was the butcher's shop. I don't know if this had always been a butchers shop, but I knew that the same butchers had been there for many years when I lived in Bowland.

Coach House

Smithy and Stocks

The building next to the butcher was the smithy, where all the farmers in Bowland took their horses to be shod. The blacksmith was quite a character, a small, stockily built, old fellow, who probably had been shoeing horses all his life. I used to get involved, in more ways than one, with the old blacksmith. When I was passing, he would always want me to pump the bellows to his small forge, where he heated the metal to make the various sizes of shoes, for ponies or horses, large and small. He always gave me a few pence for my services.

Often, I would stay away from school to take the carthorses to the smithy, or blacksmith's shop. I would normally ride one horse, and lead the other horse on a loose halter or headpiece. The horses were a good 16 hands each, so you can imagine what I looked like, at eleven or twelve years old, astride a large carthorse. The blacksmith used to remark, 'Tha' reminds me of a flea on a bull's arse perched up there.' I often wondered how these two large horses allowed me to take them to the smithy, with me in control of at least two tons of horseflesh.

The old blacksmith was very inquisitive, always wanting to know what was going on, in and around Bowland, so he often questioned me about everything. I gave him the perfect answer one day when I told him, 'Them that ask, don't get to know, and them that don't ask, don't want to know.' He gave me a belt round the ear and said, 'That will learn you not to be such a cheeky young bugger in future.'

Market Cross and Stocks

In front of the blacksmith's were two of the more historical features of Bowland village, which had, obviously, been there many hundreds of years. These were the market cross and the stocks, where the local villains, poachers and hen thieves would be placed and supposedly bombarded with rotten eggs.

The market cross was square with layered steps of sandstone, where, most likely, the locals placed their goods for sale, such as eggs, butter, cheese, poultry, etc. There was also a fence around the area of the stocks and market cross. This fence consisted of extra strong, solid oak posts with chains connected between each post. Probably, cattle or sheep would have been tethered to these posts on market days.

Adjacent to the market cross was the coffee tavern, or coffee house, as it was called in my days in Bowland; this coffee tavern, I can remember, was always very busy during summer months, and at weekends during the winter, serving a hot pot of tea or coffee to the many Bowland day-trippers. The coffee house was also famous for its cold beef sandwiches and currant pasties, which everybody seemed to buy. Above the coffee tavern was the reading room. Most of the Bowland men visited this at least two or three times a week. It contained a full sized snooker table.

Coffee Tavern

Behind the coffee tavern was a fairly unique toilet. I can remember this toilet was a communal type, in so far as it was a three seater. This was a long wooden seat with three holes side by side, without any divisions. There was no sign to indicate whether it was male or female or simply multi occupancy.

At the bottom of the village was the joiner's and village undertaker's workshop. The joiner was always called 'old Eddie' even though he wasn't very old. He was well known for his undertaking services and if you visited his workshop, he was proud to point out the many sets of oak coffin boards drying for different clients in Bowland. He also used his home for the doctor's surgery. This was a strategic move because he always knew when the villagers or farmers were poorly. He would always make sure to visit, conveniently, when he was supposedly passing the farm or cottage to keep his clients 'warm.'

Another character in Bowland village was the postman. He was a small, round shouldered, old fellow, who had pushed and ridden his red postman's bicycle many thousands of times around Bowland village and farm roads. The postman's name was Billy Bennett, everybody called him Bill. Bill was not only postman, but messenger boy for villager and farmer alike, conveying messages, sometimes misinformation and scandal in many cases. He would also find spare lambs for the farmers in spring, arrange doctor's visits or even take your grocery order to the village Co-op. Bill was noted for his Woodbine cigarettes and his whisky. Whisky he never, ever, refused and on many occasions, this would lead to late or sometimes, no delivery, of the daily post.

The farm, where I was born, was of unusual design. Probably one part was very old, with an extension being built at a much later date. The old part had quite a unique porch attached, with dove nesting holes over the entrance to the house. I never saw any dove occupying or nesting in these many holes whilst I lived there for twenty-three years. I suppose when they were occupying the holes there must have been an unwritten rule, 'never to look up, and don't stand in the dropping zone when leaving by the front door'.

Higher Fooden Farm

20

Fooden Hall

The farmhouse below where I lived was much older and was called Fooden Hall. This belonged to another estate and was of a very different design, built to a much higher standard, and quite a magnificent house in its time. Just below the far corner of the garden of Fooden Hall was the fairly famous sulphur well which attracted people from miles around. They would take bottles of this stinking water, which was, supposedly, a cure for almost every ailment.

All these different houses, places and personalities made Bowland, in the early forties, one of the most interesting villages to live in for a young lad, where there was seldom a dull moment.

Sulphur Well

The Farmers Boy

Bowland was a small picturesque village, more or less unchanged over the centuries, tucked away in the Ribble valley amongst the hills and fertile farming land.

The main industry in Bowland and most of the Ribble valley was farming of various types. In the Bowland area there were mainly mixed farms producing milk, rearing a few calves, sheep and poultry. There was normally no grain grown in Bowland, because of the higher than average rainfall, due to the many hills in the Pennine range, the highest in our area being Pendle Hill, which is just below two thousand feet above sea level.

Most of the population in Bowland village and surrounding villages were employed on the farms, large estates and in the big houses of the estate owners. There were many jobs for the villagers to do. The maintenance and upkeep of the villages and estates of Bowland was of great importance. Jobs could vary from the estate worker gardeners, gamekeepers, grooms, stockmen and forestry workers, to kennel men looking after horses and hounds. The young girls would work as cleaners, cooks and nannies, caring for the children of the estate owners.

There was also the odd person in the village who never worked, or had no intention of working, unless absolutely forced to. I remember when I was six or seven years old, just such a man, who was called Bill. I often saw Bill when at junior school loitering about the school doing absolutely nothing. We would shout and taunt Bill with the words, 'Lazy Bill, never worked and never will,' and then run for cover. One day I couldn't, or didn't, run fast enough and Bill caught me. He gave me a dammed good hiding with a stick he was carrying, leaving large bruises on my back and backside. I remembered the hiding I got from Bill for many years after, every time I saw him in the village. I told my parents when I went home later that day, about the good hiding Bill had given me but I didn't get any sympathy. I was told that I deserved it and in future it would teach me to respect my elders and to not give cheek.

Nearly all the farms in Bowland were rented from various estates. Many farmers had farmed the same farm for generations, paying the landlord an agreed annual rent for land, farm building and farmhouse. Most farmers would only move farm if a larger farm became vacant in the area, or when marrying into another farming family, or through bereavement.

Farmers in the hills and villages around Bowland were noted for having large families and six to ten children was not uncommon. The local schools were always full to capacity with pupils from the farms. Our family was no exception with seven children consisting of two girls and five boys. Most of us went to the same junior school at the same time, except the older members of our family, who had left to go to a senior school seven miles away at Clitheroe. The teacher always passed comment on how many more of our family was still to come.

Our family of two girls and five boys was about the right balance, a good sex mix for a farmer, just enough girls to help with the many household chores, and plenty of lads to work on the family farm. This provided low cost or no cost labour, a must when farming in the forties with farm incomes exceptionally low. It was also much more expensive for a farmer with all daughters when they got married, as it was a case of doing the best for the bride. The wedding dress and bridesmaid dresses would nearly always be home made, or made by a dressmaker in the village and all for a single day. Whereas, when a farmer's son got married his new bridegroom attire would last him for many years. It was not uncommon to hear a farmer telling about the suit he wears was the one he got married in twenty years ago. Many would have outgrown their wedding suit especially around the waist. There was an easy solution to that problem; a simple V gusset in the back of the pants and the buttons on the jacket moved a few inches.

My father always wore long striped shirts with removable collars. This saved my mother lots of washing, as one shirt would last a week with possibly only a couple of collars per week. One well-known farming family in Bowland, who had plenty of money, used to economise even more on the weekly wash. The first week the wife would wear the shirt and the second week the husband would wear it just to make sure it required washing. The wife also used to wear seven-pound flour bags on her feet to save buying and darning socks or stockings.

As a large family, we didn't all have new clothes to go to school in. I was second born and the first boy, so I always had relatively new clothes, usually home made by my aunt from cast off clothes, bought at jumble sales in the village. It was more of a problem when it came to protection of clothing for protection against wind and rain when attending school. We would have to join a large umbrella or huddle under a large Gaberdine raincoat to provide protection from the wind and rain. Many times during strong winds the umbrella would blow inside out and be rendered absolutely useless.

Our footwear was always laced clogs made in the village by the local clogger. I remember this old fellow well. He was quite tall with very rounded shoulders probably caused by leaning over his last for so many years. His work implements were very basic and the only automation he used was a foot drive sanding or scouring wheel. However, he could make the most exquisite clogs with the scant tools at his disposal. He would make the clog irons out of a straight piece of metal, just like a blacksmith made horseshoes, but without heat. He would form the clog soles out of a single piece of elm with a huge type of splitting knife and the top of the clog would be cut from a large piece of suitable leather. The name we always called him by was John Willey. He was almost stone deaf; so many times we kids would call him a very different name. Fortunately, he never heard what we called him.

We would literally wear these clogs from leaving the cradle to starting to walk. We would only get a new pair if the others were totally worn out. They were always handed down when they were too small for the older brother or sister. If they were too big, the toes would be packed with sheep's wool.

Clogs didn't provide the best footwear in bad weather, so we had to wear a pair of button-up leggings. These went from ankle to knee buttoned with about a dozen buttons on each leg. It was almost impossible to fasten them without a buttonhook, so there was always trouble if the buttonhook was lost or misplaced. Often you would arrive at school with soaking wet feet. The teacher would always insist you remove your clogs and socks and let them dry in front of the large coal fire in the classroom. It was not so bad as long as it was only your feet that were wet.

Old Daisy Price, our schoolteacher, made sure you didn't sit in wet clothes for long. The first person to remove their wet clothing got a small towel to cover up with and keep warm, the later and more unfortunate, got landed with a pair of old Daisy's knickers. She always wore the long knee length type knickers in either pink or blue and could probably hold three kids at once. These stretched from under your armpit to ground level, a bit like a Cossack dancer outfit. It was always a laugh if you got landed with a pair of old Daisy's passion killers, including stains!

At only four years old it was a long day from leaving home at quarter past eight to returning at quarter to five in the evening. There was no bed or cot for you to have an afternoon sleep, and many times I would just flop down on my way home and fall asleep, until I was woken up by my older sister. My parents never worried about this happening, as out in the country there was no one about and nothing to hurt you. Sometimes it would be a couple of hours before finally arriving home for tea, by which time I was always very hungry.

During these days at school, no school dinners were provided, so all food had to be home made and carried in a small shoulder strap bag. There was never much variation in what was packed into this small shoulder bag and was almost always sandwiches. These could vary from egg, from our flock of hens, or it could be potted meat, from our own pig. Sometimes it could be very tasty potted meat from a sheep's head that would be bought from the local butcher for a few pence. They split and boiled the head until all the brain and meat left the bone. This was then seasoned and all the small and large bones removed, then put into a large porridge basin to set, then used as a sandwich spread. There was also fish paste that was bought at the local Co-op shop. This was always made by the same company, Shippams', packed in a small glass jar. The cake my mother packed with the sandwiches never varied much. It would range from a huge chunk of gingerbread to a slab of jam pasty, or, if you were lucky, an iced bun or rock bun.

Drink was always a problem, very little to choose from, and was always in a small orange juice bottle which had been supplied by the Government and distributed at the local Doctor's surgery for infants, and all under five. It could be orange juice but it was nearly always milk, or it may be a home brewed soft drink made with a bought in recipe, such as Robinsons' lemon and barley crystals.

Soon after starting junior school we had to go to Sunday school, yet another long walk to and from the village. The Sunday school teachers were not the same as those who took our day school lessons, as I suppose they had seen enough of us during the week. Our teacher was only in her early twenties and one of the huntsman's daughters called Miss Heaton.

The village was a close knit community. The centre of all activities was the Church and school. Many annual activities were organised by school and Church in the village. My auntie was also a Sunday school teacher and after Sunday school played the Church organ. As I grew older I was expected to go to Sunday school and Church afterwards, and was soon promoted to the Church choir that meant more time away from home. Once in the choir there was choir practice that we had to attend every Wednesday evening. This I never liked because it was dark, wet and cold in winter and in summer there was lots of other activities going on at home on the farm.

I was also promoted to organ blower. This entailed pumping the large type bellows by hand; these were rather similar to the blacksmith forge but operated in better surroundings. I used to get told off almost every Sunday when blowing the organ for my auntie. This was because I would always want to see who was at Church. This meant leaving the organ and moving to a position where I could see almost everybody who was present. The signal to return to the organ was when the music started to fade, then I would rush back to the organ and pump like the blazes until the bellows were full of wind. After all the Sunday school, Church and organ blowing it was a long walk home. By this time you were more than hungry. Once back at home we had always to change our Sunday clothes and put our playing out clothes on before dinner.

Always on a Sunday dinnertime it was a large roast of beef or lamb. It always had to be a large roast because there were such a lot of mouths to feed. A normal sitting would be eleven, this included two farm men, seven kids and my parents. It was a problem getting a table big enough to seat us all. I remember the table well, as it was a large one with extended leaves so as to give maximum size. The top was covered in a lightweight oilcloth so that it could be easily wiped clean after every meal, as there was always plenty of slopping and spilling with such youthful diners.

After dinner it was up to us to provide our own fun and playthings. We seldom had any toys bought, except at Christmas, and these could range from a clockwork mouse to a sugar pig. Usually by dinnertime on Christmas day the clockwork mouse would be broken and the sugar pig devoured. My father would always do his best at Christmas to make a few extra toys. These would range from building blocks that he had cut out of solid pieces of ash tree logs with the circular saw used for making the fencing on the farm. The blocks were always miles out of square so it was easy to build a leaning tower of Pisa. It was always a last minute thought when my father made toys, then on Christmas morning they couldn't be used because the paint was still wet. He would also make trucks, these he would soon make, once again on the circular saw, so weight and daintiness never entered his mind. They were usually very heavy and nailed together with two-inch nails; glue had never been heard of. The wheels would be cut from the bough of the tree and was some six inches in diameter. He would strip off the bark then burn the tyre thread into the wheel with a red hot poker from the kitchen fire then burn the hole through the centre of the wheel where another huge nail would be used as the axle. He never got these holes in the centre of the wheel so the truck, when being pulled, had that up and down motion. One thing was for sure, his toys always lasted a long time.

Other methods of entertainment were when we used my mother's rocking chair. We would lay it on its back and use it as a cattle wagon. I would sit in between the rockers and pretend to be the driver, while my brothers and sisters would pretend to be the cows riding in the back. We always had one of my brothers to be a bull. This was always more difficult to load onto the wagon and more vicious. Other times, we would play hide and seek in the house. A favourite place to hide was down the long passage where the many coats were hanging and the long bench type forms were stored after every meal. My mother always scrubbed these benches clean weekly.

From an early age we were always busy with various livestock and pets. Some were bought or swapped or even caught in the wild. My first pets were guinea pigs, which I was given by my mother's Uncle William, many miles away in Cumbria. I was very proud of these as there was nobody in Bowland who had any. They were only small when I got them and not old enough to breed, so I always fed them with my fathers best cattle food to make them grow quick, hoping they would mate and have young much sooner. I had to make the hutches for the guinea pigs myself. These I made from old egg and orange boxes which I had been given by the Co-op shop in the village. We had to manually carry these back from the village after school, no mean task for a six year old. The first half-mile wasn't so bad, it was the last three quarters when your arms started to ache and your legs gave way. Sometimes we would hide the boxes behind the hedgerow or in a deep ditch out of sight, then take them home another day.

Once back at home it was a matter of urgency to get the hutch completed. I would borrow my father's limited tools, mainly a large handsaw and a claw hammer, plus nails and staples. I borrowed the wire netting from the roll which he used to make his chicken runs. I made a slide type door as there was little chance of buying any hinges. All this taught me how to create and build objects, even at that early age. Once the hut was complete with legs the two guinea pigs were then introduced to their new living quarters and nesting place, which was to be their permanent home for the immediate future.

They were soon fully-grown and mature enough to breed. There were signs that they were interested in multiplication; this was nothing unusual on the farm. For myself, I knew a fair lot about the birds and the bees. I was told never to hold the guinea pigs up by their tails or their eyes would drop out. I soon realised this couldn't happen, because guinea pigs had no tail. The female pig soon started to expand around the waist so I was pretty sure a successful mating had taken place. Just how long after mating the female pig would give birth I had no idea, so I was always inspecting the hutch to see if my guinea pig family had increased. I put newly harvested hay in the nesting side of my cage, where I hoped the young pigs would be born. I had not long to wait before the mother-to-be pig started to form the nest in anticipation of the new arrivals. I was told never to look into the nesting part for at least a week or the mother pig would worry and kill all the young ones, so I kept the door to the nesting part firmly shut.

The week soon went by and I investigated the nest box. There were six fine young guinea pigs all thriving well, but still with their eyes shut. I was in luck, soon I would have some stock to sell, or so I thought.

The pigs, after eight weeks, were all very healthy and thriving well. They were red and white all with a rich satin coat. They were by now leaving the nesting part and feeding from bread and milk, which was ideal food for the young pigs. The news soon spread at school that I had some young guinea pigs for sale. This brought prospective buyers for my first lot of young. I had no difficulty in selling my first six when they were old enough to leave their mother. The trouble was that between selling and delivering those fine specimens, the neighbour's sheepdog got into the shed where my hutch was and worried my entire stock of guinea pigs, so I had no parent stock or young pigs to sell. It took many days and lots of tears before I could believe what had happened. The farmer did give me a few pounds for my loss, but I would much rather have had my pigs.

It was many months, or maybe up to a year, after my guinea pigs had been worried, before I could anticipate any other pet rearing project that I thought I could possibly make a profit out of.

During my youth there were so many unusual activities on and around the farm that swallowed up those long hours. Once again, it was up to yourself to make your own pleasure, collecting bird eggs in the spring was a big killer of time. You would walk many miles a day to areas where you would, hopefully, find an unusual bird's nest. In those days there was such a vast array of different birds that it was a challenge to beat your pals at school with an unusual egg. Once we had found a nest, only one or two eggs would be removed, leaving the rest to hatch and grow into the next generation of that particular species. We were always very secretive as to where we found the rare bird's nest so as not to allow the other egg collectors to obtain an egg from the nest. This left them with a less important collection than myself.

During the nesting season, the lapwing and curlew were the easiest eggs to collect, as they almost always nested in open ground. With a little patience watching the female bird, you could soon pinpoint the nest. Lapwings mostly nested on the newly ploughed furrows that meant they nearly always got destroyed when discing or harrowing took place. In such cases we would collect the eggs and take them home and boil them for breakfast or tea. They tasted completely different from the normal fresh farm eggs from our own hen flock.

We would sometimes even take a well-developed young bird from the nest for a pet. Rearing these birds was a challenge and many times our newly acquired pets would die. Jackdaws were the easiest to rear and they also made good pets. They soon got accustomed to what you did and where you went. The one I reared would follow me to school each day and then return to the farm once I was in class. This particular Jackdaw eventually became a nuisance and if a window was left open in the bedroom, it would fly in and pick up anything that glittered or had a silver shining effect. Teaspoons were one of its favourites. One day, while I was at school, it suddenly disappeared without trace. I never knew whether it was my father or farm man that shot it, or if one of the farm cats had it for lunch.

One other bird we successfully fed and reared was a tawny owl. This we took from a large oak tree where, probably, the same owls had nested for many years. The nest in this large oak tree was in a hole well out of reach from the ground. So, to scale this tree to the nest, we took a few large six-inch nails from my father's nail bucket to form a ladder. Fortunately he never missed them, so trouble was avoided.

Once we had taken the owl back home and made yet another cage for it we soon found out the amount of food it could eat. The trouble was that an owl didn't like bread and milk or grass or anything our other livestock ate. An owl only ate meat, so it made it more difficult to feed. Fortunately it was the time when there were lots of new arrivals on the farm. There was the odd chicken that was squashed to death by its broody mother. There were young rabbits in plenty, also lots of young rats about the farm, and with a little help from the farm men adequate meats were obtained to feed the owl. If we were really low on meat the local butcher would give us trimming off one of his joints when visiting the farm each week. Sometimes we may just trim a slice off the Sunday joint ourselves, unbeknown to my mother.

We soon realised that keeping this owl was going to be a difficult proposition, so we decided to release it back into the wild. It was many days before it totally left its surroundings, as we left a dishful of food each day. To begin with it ate every particle, but as time went on the food was left. Probably the young owl had decided that the freshly caught food was much more palatable. For many months the young tawny owl lived around the farm and, I suppose, eventually paired with a partner and nested.

Still only young, I had been found many jobs to do around the farm. I was commonly known as Guffer, which was short for somebody who had to 'go for this and go for that'. I remember my father was a very good hand at delegating work. Saturday morning was always the day to go to the village for the papers that mainly consisted of a local farming paper for telling you of cattle market dates, farm sales and local news. There were never any scandal columns, because everybody in the village knew the day it happened anyway!

The paper shop was the first call on a Saturday morning. Besides collecting papers it was also the place for sweets. We had to get these with the coupons issued during the war, so many per week for each person. We never used our allocation, not because there were too many, but because there was not enough money. There was only a poor selection in those days, the best were Bassetts' liquorice allsorts. There were also Spanish buttons, Victory V chlorodines and arrowroot sticks, a type of tree root that you chewed.

This always left a tide mark in gingery brown around your mouth. After the paper shop the next port of call was the Co-op shop. This was where bread and other groceries were purchased. All the items purchased would be put into large cotton flour sacks before placing in the small two-wheel truck I had made to transport the shopping home to the farm. The truck was basically an orange box with two long handles on it that were similar to the shafts on a horsecart. The wheels and axle was taken from a worn out pram. I think there is a saying, necessity is the root of invention, which was certainly the case on our family farm.

From an early age there was always a lot you could do on the family farm, and it was no surprise when my father gave me the job of giving six young cows their first meal of the day on my way to school. The six young cows, or stirks, which was their proper name, were two years old and had been given their winter accommodation in an outbarn some quarter of a mile away from the farm. This was just off the footpath on which we went daily to the junior school in the village of Bowland. The problem was, there were no lights in the out barn, neither where the stirks were tied up, nor on the hayloft above, so I literally had to grope about in the dark. I knew that rats resided in this barn because there were lots of fresh droppings, and a run from the barn to the ditch just a few yards away, where the rat family went for liquid refreshment. So, I was terrified of putting my hands on a rat when taking hay from the small hayloft.

The farm men also pulled my leg about owls that roosted in the hayloft, which, I believed, could maim or kill you, so I was even more frightened of them. There was also the chance that a tramp may have decided to take shelter for the night in the comfort of the sweet smelling hay and the heat from the cows that helped to warm the hayloft.

You can imagine my feelings at seven years old, when entering the barn each dark winter morning before school. Would I be bitten by a rat, mauled by an owl or murdered by a tramp. I can assure you it was a quick visit to the outbarn and, on occasion, the stirks didn't get a full breakfast. Feeding the cows wasn't the only job I was delegated before school. My other early morning job was to deliver three pints of milk to my Aunts' and Grandma who lived in a row of cottages at the bottom of the village green. The cottages were very old and, most likely, were built for estate workers. The one my Aunts lived in was different in that it had a slate slab porch, which was limestone and most unusual for the Bowland area. The cottages faced the palatial entrance to the large estate farm and Bolton Hall. My sister Amy was supposed to help me with this delivery of milk, so we had a type of rota where I would carry the milk tin for the first field and she the next field. Most times she complained it was too heavy and I had selected the shortest field, so I had to carry the milk myself. I doubt whether the old folks, as they were called, ever got a full delivery. On most occasions there was the loss either by swinging the milk can or by having a drink myself. Sometimes it would be nearly butter if I was in a silly mood and swung the tin about. On occasions I would spill a fair proportion of the milk by accident, so, to rectify the loss, I would top up the loss at the nearest stream with water. They never complained about any shortage, this was because they never paid a penny piece for one drop of milk all the years I took it for them. There was never a tip or birthday present from them for my services rendered.

I did on many occasions stop for dinner at the cottage. The dinner was always the same, week in week out, and mostly a single sausage and mashed potatoes. Then, to finish, the pudding was always thin semolina with a spoonful of jam of the day to make it taste of something. My nickname for my three Aunts and Grandma was; boney Bessy, skinny Lizzy, fussy Fanny and grumpy Granny. They certainly didn't need to lose weight with the scant food they lived on.

Learning at school or even going to school was something I didn't particularly like. If I could get a day off school or pretend to be sick to avoid schooling, I always tried it on. My parents always knew when I was pretending to be ill, so pulling their leg was difficult.

During the summer months, when at junior school, I would play truant many times. I would simply pass time in the large woods adjacent to the farm where I would build a hide or maybe a tree house. Sometimes I would go bird nesting or even fishing in the small stream adjacent to the school. The signal to return home was when I observed all the other farmer's children and my brother and sisters heading back to the farm. I then returned home as normal with my parents none the wiser. My brothers and sisters never told my parents of my day playing truant.

There was always a day of reckoning that I always seemed to forget about. That was the day the school bobby or attendance officer visited our farm on his bicycle, simply to question my parents on why I had been away from school for so many days. The final outcome to my unauthorised days from school was a good belting or getting my arse tanned for playing truant. It always taught me a lesson, but somehow I soon forgot. My urge to wander the valleys and woods around Bowland far outweighed my enthusiasm to go to school so it was not long before I was in trouble again with the school bobby.

Even when I was at school, one or two other farm lads and I would always be asking 'Old Daisy' the headmistress, if there were any jobs to do. Old Daisy was good at delegating, a bit like my father, and she always gave us lots of various jobs. One in particular was putting coke onto the large central heating boiler in the cellar below the school. This was not a long or hard job and we could always make stoking the boiler last a good ten minutes instead of five. This all resulted in time out of class.

Another job was after a delivery of coke. The coke had to be barrowed to the cellar, where the boiler was sited, and was just the job for another school pal and myself. I was used to shovelling and barrowing back on the farm so I found it quite easy work. The bonus was also that the coke had no smell, unlike the barrowfuls of cowmuck back on the farm.

Old Daisy would also have us dig her garden. This, I suppose, could have been classed as a gardening lesson, except during spring, when it could be days before we even went into the classroom. I don't ever recall writing anything about gardening in my small green exercise book I had at school. Part of the gardening lessons also included barrowing manure from the local farm that was adjacent to the school at the top of the village green. We would have to spread the manure around the rose trees in front of the schoolhouse and also dig it into her vegetable plot. I believe we were the most suitable lads at school to dig her garden and spread the muck, because we didn't have fancy clothes. Also, we always wore a sturdy pair of clogs, and my parents wouldn't complain of me smelling of farmyard odours.

After school and weekends during the war, many times I would visit the local army barracks or camp. One camp in particular was sited just at the end of our farm lane. This consisted of a searchlight, battery, anti-aircraft guns and radio communication.

Even though I was only eight or nine years old at the time, I was more than welcome at this Bowland army outpost. The army lads would make a fuss of my brothers and me as though we were part of their family. As soon as we arrived at the large wooden army hut they would ask us if we were hungry and immediately proceed to the somewhat basic kitchen to make us a large jam butty. The butty was always camp baked fresh read, cut about one inch thick then plastered with butter and topped with a more than generous coating of jam from a huge 'army issue' tin, finally topped with an identical slice of buttered bread to form a massive jam butty. We always called these butties 'camp gobstoppers.' They really did fill a fast growing, ever hungry country lad.

Bowland and the surrounding villages at that time, around 1940 to 1945, was a well-fortified area. No persons or traffic were allowed in, or out, without permits, the reason being it was one huge bomb and ammunition store. All the woods were packed with ammunition and the roadside piled high with stacks of bombs every 50 yards.

There were sentry posts with armed guards and Alsation dogs. We were never frightened of the guards, it was the Alsation dogs that terrified us. They were always tethered on a long chain that stretched almost all the way across the road, leaving about six-foot spare for you to pass and not get torn to shreds.

One farmer I knew got fed up with one of these dogs when looking or checking the health of his cows each day. So on one occasion he went prepared with his favourite knob stick. He knew exactly what the dog would do, that was, leaving the kennel at full speed and attempting to attack him. He just got close enough not to be bitten but close enough to deal a heavy blow on the savage dog with his knob stick. This he did with such force he thought, and the sentry also thought, that he had killed the dog.

Fortunately, the dog did regain consciousness and live, but ever after that day it always stopped in its kennel when that farmer approached. The bomb and ammunition from these sites was always transported by road to Gisburn station where they were then packed onto the rail trucks for their final destination, either an airfield in Lincolnshire or a ship at Dover. During the war period there were little or no luxuries on the family farm for a large, fast growing family of seven. It was a classic case of 'what you never had you never missed'. Birthdays were seldom remembered, because there were so many of us. At best, we might have cakes with icing sugar on, and, if lucky there may be a few candles to adorn the top of the cake.

Entertainment on our farm was all self made. During winter months it was far too cold to play outside and, as there was no electricity on the farm, we couldn't see anyway. We would play about in the kitchen before my mother got fed up with us and bundled us off to bed. During the summer months there was a better chance of finding something to pass the time of day. We would go on long walks, mini rambles, exploring areas of river and woodland not previously visited. We would see how many different species of birds we could count, or go fishing in the river with various home made fishing tackle; bent pins and string, all attached to that long hazel branch we had taken from the adjacent wood. We never had fish for tea when using our own crude fishing tackle and methods. The wild brown trout in the Ribble was far too smart to take our bait.

Also, in summer months, we would prepare to hold a concert. This was in a loft over wood and coal store up a flight of steps out of the farmhouse backyard. Normally, this loft contained all sorts of unused and unwanted items, so before a concert we had to totally clear out the loft. Once the loft was cleaned it was a case of getting curtains. These we made from the large cattle feed sacks. There was carpet for the stage floor; this we had recovered from the many items discarded in the loft. In fact it wasn't carpet but old pegged rugs from the farm kitchen. The rugs were full of holes, not through wear and tear in the kitchen, but because the mice over the winter months had found it was a cosy place to reside, out of wind, snow and rain.

We made signs with dates and times of our first floor show. Benches would be assembled from bricks and fencing timbers. We also used orange boxes for the back seats of our concert hall. Clothes would be sneaked out of the house for costumes. My mother's old hats, shoes and boots; you name it, we had acquired everything. All we were short of was a programme of events. This was most difficult, and could be best described as a cart without a horse.

My sisters would sing the popular songs of the day, all out of tune. I would try and mimic the many village caretakers without much success; in all it was a complete flop. My mother did make plates of cakes and pots of various soft drinks for the twenty strong young audience who at least had had an afternoon on our family farm.

I was about eight or nine years old before I anticipated breeding any more livestock. At that time I had three of four options. I firstly considered white mice as they were cheap to buy and very prolific breeders. Two mice could soon become twenty-two and they would eat almost everything and didn't need fancy nesting boxes or cages. After careful consideration I decided against mice. I knew they were cheap to buy and I therefore knew they would be cheap when selling and my potential customer base was small.

There were pet rats that I could have bred, but I was pretty certain that should I dare to take rats to the farm they would soon have been a statistic; two rats bought Monday, two dead rats Tuesday. The farm men and my father absolutely detested rats and they were very unpopular with the farm dogs as well. Bantam chickens I considered. These were a small breed of hen so they would eat only half as much food as the large breeds of hens normally kept on the farm. Unfortunately, they only laid eggs half the size of the normal hen, which I knew I would have difficulty convincing my customers was extra value for money. I also knew that the bantam had little or no meat content and, with being so small, selling an aged bantam would be impossible. So bantam breeding was out.

There was only one other feasible option; I would have to breed rabbits. I had studied how many rabbits I could breed from a single male rabbit and four female rabbits. If I could sell all the young rabbits I would make literally hundreds of pounds, unheard of for a lad of eight years old. It could even put our family farming enterprise in the shade.

I decided on rabbits; it was all go from now on. As soon as I got home from school I was straight upstairs to get into my old clothes, so I could get to my rabbit breeding project as soon as possible. I was bringing orange and apple boxes home almost every night from the village Co-op to produce more and more rabbit hutches to cope with my fast growing rabbit population. My brother and sisters were busy collecting grass and mixing a selection of rabbit food. They took rolled oats from the stable where my father stored it to feed the farm work horses, and oatmeal from a large bag stored in the farmhouse for the every morning bowl of hot porridge for all our family.

Our young rabbits were growing exceptionally fast and prospective customers from school came to look at my stock. I was taking orders and delivering the young rabbits after school to the new owners. My old cast iron money box was fast filling up with the silver half crowns. My livestock dealing was doing well at last.

Prospects of making a fortune were rapidly looking better. There were new arrivals almost every week and more hutches and food was required. Then, one day, I found one hutch of rabbits didn't come out of the nesting box to feed as they normally did. They had totally lost their appetite for our freshly made food and freshly picked grass. I noticed there were small particles of blood in their droppings and I was really worried about my rabbit's health. I told my father and farm men about the problem and they came round to look at the hutch of sick young rabbits. They had not seen anything like my rabbit's problem before and had no idea of how to cure the problem.

My father remarked, 'They rabbits don't look so weel, tha'l soon 'ave some of 'em deed, if thee don't buck up.' He was right. It was so serious, the disease ravaged through both my young and adult rabbits until four weeks later I had literally no rabbits left. The few rabbits that survived, I took to the woods adjacent to the farm and released them into the wild where I knew they would not be living in a diseased environment. These rabbits certainly survived, because there were rabbits of all colours around our farm for many years.

I later found out from our farm vet that my rabbits had suffered from an attack of coccidiosis, a bowel disorder which was very contagious and with no cure at that time. This was a result of intensive breeding and over stocking. I learnt a costly lesson. I emptied my old cast iron golliwog money box to check my net profit balance. There was thirty eight half crowns, just under five pounds left for all my entrepreneurial efforts and hard work. My father told me it was a good lesson and in future never to count my chickens before they had hatched. In other words, wait until you have actually got the money before you count it.

Undeterred by the sudden failure of my rabbit-breeding project, I decided to go into breeding geese. Geese were one of the more sturdy and resilient feathered species, requiring little personal work and interference from myself. I had just short of five pounds in my money box so purchasing a pair of breeding geese was within my financial budget.

I found a local farmer who bred and reared geese and had a breeding pair to sell, a goose and a gander, the male of the species. The farmer wanted five pounds for the pair of geese, which I knew I couldn't afford. I had to barter, just like my father did, when buying cows, and after a few minutes bartering I bought the pair of geese for four pounds. Together, we soon caught the geese and placed them in a two compartment orange box on my two wheel truck to transport them some two miles back to the farm.

Once back at the farm I released the pair of geese in the farmyard and closed the gates hoping the geese would not escape until they were fully conversant with their new home. What I didn't realise was that my newly acquired geese could fly and escape. They did fly out over the farmyard gate into an adjacent field where they decided to take up home with our flock of free-range hens and cockerel. After a few days feeding with the hens, the geese settled down to a normal life on the farm.

It was late March, early April, when the female goose started to form a nest out of loose grass and straw collected from around the farmyard. Lined with downy feathers from her breast, this made a perfect camouflaged and insulated nest. It was almost immediately after forming a nest that the female goose started to lay and in a short period of time there was at least a dozen eggs. This was the perfect number of eggs for a goose to cover and incubate over the next month. A goose had to sit and incubate an extra seven days compared with a hen, I suppose this was because their eggs were at least twice the size of the hens.

After ten days when the female goose and gander were well clear of the nest I decided to test, or candle, the eggs for fertility. I was over the moon with excitement when I found twelve fertile eggs. Testing, or candling, the eggs was done by a candle or flashlight. If the light passed through the eggs you called the eggs clears, if there was a dark section in the egg, plus air cavity at one end, you knew the egg was fertile and contained a gosling or young goose. All clear eggs we would normally remove after testing. These would then be used for feed during the first few days of life for the young goslings. During incubation period it was as much as your life was worth even going near the brooding goose, let alone trying to interfere with the nest. You certainly would have got a damned good thrashing with the gander's extra large wings, plus a few savage bites as well.

After twenty-eight days, without any assistance from myself or farm men, the young goslings appeared. All twelve eggs had hatched leaving just the empty shells in the nest. From day one, the young goslings started plucking the new shoots of spring grass continuously, enabling them to grow at a fantastic rate. It was quite a sight seeing the female goose leading her young clutch of goslings in a military formation, one behind the other, in a perfectly straight line. Father gander was always close at hand, just to ward off any unwelcome attention from farm dogs or cats, or even myself. The gander was exceptionally proud of his wife and newly acquired large family.

There is a saying that they grew like mushrooms. This was the case with my young goslings as you could literally see them growing. Once hatched, the goose and goslings totally left their nest. They then decided that the best place to sleep was on the footpath leading to the front door of our farmhouse. This meant that every morning there were fourteen large piles of goose turds, or droppings, that my mother played holy hell about when she had to sweep them up.

I was really proud of my fast growing goslings that soon started to cast their golden down birthday suits to be replaced by their more permanent coat of feathers. This was when they were about six weeks of age. I was now having potential customers for my geese for their Christmas dinners and was fast selling up of my entire flock. I knew I could get at least two to three pounds each when they were fat at Christmas; my best prospect of making a small fortune, barring an accident or misfortune.

Once again, I was proven wrong. A major disaster occurred; it was not the neighbouring dog, or the cunning wild fox, or any other predator; it was just a one in a million freak accident. What actually happened was our neighbouring farmer left his farmyard gate open and my by-now-curious geese decided to stray into the farmyard. There was ample fresh grass growing from between the joints of the cobble stones in this farmyard, and this was just what the young goslings enjoyed.

In one corner of the farmyard was a sunken stone cattle drinking trough which was more than ideal for my goslings to swim and splash about in. Being mid summer there was little or no water coming into the trough to replace any water displaced by the goose and goslings splashing around. What actually happened was the goslings jumped into the trough splashing around forcing water from the trough until they couldn't jump out onto the farmyard. The goslings, not being in full feather, soon became waterlogged and drowned. All but two died, a total disaster. I then decided to get rid of my remaining stock and memories of my unsuccessful geese-breeding project. I sold them to the local stock dealer for a few pounds each.

I was fast approaching eleven years old and facing the change of school after the summer holidays. This meant a lot less time at home and little or no time to pursue my stock breeding activities. What I learnt during my young life to date was never to get too attached to animals, be they large or small, and never to count my chickens before they were hatched.

I had certainly had a very interesting time at Bowland junior school. I certainly did not come top of the class except in marks for being absent. I had learnt so much through practical experience about farming and village life, which would be more than useful in future years.

My father had instilled into me how to save and try and make money out of livestock farming. He always said, 'Try and make two and two into six, and if possible, eight.' Fortunately, during my youthful dealings I was lucky, retaining my initial investment. It was all a great experience, which I enjoyed immensely.

After leaving Bowland junior school, I had to seriously adjust my youthful life. I found there was little or no spare time to go my own way after school and at weekends. The new school I had to attend was seven and a half miles from the farm, so there was at least two hours a day travelling. It was always an early rise every school day to catch the bus to Clitheroe, where the new senior school was situated.

To go to this school I had to have a new set of clothes, very unusual in our family. The school insisted that long pants had to be worn, for all ages, so I had to discard my short knee length pants for the first time in my life. I also had to discard my well-used pair of clogs, as they were not allowed on the polished floor and tiled corridors at the new school. You could imagine the noise of five hundred pairs of clog irons clattering down the corridor, let alone the damage they could cause to a highly polished, ballroom type, floor.

With so many pupils at the new school there were many more classes and obviously a lot more teachers to cope with the mass of pupils. The first year pupils were all graded into four different classes. I suppose this was to separate the really brainy kids from the less able kids from less fortunate homes and families.

I didn't do too well in the grading selection and finished up in B2, which was next to the bottom grade out of four. My parents didn't complain about my grading. The only remark my father made was that I could only drop down one class into the bottom, whereas I might go up two classes into the top, if I was allowed the time at school from my usual farm activities.

At first, it took me a long time to get accustomed to the school timetable, where, after every lesson you had to change class to a different room and teacher. Being a large school complex, I often got mixed up with different classrooms and teachers and found myself late for class on many occasions. The classes were much bigger than Bowland school, with between thirty and forty pupils per teacher.

The teachers, I found, were far less tolerant than old Daisy back at Bowland school. The slightest infringement of the rules, like talking, not paying attention or poor work would get you a hefty whack round the head or even a beating with the cane. It all depended on which class you were attending and which teacher was taking the class. They all had their different methods; it could be a classroom ruler, a rubber pump or plimsoll which really hurt, strap, or just simply writing lines at playtime, lunchtime, or sometimes at home, when you got a good dose of lines for a major offence.

I was never bright in class, mainly because I found the subjects boring and of no use in a future farmer's life. What did I want to know about history for? What date certain battles took place, which King ruled which country and when? This information was totally useless to a farmer in Bowland, so I never got many marks when history exam results were published on my annual school report.

The teacher's remarks were always the same. "Peter could have done better," "ample room for improvement," "could have worked harder." It was true; there was ample room for improvement as I was always in the bottom three.

Geography, once again, was the same story. I had no interest in knowing where the many different continents and countries of the world were and had not the slightest chance of ever visiting the many interesting places I was hopefully being taught about. On geography lesson days I would try and avoid the lessons by missing the school bus or pretending to be sick. My parents took quite a while before realising it was always the same day every week when I was feeling sick.

My sister was fairly good at geography so I decided that because she knew so much, I didn't need to worry about learning it. My exam results were the same old story, bottom or near the foot of the table.

English was, yet again, one of my weakest subjects. I was a terrible speller, my English was worse, with no full stops, punctuation marks or commas. When the English teacher marked my exercise book there was more red ink crosses and sentences almost re-written than any other pupil in the class. I would often have to stay in class during playtime and lunch break to re-write, many times, the simple words I had spelt wrongly during an English lesson.

Mathematic lessons I used to like much better. It was a subject I was much better at, especially mental arithmetic. I had no difficulty at gaining top marks in the class. Often I would have marks in the high nineties out of a hundred, way ahead of my classmates. I suppose this was because of my wheeling and dealing in the various livestock during my early youth, albeit, my dealings were not very successful, but it gave me experience. My father always told me that if I was successful, I would get too big in the head. Therefore, when my dealings went wrong he said, "That will be a lesson to you. Hopefully you won't make the same mistake twice." I didn't.

Woodworking class was one of the classes I really looked forward to. Simply because I thought I was a good joiner and used to making all sorts using bits of wood and nails from my father's nail tin. Again, I was not as good as I thought. This was because the school woodwork teacher was not making rabbit hutches, buggy-type 4 wheel trucks or hand trucks. He was teaching the class how to use various woodworking tools which I had never seen before, let alone used.

The woodwork teacher could talk for a full double lesson on a selection of different wood tools. This I found totally boring. It was at least 6 months before I saw a piece of wood that I could make something with to take home and show my parents. The first completed items I took home were a pair of bookends. This was the last item I required at home, because I never read any books due to the other activities that took place on the farm and countryside.

PT or physical training was another subject I was fairly good at, simply because it was a fairly physical life we led in the country. We walked so many miles per week just going to school, let alone all the other activities we did on an every day basis, plus all the different jobs my father gave me to do on and around the farm and farmhouse.

I had to do homework on a few occasions. This really was a total disruption for me at home. It interfered with the many jobs my father always found for me to do at night and weekends. Many times, my father would write a note explaining that I had been unable to do my homework, because of certain jobs. On many occasions I would write my own note, unbeknown to my father. The teacher always pointed out the writing was of poor quality. I explained that my father always wrote them while he was milking and the cowshed wall was very rough and far from an ideal writing desk.

During my secondary education, I had lots of days off school helping my father with so many different jobs. My father was a cattle dealer, so he was away from the farm at least 3 days per week, either buying or selling cows.

My job, when away from school, was to travel to market with the cattle wagon and the first load of cows and then clean them from top to toe. This was to ensure they were presented well in the sale ring before the prospective purchasers. It was no use trying to obtain top price for a cow that was literally covered in manure. You can imagine the state of the cows after being crammed in a cattle wagon along with six or seven more cows, gorged with grass. Many times, the cows were totally green, so it was no mean task cleaning up to half a dozen cows on auction day.

My cleaning services also saved a considerable amount of money. The auction cleaner charged two shillings and sixpence for regular customers, and up to five shillings for the farmers that only took cows to the auction a few times a year. The same cattle cleaners also used to milk the cows after they had been sold. The normal charge for milking a cow was sixpence. These professional milkers would milk a cow in a matter of a few minutes. It was a really tough job cleaning and milking cows on a midsummer day, when the heat in these market sheds was probably in the high nineties. They were literally wringing with perspiration and were heavy drinkers, so all the money they sweat and toiled for, ended up in the nearest pub. The cleaner would be far the worse for drink, normally finishing up in a horizontal position instead of upright. They certainly were individual characters and part of the cattle market scene and heritage.

Another job I always had to do before market day was to go to the small booking office of the local cattle wagon, in the village of Bowland, to report how many cows we would be taking to market next day.

There may have been six or seven local farmers requiring the services of Tim Robinson's cattle wagon, so collection times had to be arranged at each farm. Many times this caused a problem because the farmers always wanted their cows on the first load to market. The regular users, like my father, always got cattle on the first load, whilst the farmers that only used the haulier on a few occasions a year, on the last load. It was always about eight o'clock before you got the collection times for your cattle, so one or two nights a week was taken up going to the village.

During my early teens, we still had our ponies to look after. This took up spare time at nights and weekends. I occasionally went hunting but I had to share the pony with my brothers and sisters. I was never too enthusiastic about hunting, because I was only riding a small pony and felt it was a bit unfair to the pony. The jumps and ditches were far too big for a small pony, so I was always left at the back of the field. When my pony was able to jump, it was when the jumps had been partly demolished by the larger horses.

The weather in Bowland was always against hunting, as most days it was raining, or frosty, or the ground was just too wet. They seldom ever caught anything because of the many small fields which were either divided up by thorn hedges, stone walls or wire netting, so the hares always had the upper hand. All I ever seemed to get when I went out hunting was either wet through to the skin, or half frozen to death.

I was classed as a fairly good rider, for my age, not particularly for my style of riding, but for the capacity for riding any sort of pony. During my early teens I had many requests to ride ponies solely kept for racing, or flapping, as it was commonly known in Ribblesdale. I always rode quite a big silver grey pony for a local farmer.

Riding ponies was always a summer sport when, hopefully, the weather was near perfect. I spent a lot of my spare time exercising and training this pony. You could say I was both trainer and jockey during summer months. It was almost every night of a job cycling a couple of miles to the farm to ride and train the pony. Pony racing usually took place only at weekend. The races were usually part of the programme of the many local shows held in Ribblesdale.

There was always a large crowd at the show when horse and pony racing was taking place. Bookmakers would be there, all lined up on their folding stools, shouting out the odds to the many punters. They were all hoping to make a profit, or as they said, "An honest bob or two."

Even though it was a local village event, the pony and horse owners were slight rogues. I never knew, until the very last minute before the starter's pistol, whether I had to race to win, even though I knew full well my pony was the fastest in the field. It was always down to what odds the bookmaker was offering on my opposition. I was always told to ride like hell when in full view of the crowd, use the whip but don't hit the pony, and flap my legs so every punter thought I was really trying to win. I would then have to lose by the safest of margins, in other words, not too close to the winner.

There were many arguments if the owners hadn't placed their bets before the starter gun went off. On some occasions a brawl would break out. This all added up to a good night at the races and gave that little extra to talk about the following day.

I was always paid a flat two pounds fifty for riding at a race meeting. This included training fees and travelling expenses, to and from the farm. It would have been useless, being paid on results, because most times I was instructed not to win.

It was during the late forties that the Bowland Young Farmers' Club was formed with myself as one of the first members. This was another drain on my spare time at home and around the village. The idea of the Young Farmers' Club in Ribblesdale was to exchange knowledge through visiting other clubs and seeing different farming methods, also holding competitions between clubs, and, in general, getting to know young farmers of your own age in the many villages of the area.

The competitions would vary, but were mostly held in connection with the regional organisation. Our region was centred in Settle. The competitions could vary from stonewalling, hedge laying, sheep shearing, public speaking, etc. On competition days, proficiency certificates would be awarded to competitors who proved themselves capable of doing a professional job in their class. Through the club within the Settle region, there were always social activities taking place. Dances were probably the most popular and mainly held in school classrooms in the many villages around the region. I believe the Bowland Young Farmers Club was the first to hold a barn dance in aid of young farmers' funds. This was held at our family farm and proved a more than successful event, attracting hundreds of revellers from over a wide area. Through these events, many romances started which eventually led to marriages in the many farming families of Bowland.

During the summer months on fine evenings, there was a local assembly point for almost all the teenage lads of Bowland. This was on the bridge at the top of the village. There was always a good selection of bicycles and the older farmer lads would have various brands of motorcycles. There was no particular reason for the evening meetings. The normal discussion was farming and what was going on in the village and surrounding farms.

During the winter there would be the occasional picture show in the main hall of the school. On picture nights the hall was always packed to capacity, with standing room only if you arrived late. The pictures were always in a faded black and white, with a poor soundtrack. On a normal evening's film show, the film would break at least two or three times and the sound would be very intermittent.

For many years, when I was young, there was always a concert held in Bowland school. This was not for any particular fund, simply for light entertainment, and held just before Christmas. The entertainers were the same from year to year, with a few good singers from the village. Comic acts were always part of the show, my father being the star turn.

Different classes from the school would have a part to play. My only part was as one of Snow White's seven dwarfs, as I was only young at the time. The school hall, at that time, was totally blacked out to comply with the war lighting regulations, as were all the farmhouses, and every cottage in the village. In most cases of a total blackout, the local council supplied the dense black cloth. It was also a job for the local bobby to visit the many properties checking that the total blackout rules were being observed. If not, a hefty fine would be imposed by the local magistrates.

When I left school I had no option but to work on our family farm. This, once again, totally disrupted my social life, and wheeling and dealing, as I did when at school. It was a case of getting up early, mucking out the cows and then, once clear, it was time to get your bucket and stool and begin milking. This could take up to an hour for three men.

I never liked milking by hand, so it was not long before I persuaded my father to invest in a milking machine. This saved both time and wages, cutting one staff from the payroll. It also allowed the dairy herd to increase, with fewer staff.

It was a time of major changes in farming around the many villages of Bowland. Tractors were fast replacing farm horses. I had one hell of a job persuading my father to buy a tractor. He insisted that it would cause too much damage to the surface of his meadows and pastures, also use expensive fuel. He pointed out that all his farm machinery would be outdated and scrap, after he had preserved and maintained them in good working order for so many years of his life.

The cattle dealing business was fast growing into a full time job, so he was away from the farm most days. He had, by now, decided to buy a car to commute around the many farms where he bought the cows for re-sale. The car he bought was a 1935 Austin 12hp 4-door model, literally unused. This was because the owner, who was a well-known jeweller in Clitheroe, couldn't obtain any fuel to run the car because of the war and petrol rationing throughout the country. Farmers had petrol coupons, so fuel could be purchased, although in very limited quantities.

The car soon lost its pristine condition when it literally became a small cattle wagon. My father used the car to transport the newly born calves to market along with food and hay for the cows he sold at the cattle auction. I remember quite well, the day the car was delivered. It was a real family gathering. The owner had to show my cousin how everything worked because my father had no knowledge of anything mechanised. The ex-owner drove the car up the farm lane into the first meadow, before giving final instructions on how everything worked.

It was only minutes after the owner left the farm, literally in tears at having to sell his car, that driving lessons commenced, my father in the passenger seat, my cousin driving. The meadow, being seven acres and quite large, was ideal for the first lesson. The whole family was instructed to stand well back on top of the banking, on the perimeter of the meadow, just in case the car got out of control.

After, maybe, half an hour, the car stopped, to allow passenger and driver to change seats. This left the, by now instructor, reasonably sure of how to stop and start the car, with my father in full control. The car revved up, stopped and started, many times before any forward motion took place. It was definitely kangaroo juice, or Australian petrol, that was in the car. Alas, after many attempts and a nearly burnt out clutch, the car moved forward, very erratically. It was not long before the car came to a complete halt, through lack of petrol. To get more fuel was no major problem, only a 4-mile walk to the other side of Bowland village to the petrol station.

After two days practice round the meadow, my father decided to abandon catching the village bus to Clitheroe and take the car. He was far from safe. He managed to arrive back at the farm with no damage to the car or himself, and never caught the bus again. In fact, he never took a driving lesson or test in his life.

It was not long after that he went even more mechanised, and bought his first cattle wagon. This was an ex-army guy, capable of carrying three large cows or four small ones. This cattle wagon was made at the farm using trees from the estate, cut into slabs on the circular saw bench. The steelwork was made at the local blacksmiths. It was far from a professional job but didn't look too bad after a couple of coats of dark green paint.

Gradually, I was convincing my father of the advantages of modern implements that could save time on the farm, and do as good a job, if not better, than hand. I had great difficulty in persuading him to buy a power driven grass mower. But once I had chosen the right model he was soon asking neighbouring farmers to come and look at the speed it could work, without getting tired like the horses. He also pointed out that it didn't need grooming or taking to the blacksmiths for new shoes.

The old twin horse-mowing machine stood unused for many years before he decided to sell it to a local scrap dealer. The era of the horse was fast coming to an end.

The hardest job on our farm was manure spreading. This job was definitely a backbreaking job and was an endless task. During the spring months it was a full time job loading muck by hand onto a trailer or horse and cart, and dumping the muck in small heaps in rows at equal spacings. Literally every square foot of meadow received a generous covering to promote growth of grass for next year's hay. The farm man and myself could spread muck for weeks on end with our own five pronged lightweight manure fork. It was always the case, when returning at night, complaining to my father about backache. He had no sympathy and his reply was always the same, "It will be a long while before it breaks, lad".

Once the tractor had been accepted on the farm we decided the first implements we would purchase were a plough, discs, harrows and a roller. These we would use to plough and re-seed many scores of acres of the poorest land on the farm. By doing so we would increase grass production and quality. There would be more hay for winter feed, and better quality grass meant more milk and less bought-in protein feed, a saving all round.

By the mid fifties we had more or less modernised our farm machinery. We had as many cows and sheep on the farm as the land could feed and support.

I had decided to keep poultry for egg production, also for parent stock to replace the older hens when they gave up laying. I had many hens, all in poultry cabins placed around the farm in different fields.

I was making quite a useful profit out of my poultry business, so I decided that I would hatch my own produced eggs and sell the day old chicks. First I bought a fairly large incubator, capable of holding fifteen hundred eggs when full.

Hopefully I would have a fair amount of day old chicks to sell if I was lucky. Normally fifty per cent of all chicks hatched are cockerels, so in a good hatch I could have in excess of two hundred to sell each week.

There was another problem. How could I tell at a day old, the cocks from the pullets or females? I needed them sexing. The only sexer I knew was a member of the pony club who used to visit our farm at most pony club events. She was a good rider and much better than the average female member of the pony club at most events. In fact, we had a fair amount in common. Her father hatched tens of thousands of chicks per week, a good source of supply, if I should oversell my production.

With my chicken breeding I had to visit the small village of Barrowford every week with my newly hatched chickens needing sexing. This was about eleven miles from Bowland, quite a long way to travel just for a few hundred chicks sexing. I was fortunate selling chicks, so every week I bought more chickens from the chicken sexer's father, in fact many more hundreds than my incubator could ever produce. No one ever realised that I was buying-in chicks to supply my ever expanding market.

The young chicken sexer was quite an attractive and hard working lass, more or less running her father's chicken farm. During my early visits to their farm, to require her services sexing my chicks, she would never be paid. So, one day, I decided to ask her to the cinema in Nelson, as a gesture of appreciation for her services rendered.

The first night we really enjoyed. I can't remember the film, but I can remember we had fish and chips afterwards, something not available in Bowland. The date was the start of many dates at weekends, plus my many visits at night during the week, when she sexed my chicks or when I bought chickens to re-sell.

She never charged me for her chick sexing. Most times she was rewarded with an extended kiss or hug.

There was one major problem visiting Barrowford, and that was travelling. At home I had a few brothers who also required transport for courting or recreational activities, so many times I had to stop at home. A few times I would take the cattle wagon to see her at weekends, not the most romantic passion wagon in the world, but she never complained.

Often I would tell her I was coming over at night and then never arrive. Many girls would have told me to go to hell but she never did. I suppose, with living on a farm, she knew that frequently things didn't go to plan, so I couldn't keep my promise.

Over the next couple of years I visited her regularly at her home in Barrowford. Likewise, she came to our farm in Bowland. My sisters were both good horse riders so there was plenty in common between both families. I was a good horse rider also, but never in the same class for style as Margaret, my girlfriend, and my two sisters.

Eventually, Margaret moved to Clitheroe, a much more accessible place to reach by car, bicycle or bus. Soon, we became engaged and married. That is when I left the family farm to start up business, in partnership, with my father in law, hatching chickens, milking cows and breeding sheep.

The partnership was short lived and lasted about twelve months.

I then started farming back in Barrowford, all on my own, with a young wife and family plus a large bank loan, a large family loan and a pair of hands capable of hard work.

We had to work hard to survive.

Farmers Story:
Young Jimmy Robinson was courting Mary, the neighbouring farmer's daughter. They had been going out for a short time when Mary became pregnant. Mary's mother was concerned about the relationship, as Jimmy didn't seem to care about Mary being pregnant.

One day Mary's mother decided to visit young Jimmy's parents, to get clarification of young Jim's intentions regarding Mary. Mary and mother walked across the fields arriving at Jimmy's house. She knocked on the farmhouse door which was opened by Jimmy's mother who asked, "What can I do for you?" Mary's mother said, "I have come to see young Jimmy or his Dad to ask what he is going to do about our Mary being pregnant". Jimmy's mother replied, "Jim's Dad isn't in at the moment. I know he charges ten pounds for his best Freisian bull, but I have no idea what he will charge you for our Jimmy".

The Outing

It was a rare treat for our family to have a day out, taking time away from the farm, even for a short period, was not that easy. The unexpected, always lurked around the corner, and any hopes of an outing that we children might harbour could suddenly be dashed if the sheep wandered off, or the favourite Jersey cow decided to drop her calf earlier than expected. Since my father was not that keen on taking time off, the mere suggestion of an outing would bring forth a list of urgent jobs which just couldn't wait. So the odd day off was all we ever seemed to get each summer, and even then, we didn't' t spend it far away from the farm. There was a limit to how far you could travel in a cart drawn by a farm horse and a distance of six or seven miles was about the maximum.

Once a day out had been agreed upon there was much preparation to do. If we were to embark on such a venture, then my father was insistent that our transportation would be at its best and the family would be well turned out.

The day before we were due to set out, the cart was scrubbed clean so that not a speck of dust remained. The leather seat which was normally kept in the cart shed was retrieved, cleansed of the bird droppings, and polished with a leather dubbin mixture to make it look like new. The best trap harness was fetched from the big cupboard in the pantry where it had been stored since our last excursion. So long had it been there, that the buckles and horse brasses had lost their sheen and become tarnished, with a finish reminiscent of silvery green mould. With much hard work and elbow grease we buffed them until they sparkled and glistened in the summer sunlight. The dull leather straps had deteriorated in storage, but my father knew exactly what to treat them with and it wasn't long before they, too, were returned to their former pristine condition. Finally, the best driving whip was brought out of store and thoroughly cleaned and polished. The whip was only there to put the finishing touches to our image. My father would never have used it on our well trained and willing carthorses. The preparation of the horse had to be left until the next day, since today she was needed on the farm.

A family outing was a good excuse to bring our clothes out of the wardrobe. My father would wear his best brown boots and leggings with pride. His boots were taken from their box and polished until he could see his reflection in them. My mother brushed and pressed his knee breeches, making sure that there was no trace of any cow muck or cow hair, and she washed, starched, and ironed his striped union shirt with the loose collar, hanging it carefully overnight. His favourite spotted tie was brought out of mothballs for the occasion and hung with the shirt, then reverently, my father would lift down that special box where he kept his best bowler hat. This he gently brushed until the pile lay smooth and velvety around the crown and along the brim.

This was quite a performance for a day out, but it was only the beginning. There were still the seven of us to see to and my father was not going to let us get away with being badly turned out. First of all he checked to see whether we needed a haircut. This was always his decision because there was nothing he hated more than to see us with long hair. We kept our fingers crossed that it was short enough as we hated having our hair cut. We didn't just go to the barbers in the main street or down into the village. This all cost money and his opinion was that it was money wasted when he was perfectly capable of doing the job himself. So we had to put up with his standard of hairdressing. We would sit on the tall wooden stool in the middle of the back yard, our hair falling onto the rough ground, as he shaved us first with the hand driven horse clippers which were far from sharp and tore the hair rather than cut it. He always finished off with the comb and the scissors, but in truth there was little finesse about it, and we often looked worse after the cut than we did before. We tended to resemble a monk or worse, no hair and all ears. "There's only a week between a good haircut and a middling one", he used to say.

My mother examined our clothes, checking first that we each had a pair of shoes that fit. It didn't matter if they were too big, because a little sheep's wool in the toe made them fit snugly. It was more of a problem if they were too small, as someone's' shoes had to be handed down and that meant finding another pair from somewhere else. We each needed socks, and those with even the smallest hole had to be mended and then the pairs matched up. This didn't cause too much of a problem either because most of them had been knitted with black and red wool and the majority matched, although they were often too big for the younger ones amongst us. However, a day out did demand that we wore garters. My mother was always providing them for us but we tended to lose them and were usually to be seen going to school with our stockings stowed in a concertina fold on top of our clogs. But for this occasion garters were a must, and for those of us without, my father provided a piece of string, which we tied around the top of the stocking, folding the welt over to hide the crude fastening.

My sisters had to wear a frock and a ribbon in their hair, whilst the boys were decked out in short pants, a white shirt and a jacket. Each boy also had his own neb cap, which my father insisted we wear on the excursion. In most cases our clothes were home made by my aunties, purchased at the village jumble sale, or handed down from our relations and friends. Either way once the garments had been washed and pressed they looked reasonably smart and my father was eventually satisfied with our appearance.

The outing that sticks most in my mind took place one Sunday in late June. The night before, we had been sent to bed earlier than usual so as to be ready, fully wakened, for an early start. We were awakened to the sound of my mother raking the ashes out in the kitchen fire, so that it could be re-lit to provide hot water for baths and washes. The younger ones had the baths, and the older ones, the washes.

The farm workers were up and about carrying out the daily chores, and my father was dashing around preparing everything which hadn't been got ready the previous day. He had already caught Betty, one of the Clydesdale farm horses and was hard at work, plaiting her mane, combing her tail, washing her legs and feet and greasing her hoofs to make her look that bit more perfect. Even Betty could not escape my father's attentions. Her hair shone like a raven's feathers after a thorough grooming.

As we lay in bed, the smell of the home cured bacon frying in the pan was percolating upwards into our nostrils. This meant that milking was finished and the farm men were about to eat their first meal of the day. The eventual scraping of chairs as they left the table was a signal for us to get up. At a shout from my mother we clambered out of bed, leaving sheets and covers piled high on the mattress. We had no fancy pyjamas to side or to fold, since we slept in our vests or nothing at all.

By the time we got downstairs the table had been cleared of porridge basins and greasy bacon plates and re-set for the rest of the family. The long bench seats had been brought in from the lobby to seat us all at the table at once, the youngest nearest the warming fire. The porridge was still piping hot in its pot above the red coals and the toast was ready to eat. A large jar of damson jam stood centre table awaiting the arrival of seven hungry mouths. My mother always asked us what we wanted, although I never understood why, since there was no selection, only porridge and toast. But it was a case of if you didn't like it; there was nothing else. "You can eat that or nowt!", my mother would say to us.

Once we had eaten our fill it was our job to clear the table and wash up. When we had finished we were ordered to play outside for half an hour whilst my mother prepared the food for the picnic. She made sandwiches from the batch of bread she had baked the previous day, cutting good thick slices. These would then be spread with well-salted farmhouse butter and topped with our favourite damson jam, or with mashed up hard-boiled egg. She also included squares of homemade currant pasty, spread with a generous coating of the farmhouse butter. My mother's favourite cakes were butterfly buns and she had made some for this special outing. These were small buns in paper cases with the centres scooped out and filled with jam made from the raspberries growing wild in the woods. These were topped with fresh whipped cream and finished off with the scooped out cake cut in two and placed in the cream, to resemble the wings of a butterfly.

To quench our thirst she had prepared oatmeal brew. The oatmeal was first scalded with boiling water then sweetened with sugar, allowed to cool, and sieved into a couple of bottles. It tasted good, although for us a real treat would have been pop or cordial, but my father couldn't see any reason to waste money on that. The alternative drink was tea, brewed in the huge brown enamel teapot. It was sweetened, and poured into bottles which had been warming in the side oven, so that the heat of the tea would not crack them whilst they were being filled. Finally, the sandwiches were wrapped in a newly washed cloth and the buns put into a used Crawford's biscuit tin. Everything was put into a straw box and stowed under the seat of the cart ready for transportation.

This was our signal to get ready. Had it not been for our mother's organisational skills this part could have descended into chaos. She used a combination of rotation and method, the rotation meant that we all went into the kitchen together, oldest first. We sat on the oak settle and method took over - one at a time, moving along the wooden bench until eventually we were all back in our original places. No one dared move away for fear of a good whack with a leather strap which hung on the end of the pot rail - that also, was part of her method! Once we were all dressed and ready it was my mother s turn. Like the rest of us, she used the washing up bowl in the stone sink in the kitchen. New warm water replaced the colder dirtier water used by the seven of us and, like us, mum washed herself with the carbolic soap taken from the block.

When my mother was ready, my father entered the kitchen to wash and shave. He had been working hard since early morning preparing Betty for the days outing. My mother went upstairs to get dressed whilst my father kept an eye on his offsprings looking like new pins in their Sunday best clothes. Still, not one of us dared move.

Fascinated, we watched him shave. He filled a cup with hot water and carefully placed it on the edge of the sink near the mirror. Next to this, he stood his shaving soap in a cartridge type dispenser and his shaving brush, with which he rubbed in the soap and then brushed across his chin. Soon he was lathered up, looking just like Father Christmas. He angled his sharp, cut-throat razor, and with effortless strokes removed the two days' growth of beard. Finally, he swilled his face in the fresh, cold tap water just as my mother returned, dressed in a frock, patterned with large flowers. She looked very summery, but the dress smelt strongly of mothballs. Her shoes were of good strong brown leather tied up with laces. Leaving us in the capable hands of my mother, my father went upstairs to get ready. It didn't take him long and when he returned he studied the effect in the small dual-purpose mirror and brush rack hanging on the wall. Taking hold of the stiff bristle brush he made a dead straight parting in his thick brown hair and then carefully placed his beloved bowler on his head. We were ready!

Father left the house by the front door which we used only on special occasions like this, or when visitors came. A few moments later we heard the clatter of horses' hoofs on the pathway and Betty appeared, to be harnessed to the cart. What a difference the few hours grooming had made to her. I was sure the household cavalry horses didn't look so smart. She was as excited as the rest of us. Her ears were aware and erect and her tail was pronounced with the graceful, long, black hair floating like silken strands in the warm breeze.

Betty stood patiently whilst everything and everybody got on board. There was a lot of freight and a lot of bodies, but somehow there was plenty of room. My father made a last check before urging Betty on with a, "Girrup", a signal the horse understood well. We were on our way at last at a steady trot. At this stage we had no idea of our destination, probably only our father knew that. A lot depended on which way we turned at the end of the drive, left or right.

This time we turned left and headed for the local village of Bowland. The road was smoother than the farm track as there was a marked absence of potholes and rough stones. The cart was moving smoothly and the passengers were not getting a rough ride.

The day was of the type that made up the memories of childhood, lovely and warm, with a clear blue sky overhead and a gentle summer breeze. The smell of honeysuckle pervaded in the air and the hedgerows were covered in an abundance of wild flowers. The growing lambs seemed to be racing us along the inside of the hedgerows. I could hear a lapwing and a curlew in full song and sighted other birds flying freely in the country air. It was on days like this that I realised how much wild life we country folk took for granted. Yet, there were town dwellers who had never heard the bird song or knew what a lapwing looked like.

From my elevated vantage point on the trap I could see things that I never saw when I walked the same road. The trees were in full leaf in a multitude of shades of green. The meadows were nearly ready for cutting and the long grass was waving in the summer breeze. Young rabbits, probably only a few weeks old, popped in and out of their nests trusting nature as only the young can. The hen pheasant with her brood sauntered in the rough grass whilst the splendidly coloured cock pheasant stood guard only a few yards away. We passed the tall pine trees in one of the estate woods and, looking closely, we saw a seka deer with her young, probably newly born and not fully aware of what was around. I relished the moment, and let my eyes take in the sight of the farmsteads, the cottages and the beautiful country landscape, which I could see now, over those same stone walls and hedges that hid them from my view when I was on foot.

Betty was enjoying her day out and pulled the cart and its contents with ease. In the distance we could see the village of Bowland and the steep hill which led down into it. A fully laden cart was too heavy for Betty to manoeuvre down the hill. There were no brakes and there was always the danger that it would run away with her. So, as soon as we arrived at the top, my father brought Betty to a halt with a loud, "Whoa lass". To ease the load on the horse, some of us climbed out, and walked alongside the cart down the hill. At the bottom, my father uttered another, "Whoa lass", and Betty pulled up to let us clamber back into the cart. With a "Girrup", we were on our way again, passing the school, the village green lined with horse chestnut trees in full bloom and the small church standing serenely, as it had for the last few hundred years.

The village of Bowland was busy with hikers who had probably arrived by the local bus, and day visitors pedalling their tandems. The coffee house was doing a roaring trade selling pots of tea and sandwiches. It was our father's intention that we should stop by the river Hodder in Slaidburn, the next village along, where we could paddle and later eat our picnic. But, on this beautiful sunny day, so many other people had had the same idea that there was hardly a spare yard of ground along the river bank, certainly not enough for our large family to sit or play comfortably.

We decided to carry on and take the moorland road, leaving behind the thorn hedges and the leisurely grazing cows. The landscape now became a patchwork of forests and rough brush land sprinkled with clumps of purple heather, separated by dry stone walls. We had to travel quite a distance before we found a suitably level stretch of soft, grassy ground, which had not been too heavily grazed by the farmer's sheep. Once off the road, Betty was released from the cart and tethered to a tree, where she could relax and munch grass until we were ready for the homeward journey. The country here was different from that near home, and the seven of us were soon off exploring whilst my mother set out the picnic.

We were called back eventually, to find the food and drink laid out on an ex-army blanket, which my father always kept under the seat of the trap. We were ravenous by this time and made short work of the damson and the egg sandwiches. Since there was only one piece of currant pasty per person, that too, soon disappeared. But the real treat was left until the last, the favourite butterfly buns. Two each!

After we had eaten we thirstily drank the oatmeal brew, leaving none at all for our parents, who had to make do with the tea. It seemed a bit mean, but outdoors the tea probably tasted better than it did in the farm kitchen

When there was absolutely nothing left in the tins or the bottles, my mother told us to go and play. We ran into the forest where we played hide and seek behind the rhododendron bushes, or climbed trees, trying, as we did so, not to tear or snag our Sunday best clothes. Eventually I tired of these games and wandered off to the side of the road to watch the motor cars driving by. None of them stopped to picnic where we were, so I supposed they were travelling to the picturesque village just a few miles away.

Adjacent to the picnic site was a gate. There were many of these gates in this area and they were there to keep the sheep upon the moor, to stop them from straying onto the lowland meadows where they would eat the grass waiting to be harvested for the winter fodder. The motorist probably disliked them even more than the sheep did. There was no way round them so he had to stop his car. get out, open the gate, get back in, drive through to the other side, stop again, get out, close the gate, and climb back in before he could continue his journey.

It occurred to me that instead of watching each driver go through this procedure I could open the gate for him. The first motorist stopped his car to thank me as he passed through the gate. He wound his window down, stretched his arm towards me and to my surprise dropped a three-penny piece into my hand. I looked at the coin. A three-penny piece was something I never saw at home and, even more amazing something for which I had done very little work. This was going to be a worthwhile day out.

I promptly closed the gate. It was badly hung and dragged along the ground as I pulled at it. I fastened it to the gate post by hanging the chain over a bent nail; a typical farmer's fastening! Almost immediately, a huge black and silver motor bike with sidecar came into view. Squashed into the sidecar were four children with mother and father astride the bike. The woman was wearing only a summer dress, which she was attempting to hold down with one hand, whilst supporting herself round her husband's waist with the other. I sniggered at the thought that she might not know where the wind was coming from, but she certainly knew where it was going. They said, "Thank you", as I opened the gate for them but didn't give me any money, probably they weren't as well off as the motorists.

The strike rate of cars coming up the road was improving and I was fairly busy opening and shutting the gate. Most drivers gave me something and the pennies were adding up. I missed the odd one by not shutting the gate in time, but I soon sorted that one out. I didn't know how much I had made, but my jacket pocket was feeling heavy by the time Mum called to say that we were returning home.

When I arrived back at the clearing the army blanket had been folded and stashed under the trap's seat, together with the empty picnic basket. Father had un-tethered Betty and harnessed her to the cart. We clambered in and within minutes were on the homeward trail. Betty seemed to know instinctively that we were heading home and was soon into a brisk trot.

By the time we arrived back in the village of Slaidburn, the day-trippers had gone and the riverbank, which two hours earlier had been spilling over with folk, cars and carts, was almost deserted. There were still several miles to travel, and the roads were busier than they had been on our outward journey. It was milking time and farmers were driving their herds of a dozen or so cattle, back to the milking sheds. A sheep dog was running from left to right, keeping the beasts under control. Every so often the farmer would instruct the dog to drive them on a little faster and with cunning skill it would bite the cow's back leg, retreating hastily to avoid the full force of a nasty kick from the stricken beast. My father knew most of the farmers along the road and would often pass comment on their herds. Some would retaliate by jokingly asking what he did in his spare time and winking at the large number of children riding in the trap.

When we finally arrived at the village of Bowland we met the local bus, a big blue and white Leyland, coming in the other direction. This posed a problem because the road was too narrow for us to pass easily. I suppose it was like the law of the sea and the smaller of us was allowed to pass first. The bus drew as far into the side as it could, and, urged on by father, Betty nervously but sure-footed, negotiated us past it. The time was 4.45pm and the bus only ran through the village once every two hours. It was just our luck to meet it, particularly as Betty had never before encountered a large belching machine like this.

Bowland was almost deserted. The day-trippers were returning home by the 4.45pm bus, the pub was closed and the coffee house was clearing up after its last customers. There were a few local children playing on the old market cross which, having stood for hundreds of years, was the focal point of the community. We passed by the church and the school and were back again at the bottom of the hill leading out of the village. Quietly, my father ordered Betty to stop, "Whoa lass!" He rarely had to use the reins on the horse for there was a natural relationship and understanding between them, and a simple instruction was enough. As before, we dismounted from the cart, leaving only the five lightest ones in it to give it some ballast, but not to make it too heavy for the horse to pull. Once at the top of the hill we clambered back in and Betty set off at a tidy trot, gathering speed back to the homestead. She seemed to sense that we were not far away, but when my father gave the word, "Steady lass", she promptly obeyed. There was less of the wild life around now; maybe they had found enough food and had headed back to their roosting quarters deep within the wood which surrounded the area.

Arriving back at the farm entrance we turned right onto the rough track. Only half a mile and we would be home - our outing but a memory. Betty let out a whinny hoping that Captain, the other farm horse, would hear and gallop across the field to greet her. Indeed, he must have heard her signal for when we turned towards the farmyard, he was standing by the gate to the field. We stopped by the front door to the house and jumped down from the cart and ran to get changed. There was no question of playing out in our Sunday clothes. We were back into our well-patched, weekday garments and our clogs.

Father, by this time, had un-harnessed Betty and was preparing to give her a swill down with a few buckets of water from the farm trough. This was a good way of cooling her, and getting rid of that sweaty lather she had built up pulling trap and passengers the several miles we had travelled. After a quick brush, she was returned to the field to be reunited with Captain. Both horses were so excited that one could have been forgiven for thinking they'd been away for years instead of only hours, the fuss they made of each other.

In the farmhouse I counted my takings for the gate opening. I had reached a grand total of three shillings and seven pence. I was rich, but not for long. Once my father found out, he made me divide it up amongst my brothers and sisters. That gave us only sixpence each, although, I was allowed to keep the extra penny, as I had been the one opening and shutting the gate. Well, seven pence was better than nothing and I began to think about what I could buy with it. Alas, I soon found that it was not for spending. It had to be put into our money boxes. I placed my coins on the hand of my golliwog money box and watched sadly as he raised it to his mouth and swallowed them.

His chores finished, my father came in for a pot of tea and we were told to feed our pets and then to play out for a little while. My mother had re-kindled the fire which was burning brightly. She sat on the long oak settle, whilst my father made himself comfortable in his grandfather chair with the hood above it.

It was not long before I returned to the kitchen to find both my parents fast asleep. Soon they would have to wake up and the routine chores of the farm would need to be completed. The trap would be returned to the cart shed, the harness to the cupboard in the kitchen, our best clothes would remain in the wardrobe and my father's beloved bowler hat would be lovingly restored to its box until the next time.

So much for a day's outing. Was it worth all the hard work that went in to preparing for it? I think so, because it would be another twelve months before we had another on such a grand scale.

Old Neddy

It was approaching Christmas in the mid forties and in our family we always tried to make it a happy time of the year. We knew we wouldn't be getting very exciting presents like many other children from more fortunate families. The most we could expect was, maybe, a sugar pig or a cheap clockwork mouse, and, most likely, some knee length socks knit by either of our two Grandmas. My mother seldom went anywhere to buy toys. I suppose she told my Aunts what they had to buy with the money available. This particular year I heard my mother complaining bitterly about not being given money for Christmas presents by my father. He replied, "I have never let the kids down yet. They have always had presents of some kind to wake up to on Christmas day morning".

As Christmas drew nearer there was no sign of presents or money. I seldom saw my mother in tears, but on this occasion she was clearly worried. Farming during that period was difficult, with livestock prices low, so money was tight.

Christmas Eve came with no sign of presents and it was impossible to get anything at that late hour. There were no shops in Bowland, only the Co-op and the paper shop, and they had long since closed. There was yet another row between my mother and father, but my father promised that he had not forgotten, and was always true to his word, so we all went to bed with no idea what to expect to see in the morning.

On Christmas day morning we always awoke early in expectation of what Father Christmas had brought. There were a few surprises. The surprise we had this particular Christmas was that there were no family presents, only those from my Grandmas' and Aunts. There were hand knitted mittens, socks and helmets all in the popular red and black wool. I must say that this red and black wool was very warm to wear and matched all of our family's' drab coloured clothing. Many of us were in tears; there was nothing from Mum and Dad. My mother had a terrible argument with my father, this was something our normally happy family had seldom heard. My father, however, insisted he had not forgotten and the present would soon arrive if we waited and watched the farm lane. We watched and waited. The neighbour's horse and cart went and came back after delivering the churns of milk to the local dairy. The postman came, not so much with the parcels and post, but for his glass of whisky and mince pies. After visiting the two farms, old Billy Bennet, the postman, lost all his cycling skills and usually finished up in the ditch with his cycle on top of him.

By this time we had no idea what the exclusive Christmas present was going to be. All of a sudden we heard an engine sound, something we least expected to hear on Christmas morning. It was old Jack Gotts' cattle wagon. We thought it couldn't be stopping at our farm' but suddenly it stopped in the farmyard. My father announced, "He 'as probably landed wi' yer Christmas present". All the family rushed out of the kitchen and to the back of the wagon all waiting in anticipation to see what we had got for Christmas. At this stage we had not the slightest idea what it was going to be. My mother's face had changed from a very worried and disappointed look to an excited happy smile. She most likely knew in her heart that my father had a very soft spot for his offspring, but didn't always show it.

My father said, "Tha'd better let they door down Jack, so thee can see what tha's browt". Jack undid the fastening holding the cattle wagon tail and lowered the loading ramp onto the ground. All was revealed, it was the perfect present for all the family. A donkey, all nicely groomed with a bridle and saddle. It looked quite a big donkey to ride for the youngest members of the family, but once down at ground level it was just perfect and it wasn't long before all the family was scrambling for rides. The donkey was female and the normal grey. We were told that all donkeys carried the holy cross and normally it was in a black brown colour. We could not see this cross perfectly until the small felt saddle had been removed. Once removed the cross was plain to see. I suppose it was a perfect fitting for any Christmas day present.

My mother was more than delighted with my father's selection of all the family's' Christmas present. She remarked, "Well, you won't break this like the clockwork toys, and it won't wear out. The only thing you will have to do now is to look after it".

My father had also thought about where we could keep the donkey over winter when all the cattle stalls and horse boxes were fully occupied. He had swilled out the recently vacated pig sty, whitewashed it out, fixed a hay rack to the wall and cut the full length door in half so Neddy could look out and observe what was going on around the farm. There was a new galvanised cattle feed bucket for the fresh water, in fact there had been no expense spared with our new 'toy'.

We first had to find a name for this new arrival. Many names were bandied around. Neddy was not one of them. Finally, we decided to call her Ginney, so one of the first tasks was to paint the name on the door and also on the new water bucket.

Being nosey children, we asked my father how much he had paid for our donkey. He replied, "Them who asks won't get to know, and them that don't ask don't want to know". So none of us, including my mother, ever found out how much he paid for the new toy. On reflection, we bet my father never paid anything for the donkey, as we all assumed he had bought it in a deal when he visited other farmers to buy surplus cattle, and most likely got it as luck, or as a discount. Not only did we never find out how much the donkey cost, we never even found out where he bought it from, which was pretty unusual in a close knit community like Bowland village.

The first thing my father taught us was how to look after Ginney. He showed us how to remove all the droppings from the straw and how to relay the straw bedding. He also taught us just how much hay to give her without wasting a single wisp of the valuable fodder. He told us not to give the donkey any type of extra feed like oats or bran. This order we soon disobeyed by giving her cattle ration and nuts when he wasn't around.

Ginney didn't have a chance to get much rest when all the family were on their Christmas holidays from school. There were frequent arguments about whose turn it was to go riding. Ginney never bothered, and was always willing to transport us around the farm, although it was a different story when one of our farm men decided he would have a ride. Once astride Ginney with his legs only a few inches from the ground at each side he said, "Giddiup Ginney". But she never moved an inch; no matter how he tried, there was never a chance that he was going for a ride. He decided that a little gentle persuasion with his cow stick might work, and it did. Ginney set off at full gallop, totally surprising the jockey. She had gone but 20 yards when she suddenly stopped dead, sticking her front feet into the thick green turf. Whilst stopping dead, she decided to give a huge buck. This she did like a professional rodeo horse, with head bent between her front legs and her back end almost vertical in the air. The jockey was thrown off with surprising ease and at great speed. We all burst out laughing, the jockey was furious and decided to have another try. There was only one problem, he had to catch Ginney first. This he tried and tried again until he gave up the task as a bad job. Once he had left we simply walked up to Ginney and got hold of the bridle and then one of us rode her home. We did, however, give her a small reward, a few sugar lumps out of my mother's cupboard. Many people think donkeys are daft. I can assure you that Ginney was the wisest and brainiest animal we had on our farm. She had given us fair warning that she had no intention of conveying a 12 stone farm man around the farm.

This Christmas was probably the happiest one we had ever had and most likely also for my mother and father. My father probably thought that was the best animal he had bought in years. At this stage I had no idea of the endless pleasure Ginney was going to bring to our family.

Soon the winter passed and spring arrived. It was during that spring my father decided to make us a donkey cart. He had found an axle and wheels somewhere on his travels, which was just what he needed to make us a cart. The wheels were solid iron, so there was no cushion effect on our very rough farm lanes. He also found the perfect box for the main part of the cart which was a second hand Irish bacon box about 3'6" square and maybe 2'6" deep. He soon managed to find some 3" x 2" timber from an old poultry cabin. There was no tailgate on this cart so we had to clamber over the side when going for a ride out. The harness we required, when using the cart, was home made from some of our farm work horses' harnesses. The villagers remarked, "Who has made your harness?" and we replied, "My Dad". They said, "I thought as much, what a mess". We never bothered, as we always knew my father did the best on his very limited budget.

The arrival of Ginney soon altered my pattern of life. I no longer had to walk to the village on a Saturday morning for bread and groceries. My sister and I could now go in style, the whole set up was admired by the villagers. What with the bacon box and tatty harness we must have looked a sight. Unfortunately, we never got a photograph of Ginney and the cart.

I soon became the local haulier for the family with donkey and cart. I had to take wood to all my aunties for their kitchen fires. I would stack the small cart high with logs and then sit on top instead of walking alongside the cart with Ginney. I would visit my aunties just for the ride out, and on many occasions tipped the cart over trying to drive up the most inaccessible pathways. It was all good fun and experience.

Ginney, as I said before, was a very brainy donkey and soon found out how to open a farm gate, so we always had to double fasten Ginney's gate with a chain. If Ginney did escape from the field she never wandered off and always finished up around the house. If the house door was open she never knocked, but just walked straight in. On occasions, she would walk in when dinner or tea was being prepared and literally eat the lot. She wasn't too fussy what she ate, she always liked bread, cakes, etc. On one occasion, she ate all the sliced roast beef from the table and then decided to take up her homing position standing on the hearth rug in front of the kitchen fire, with her nose halfway up the chimney. On many occasions she burnt her whiskers from around her nose.

During haytime, we would help cart home the hay from the field to the barn. The cart was only small so we made extra supports at the back and front of the cart. When it was fully loaded it held very little hay. But we all thought we were helping to harvest the valuable winter fodder. Ginney was always happy in the hayfield, pulling the light loads and consuming small quantities of the sweet smelling fresh hay. The whole team looked a different sight as no other farms in Bowland had a donkey or cart with such willing young workers. Ginney had a very varied life whilst at our farm and, I suppose, never a dull moment. During June we always had a sports day at the school in Bowland, which consisted of all sorts of sports like the egg and spoon race, sack race, slippery pole and catching the slippery pig. I took part in many of the events and I also had another job to do. This was to take Ginney for donkey rides to raise funds for the Church. It was approximately 100 yards down the village green so every ride was about 200 yards. The cost was sixpence, quite expensive in those days, but my customers didn't seem to bother about the price, as it was for a good cause. It was a longer ride than you got at Blackpool, the main difference was there was no sea and sand. Being a bit of a lad, I always kept a few bob for myself, as I didn't see why I had to walk many miles with Ginney for nothing when everybody else was having a good time, and nobody had any idea how many miles I walked.

On most occasions I took Ginney with the cart when going to the village for papers and groceries. However, on odd occasions, my sister would venture down to the village with cart and donkey. On one of these occasions the dustcart was coming one way and Ginney the other. Ginney had never seen or heard such a vehicle, so she shied and bolted when passing. Once startled, Ginney soon got into a full gallop with cart and occupant and didn't go far before tipping and throwing my sister onto the road knocking her out and causing a large gash in her head, requiring many stitches at the doctor's surgery in the local town. During all the years, that was the only major accident we had with Ginney.

Ginney also had two companions in the large carthorses, which were almost twice her height. If the carthorse was taken from the field to work Ginney was always uneasy, and was continually ee-awing until they returned to graze. It worked the opposite way when the cart horses were left in the field alone; they would whiney and gallop around until they sighted Ginney returning to the field.

In the field where Ginney was kept all summer, there were deep ditches with the occasional large oak and ash tree. This was where I would play hide and seek with Ginney. I could easily hide behind these trees and move around them when Ginney got close, so she couldn't find me. I spent many a long hour during the summer months playing in this way with Ginney, until we were both tired out with running and dodging each other.

In this field one summer there was a bumper crop of field mushrooms which my mother would make into delicious soup, or fry with the bacon and egg, or put them in a potato pie. Field mushrooms freshly picked had a far different taste from the cultivated mushrooms of today. It was believed that, when you kept a few horses, the horse manure helped promote the growth of the wild mushroom. It was on one of these mushroom-picking days, which were always in midsummer, and after some good, long, warm rain showers, that mushrooms appeared. I was kneeling down picking when Ginney decided to play around, which, at first, I did not bother too much about, until all of a sudden she pounced on me from behind, literally flattening me. Once flattened, she started to bite me and I can assure you that a donkey really hurts when it bites, with its strong jaws and sharp teeth. It tore my shirt and brought blood in about seven places on my back leaving good imprints of her large set of dentures. I was probably very lucky to escape with a few nasty bites and bruises. I didn't bring home any mushrooms as I had to use the cane basket to fend off Ginney in an attempt to escape. Ginney must have thought she was having a bit of fun with me.

Once I got home and had my wounds bathed in Dettol, then smeared with Germolene, I went back to the field to catch Ginney. Once I had caught her I let her know my disapproval of what she had done to me. With a short hazel stick which I had just cut from the adjacent hedgerow, I gave her a sound beating. It was many days before Ginney regained her trust in me again. I always thought she knew she had done wrong.

Ginney was a well-known star when any special functions went on in the village. After most June sports there would be fancy dress competitions held on the village green, then paraded in the village centre. My father would always have a go when a fancy dress competition was held. One year he decided to dress up as Mahatma Gandhi and decided to use Ginney for his method of transport. My father was fairly thin in those days so he made the perfect size and stature of Gandhi. First, he covered himself with a coffee mixture to give himself the Indian tan. It was very effective. Next, he used a pig's bladder, which he had stored since killing last year's pig. This fitted his head perfectly and completely obliterated his dark head of hair. He took out his two or three false teeth, made himself a whiskery beard from sheep wool, then wrapped himself in a white sheet which he tied round his waist, with a short length of rope cut from the end of my mother's clothes drying line in the orchard. He borrowed a pair of sandals from my cousin, as he only used clogs and boots all the rest of the year. He used the remains of the coffee to colour his feet and legs. His final touch was a pair of old wire rimmed glasses that were miles too small for him. In all, it added up to make the near perfect Gandhi.

Ginney was draped in a small white sheet. My father carried a large cross that he had made out of a broken hayrack. He also carried a bible to complete the Gandhi image. He even coloured a red spot in the middle of his forehead, which wasn't too easy to do when my mother never used lipstick. I think he either used a red crayon pencil or borrowed a lipstick from one of his sisters. He won his class in the fancy dress competition. Many of the villagers had no idea who Gandhi was, their only clue was Ginney the donkey.

V.E. Celebrations

On another occasion Ginney was used in a fancy dress parade to celebrate V.E. Day. I can see the parade quite clearly today, even though it was so many years ago. It was the largest celebration Bowland village had ever witnessed. Sadly, there had been families who lost sons and relatives in the years of conflict. My father, once again, was the star attraction. He dressed up as a clown with suitable hat, cigar, etc, plus a large hayfork. The hayfork he used to stab, and carry aloft, a stuffed effigy of Goering, a German Field Marshall, which he was dragging round the village, tied to Ginney's tail. It was very well received by the hundreds of spectators. As the years passed, and the family grew up, Ginney was fast getting too small, so we had to look around for a pony that was capable of taking the place of Ginney. By this time Ginney was part of our family and there was no way my father could be allowed to sell her to any person we didn't know, or where we could never see her again.

It was on a cow buying trip, at a farm about two and a half miles from our farm, that my father met Ginney's new owner. He had a pony that had totally got the control of his daughter. It was much larger than Ginney and only a few years old, just what we required. The farmer and my father came to a clean swap agreement, so no money changed hands. The only condition was that the farmer who owned the pony would not guarantee, or be responsible for, any damage or injury caused by his pony, once the swap had taken place.

I knew who was going to be the rodeo rider, once we became the new owners of this untamed bucking bronco. It was mid summer when I left our farm with Ginney for the last time. There were tears from all of our family before Ginney left. She had been a true servant during our family's' youth, giving endless pleasure to us all. It was a good hours' walk down through Bowland village towards the village of Sawley, where Ginney was to make her new home. When I arrived at the farm, my father was waiting with the owner of the pony and his daughter. She decided to have a ride on Ginney, something she had not dared to do on her own fiery, bucking pony. Ginney obliged by letting her have an incident free ride in the nearest field, a relief for her father, who always expected the worst when she had a ride on her pony. He was over the moon with his side of the bargain. At least he knew his daughter was not going to be injured when riding her new acquisition.

It was time to saddle the pony we had just acquired. The saddle was a proper pony saddle, not a felt pad which I used when riding Ginney. It was much better to stick onto, which I knew full well that that was what I was going to have to do. We led the pony from the cowshed, where we had attached the saddle and bridle, to the farmyard, adjacent to a large meadow. It was time to mount the fiery-eyed pony which, I knew, was going to be a bucking handful of pony flesh. I got astride the pony, equipped with a good quality whip, that I was already prepared to use even before I left the farmyard corral.

I decided my tactic was to use one hand to steer this bucking bronco and use the other to administer a quick blast with the whip, something this pony had not encountered before. The farm gate was opened and I was now on my own with the handful of quicksilver. I had guessed right, and as soon as I got into the open meadow the bronco bucking started. I gripped hard with my knees onto the saddle and held onto the back of the saddle with my other hand, making sure not to lose my whip. The pony really could buck better than anything I had been asked to ride before. The first few bucks were so bad, normally it would have unseated most experienced riders, but I was still there, gripping for dear life, but gaining confidence all the time. I soon let go from gripping the saddle and was now in a position to teach this bucking bronco a lesson. Every time the pony bucked I administered a good swipe with the whip that I had held in reserve for just such an occasion. I probably gave it twenty swipes before the bucking stopped and I got the pony to move forward. Once I got it moving forward, I decided I would keep the pony moving not allowing it time to buck again. It worked, and after a good ten minutes in the meadow I returned to the farmyard, where the new owner of Ginney was more than relieved to see me back in one piece, and he knew that someone was capable of riding his pony.

My father said to this gentleman, "I told thee it wouldn't throw the young bugger, he can stick like shit to a blanket when riding horses and ponies". I left the farm with the new pony which we christened Molly. Molly turned out to be a pony that all the family rode without any of her bucking bronco antics. I must have taught her a lesson she never forgot.

Ginney, I believe, stopped on the gentleman's farm for many years until she died. I bet Ginney led one of the most interesting lives of any donkey born and was faithful to the end. We kept Molly for many years and all the family enjoyed riding her. She would take us hunting on many occasions, but was not capable of jumping the high fences like the large horses, so, most times, we had to use the gates to keep up with the rest of the hunt. We kept Molly, as with Ginney, until we needed a larger pony. The next one we bought was grey, and was called Silver, and we rode her until once again we outgrew her size.

Gathering Fruit

During my early life, the summers seemed to be long and sunny and there were always plenty of unusual activities to spend our leisure hours doing. There were also many jobs I had to do for my mother. One of these was picking fruit to conserve jam or bottling for the next 12 months' pies.

The first crop was gooseberries. I had to pick these with my Auntie from a farm, about six miles away, at Gisburn. It was an early rise, about 8.00am, and then a bicycle ride, with basket and boxes tied with string onto luggage racks at the back of the bicycle. We arrived at about 9.00am and started picking berries. My auntie was a very fast picker, so it wasn't long before we had filled our baskets and boxes with around thirty pounds of berries.

The farmer's wife would always make our dinner before we left. It was very different, having dinner with only four diners instead of eleven, as at home. It was also different in another way. At home we only had the one plate for vegetables and meat which was then used again for pudding, be it rice pudding, steamed pudding, or fruit and custard. We always made sure it was reasonably clean, either by scraping with our knife or mopping with a slice of bread. It was a little off-putting when fat and gravy was mixed with the dessert.

It did not trouble our family too much, because we were used to it. My father would remark that, if it wasn't mixed before you ate it, it soon would be after. I suppose he was right, and just think how much washing up it saved in a week for my mother.

When we arrived home in the early afternoon we had to begin topping and tailing the berries. This was necessary to avoid having stalks, and dried off heads, in the jam or pies. Topping and tailing was a long, boring job, especially when I could have been playing around the farm and village of Bowland.

It would be late evening before all the gooseberries had been conserved for the next year. There would be many bottles of jam all made in a huge copper jam pan on the log fire in the kitchen. There were also bottled gooseberries that would be used for pies or puddings over the next twelve months. These were always sealed in screw topped jars, so they could be resealed if all the contents were not used in one go.

The most rewarding part of the gooseberry picking was the large, plate pies my mother made. She could soon make a pastry base and top and when filled with freshly picked gooseberries, and covered with plenty of sugar, that long day's work seemed all worth while.

During the summer months there was a continuous supply of fresh, home grown, and wild, fruit that all came in rotation. When one variety finished another crop would be ready for picking.

The next crop that was ready to pick after gooseberries, was red and black currants. We picked these from the same farm as the gooseberries, but not in the same quantities. In some years there were bumper crops and in other years, if there had been a late frost, none at all. We would always make the blackcurrants into jam and use mostly when one of the family was sick, or out of sorts, as a 'pick you up' or medicinal drink if you had a bad cold or sore throat. '

After the currants it was time for picking raspberries. The entire raspberry crop that we picked grew wild, in the large woods belonging to the estate. The wood where the raspberries grew was a good mile walk away from our farm, so I had to stay with my auntie and grandma at their little estate cottage.

The raspberry, not being the cultivated strain, grew mostly where large trees had been cleared. They had been felled, died of old age, or blown down during the winter gales. The reason the raspberries grew in these areas of the large woods was because there was no canopy from existing trees. Also, all the dead and rotting tree tops, left after felling, acted as a type of mulch, controlling, to a certain extent, the weeds and young raspberry plants.

I often wondered why the raspberry always grew in this environment, so I asked my auntie. She told me that the birds ate the raspberries, then deposited the seeds in their droppings, when they perched among the fallen trees and foliage, hence new plants every year in different parts of the estate woods.

When picking raspberries it was a fairly late start, 11.00 am, on most days, was the time I had to go with my auntie to the woods. Each year she knew exactly where the best crop of berries would be, mainly on the youngest canes and in the worst possible places amongst the fallen tops of the large trees, long grass and thistles. The reason we left late when picking raspberries was because of the heavy woodland dew. If the early morning dew was not dried from the canes, and grass, it was not long before you were totally drenched. You had no chance of drying off until you returned home many hours later.

My auntie was an exceptionally fast raspberry picker and on many occasions we would pick in excess of fifteen pounds weight in one day. The catering facilities in the large wood were none existent, so we always had to take light refreshments with us. I remember, on one occasion, we set off to pick berries and my auntie had packed my favourite, extra large, home baked ginger biscuits, plus a large bottle of cold tea. It was a very hot day and I soon became thirsty. So, I checked where my auntie had deposited the ginger biscuits and bottle of tea, and, making sure she was out of sight, I decided to have a biscuit and a drink of tea, which tasted exceptionally good after an hour's picking. My auntie never seemed to get hungry or thirsty when she was picking a good crop of raspberries.

The ginger biscuits were absolutely delicious, the tea was thirst quenching and nothing more. So, about every thirty minutes, I sampled another biscuit and more cold tea until there was nothing left.

It would be about two thirty when I heard my auntie coming through the shoulder high canes and thistles, heading towards the site where the refreshments should have been. She certainly had picked a lot of berries, far more than I had. She remarked what a good crop there was, and said to me, "We will have a biscuit and a drink before we set off home". I was in one hell of a predicament. I knew my auntie would half kill me if she knew what I had done, so I had to think very quickly. I decided to move ahead more quickly, leaving ten to fifteen yards distance between us. When I approached the area where the refreshments should have been, I decided to run, shouting, "There's a bloody black cat eaten all the biscuits and spilt the bottle of tea!". My Auntie didn't doubt that there was a black cat and it had devoured the biscuits and spilt the tea. She remarked "That's a poor do! I was looking forward to a drink of tea and a ginger biscuit. We will just have to wait until we get home".

It was, maybe, twenty years later before I told her about the biscuits and tea incident. Even though she was now well in her seventies she could remember that day, and the story I had so ingeniously invented to save my skin!

As the summer came to a close, and autumn arrived, there were many more varieties of fruit to be harvested after the raspberry. There were the blackberries that were abundant in the hedgerows and the woodland areas on the estate. These were much harder to collect than the raspberry, mainly because they were a climbing bush, so the best berries were always well out of reach. We used to take my grandma's walking stick to pull back the branches to get to the fruit. We always had to remember to take back her stick, after every picking session, or we would have been in serious trouble, or certainly there would have been no tea until it was returned.

I was also called upon to pick pears and damsons for my mother's aunt, some three miles away, at a small village called Sawley. The pear tree was a large tree that always had the best pears on the very top branches, making them difficult to pick. I was fairly good at climbing trees when I was young, mainly because it was a good pastime, and a challenge. We used to see who could climb certain trees the fastest and descend the fastest.

The easiest way to collect the pears was to give the branches a good shake. The trouble with that method was that they all got bruised and soon went rotten or bad, so I had to pick as many as I could without damage. When I had a small basket full, I was instructed by my aunt to take them up to the cottage, where she lived. This was a fair distance from the fruit orchard and she would sort them, and give me a large bagful to take back home for my mum, after I had finished picking for the day.

On the first day of picking I arrived home at about three o'clock, quite proud of my achievement; no spending money, but, a large bag of pears. On opening the bag I was dismayed to find the pears were not what I had picked, but windfalls that my miserable, greedy, old aunt had collected a few days previously.

My mother was very annoyed to think I had travelled so far, and risked falling from the tree, for a bag of bruised pears. She told me I had not to go again, but I decided that when asked, I would return. The next weekend I was asked again, and I went. The pears that I had left on the upper branches seemed to have doubled in size, and I took particular care not to bruise them. I placed them in a carrier bag and then I hid them under a hollybush, adjacent to the road I would be taking to get home. My aunt came down the garden, at least twice, to ask when she was going to get the first bag of pears. I replied, "They are taking more collecting from the top of the tree. I can only get them by shaking the tree". I took her a few bags of bruised pears. She grumbled about the damage and offered me a bag to take home, but I refused, saying my mum had a lot of last weeks left. I didn't even get thanks, or a sixpence, for my efforts that day. I did, however, get a large bag of her best pears to take home that she never knew about.

The crops of wild nuts and fruit that we gathered in late summer varied greatly from year to year. This was due to the type of weather we had in the spring, when the various trees and bushes came into flower. The main cause of a poor crop was a late frost, that simply froze the blossom and reduced the crop or caused total loss.

There were other weather factors that caused loss of fruit and nuts; these were cold and wet weather. In the latter, rain totally stopped the bees and insects from their pollinating activities. They were not able to fly in wet weather as easily as on dry, sunny days. There was always the buzz of the wild bees and insects, when you stopped and listened, under a large fruit tree, lime or chestnut tree.

Not all the wild varieties of fruit and nuts grew close to our farm in Bowland. There were certain woods where hazelnut was plentiful in late summer. The best wood was about a mile away, on the other side of the river Ribble, where the trees were not too large, so you could gather nuts reasonably easily with a walking stick, or a hazel stick cut from a tree.

Before the hazelnut picking time we would walk many miles to search the woods to find the best crop. Often we would find trees totally barren of nuts or sometimes just the odd tree laden with nuts.

If there was a poor crop you knew it was going to be difficult to beat the red squirrel, and other various mammals, that gathered the nuts for their winter food store. Also, there were other villagers that knew where the best hazelnuts grew in the Bowland woods. These were mainly retired people who had plenty of time on their hands, so a walk, at almost anytime, was possible and our family was at a big disadvantage, with school, and jobs on the farm to attend to.

Nearly all the woods were on the other side of the River Ribble, so the river was a big barrier to our youthful nut picking team. The problem was the amount of water. If the weather was dry, the river would be at a very low level, so there was no problem, but, if there had been recent rain in the upper reaches of the river, the height of the water soon made it very dangerous for us to cross. Normal water level was about knee deep in certain parts of the river. We had to find the shallowest part of the river, which was not always directly across. It may be at an angle, depending on where the deep pools were. We did not have wellies, so, we had to take off our clogs and socks, and paddle across. The riverbed was far from sandy, so it was quite painful on the feet, walking on the gravel and shingle that formed the riverbed.

The place where the hazel trees grew was in one of the prettiest areas along the river, with large, fast flowing pools, and mature trees growing on the riverbank on both sides. The wildlife was very plentiful. The Seka deer, with their young, used to frequent the hazel wood. There were the badger setts, which, we could see, were well used, with the new bedding grass strewn about, just adjacent to the main entrance, and their toilet a few yards away.

The badgers' habit was totally different from the Seka deer. We never, ever, saw them in daylight; they were totally dusk to dawn animals. We could tell, quite easily, when badgers were about, on our farm, by the number of dry cowpats that had been completely turned upside down. This was so that the badgers could gather the worms and grubs that lived underneath.

There were lots of rabbit burrows within the variety of woods that stretched for miles along the riverbank. When gathering nuts, it was normal to see scores of rabbits close to their burrows or just running around under the canopy of trees. Occasionally, we would come across a fox lair. It was easy to distinguish between a fox lair and badger sett even though the entrance holes were about the same size, and normally sited on a dry, sandy bank. The difference was in the various bones and carcasses strewn around the fox's lair. There would be the bones of lambs, hens, ducks and geese that had all belonged to the many local farmers in Bowland.

One day, when gathering hazelnuts in our favourite wood across the river Ribble, we had a very serious situation. We had collected a couple of shoulder sized bags of nuts and were walking along the riverbank when we noticed a rapid change in the flow of the river. All of a sudden, ahead, there was a 4 foot wall of water rapidly approaching us. The problem for our young team of nut pickers was to decide whether to risk dashing across to the opposite bank and risk being swept away, or wait and see how high the floodwater would rise, and how long it would be before we could cross safely.

Within ten minutes the river was a raging torrent, with no possible chance of us being able to cross. In fact, we were very lucky not to be in a narrow part of the river, where there was no room to get away from the major floodwater. There were dead sheep, trees and debris flashing past at great speed, carried along by the rising, raging water, a very frightening experience. We were left in a predicament; it was about 3 miles, either way, to the nearest road bridge over the Ribble where we could then head home, back to the farm.

We decided to follow the river downstream to the village of Sawley, where the woodland terrain was a little more walker-friendly. It was still going to be a good 6 miles home, whichever direction we decided to walk. The worrying problem was how our parents were going to know where we were. It could be a more than serious situation if they started to worry about us not returning on time and much worse if they went down to the river and saw it in a full spate flood, especially if we could not be seen on the opposite river bank. All we could do was set off to walk as fast as possible downstream, then round by the main road to Bowland.

It seemed to take no time at all to walk the three miles to Sawley village, where we could cross the raging river by the road bridge. Once on the main road, we had walked only a short distance when a big, black car stopped. We were more than surprised to see a car, and we instantly recognised the driver as our family doctor, who asked us to jump on board for a ride back to Bowland. He offered to take us back to the farm but we insisted we could walk the one and a quarter miles across the fields back home.

When we arrived home my parents had not been worried or concerned that we were a couple of hours late. We then told them all about the big flood on the Ribble, and how it had cut our homeward journey from the hazelnut wood, how we had walked the many miles to the roadbridge at Sawley, and then how our family doctor had recognised us and had driven us to Bowland. They decided we had been very brave and sensible doing what we had done, and not taken the risk of crossing the river.

We went down to the river with my father to show him the extent of the flood; he just could not believe his eyes at the height of the water. It was over a week before we could cross again for hazelnuts. We were a week too late, the squirrels had literally devoured and stored the lot, so we only had a few nuts that year.

During the war years we had yet another fruit to pick in the country. This was the rosehip, a wild fruit, but not immediately edible. The government, I believe, had a rosehip collection drive nationwide where schoolchildren were asked to collect rosehips to make rosehip syrup rich in Vitamin C, which was vital for the health of many young children.

Rosehips were the fruit of the wild briar that grew in hedgerows and on wooded slopes around the village of Bowland. It was always a very sharp, thorny bush, which made picking rosehips difficult and painful if you didn't take care when gathering the fruit.

In our Bowland school, even though there was no financial reward for gathering rosehips, we always collected many hundreds of pounds in weight. It was a type of competition as to which school could gather the most. The rosehip crop depended on a good, warm spring, as with many other wild and cultivated fruits.

The elderberry was yet another wild fruit that grew abundantly in and around Bowland. We used the elderberry fruit on our farm to make wine and a medicinal drink to take when you had a cold or flu. We would only drink wine at Christmas, or on a special occasion such as Christenings, or weddings. Gathering elderberries was one of the easiest, provided you were just in time, before the pigeons and wild birds decided they were ripe. It would be only a matter of a day before the trees could be totally stripped of their fruit that hung in bunches quite close to the ground. The added bonus, when picking elderberries, was that there were no sharp, prickly branches to contend with.

We would also have to collect crab apples to make crab apple jelly conserve. The crab apple always looked very edible from the ground, when you looked at the branches laden with fruit, but once you had picked them it was a different story. They were so sour that it was impossible to eat them without sugar whether in jam or jelly.

The only other wild fruit that grew on the estate woodlands was the sloe. This was a type of damson which, when ripe was black and looked very appetising until you actually tasted the fruit. The wild sloe was so sour it made you wince after a small bite. I actually finished up spitting it out immediately, even though I knew exactly what to expect when tasting sloe. Many villagers and farmers would collect the sloes to make sloe gin to a well-tried recipe. This, again, would be used for medicinal purposes, in most cases, along with the many wild herbs that were collected in late summer.

A very popular wild berry, that we never collected was the berry of the Mountain Ash. This tree was an absolute picture when the fruit was ripe and orange. The trees grew profusely around our farm, in hedgerows and woodland. Once ripe, the birds would strip the trees bare within days. You could see wild wood pigeon gorging themselves on the abundant fruit, also blackbirds, starling and many other migratory birds.

We also knew, as school children, the apple trees that grew *en route* to Bowland from our farm. The best grew at the back of the village school, which we visited every day. We had a problem with old Daisy, the headmistress, at that time, because she lived in the schoolhouse. So, we had to keep her in class while one of us raided the apple tree for a few apples that we ate on the way home from school.

There was another fruit that was very collectable but not edible, and that was the wild chestnut or the conker. We would walk miles to collect these in the many areas around Bowland where they grew. They grew mainly in the parkland around the large houses in Bowland. There were also lots of large chestnut trees that lined the village green, beside the road between the church and the school. We were at a disadvantage with the village trees, because the villagers, who lived there all the time, could collect the conkers before we even arrived for school.

When all the wild fruit had been harvested, either by man, bird or beast, it was late autumn, when the leaves fell from the trees. This was a sure sign of the approaching winter, with long, dark nights and short days ahead.

The Great Storm

It was 1946 and a good year for farmers, both large and small. There was an early spring, just what a farmer needed every so often to give that extra boost to his income. Indirectly, the way it worked was more a saving on feed, which was expensive. It also saved on labour because the cows and calves were turned out to graze that couple of weeks earlier than usual.

The climate was much warmer during the day, with no hard frosts at night, so every field had that extra lush grass, just what was needed for the ewes and new born lambs. More fresh grass meant more milk from the ewes to feed their new offspring. It made lambing time a lot less stressful for the farmer and his family and also less hard work. The better the spring, the better the chance of bumper hay crops for the winter and spring of the following year.

In Bowland there were many wise prophets of the unpredictable weather, be they the wise old farmer of seven score years and a few more, or a villager who had lived there all his long life. They had predictions for the 1946-47 winter. Obviously, all the different predictions couldn't be right, but, in general, there was an opinion that we were in for an unusually hard winter. The normal signs were beginning to show in late summer and autumn.

There was an exceptionally heavy crop of berries; hawthorn, holly, rosehip and elderberry, also, the wild growing fruit; nuts and acorns were plentiful, with the large oak trees laden with extra large acorns. There were loads of hazelnuts on almost every tree. We collected these for our household use from the lower branches. We left the nuts on the inaccessible branches to the red squirrel, which was abundant in the woods of Bowland. Nuts were easy for the squirrel to collect and store. There were lots of beech nuts, again a desirable food for many Bowland birds and small animals.

There were many more rabbits leaving the wooded slopes of the river Ribble each evening to feed in the meadows and pastures adjacent to these woods. This was because of the perfect spring, when the rabbits had their young in short, shallow burrows in fields and bankings and hadn't been drowned by torrential rain as in normal spring weather. There were more wild hares, all in a good condition, due to the perfect spring and summer. Wild duck was plentiful on the river and surrounding ponds and ditches, unusual for the Bowland area.

The migratory birds were also plentiful, having successfully reared their clutch of young. These could be seen in hundreds, assembling ready to migrate that week to ten days earlier than usual. The swallows and house martins would be perched in rows on the wire fencing and clothes drying lines ready to take off on their long journey to a warmer winter climate. Curlew and lapwing assembled in large flocks, ready to fly away to the estuaries around our coast and the lowland marshes.

The trees turned a magnificent brown and gold and the tints in the hard and softwood plantations had great variations, unlike the large conifer woodland and forests in other parts of the country.

It was time for the harvest festival celebration in our local Church. We all looked forward to this as the various crops of Bowland were magnificently displayed by most of the villagers. There were peas, beans, tomatoes, sheaves of corn, turnip, potatoes and fruit of every variety from gooseberry to victoria plum.

I always enjoyed harvest festival not just because I was in the Church choir, but because, after the festival service, we could eat the various fruits. In some seasons we would sing the hymn "All is safely gathered in" when there had been no harvest gathered. In 1946 we had actually gathered the harvest.

Autumn soon went and winter arrived, the cows were brought from the fields and put undercover in the various winter accommodations. The milk cows would always be in the large cowsheds and the young stock in small outbarns on other parts of the farm. The large white pigs would be coming to their day of destiny, being fed large amounts of food to get them as fat as possible before killing. The sheep looked exceptionally well having enjoyed a favourable spring and summer, equipping them for the oncoming winter. The farm sheepdog had cast its summer coat and grown a new crop of dense fur to withstand the winter cold. The horses had grown their winter coat, which was at least twice as long and thick as their summer coat. The hens had long since moulted their feathers and grown new feathers to combat the cold and wet of the long, dark, winter days.

The old year soon passed and was talked about as an exceptionally good farming season among the Bowland farming community. They had all made a little bit more brass, with it being such a good year. Farming always relies on the weather. If it's too dry nothing grows, if it's too cold nothing grows, if it's too wet nothing grows, if it's too warm nothing grows. 1946 was the perfect combination. The perfect weather is enough rain and sun in the spring and summer, good weather in haytime and harvest and everybody is happy.

Unfortunately farmers cannot control the weather so you have to have what arrives, and, in general, one season balances with the next, hopefully. The spring of 1947 was totally out of balance and probably, the worst in the 20th century.

Most farms were equipped for a normal winter, which saw the odd few weeks of frost and snow, but not for the winter of 1947. The wind seemed to lock in from the North East in the early part of the New Year, drawing in cold, sub-zero temperatures from the Russian Siberian continent with persistent strong winds. This meant the early disappearance of the winter grass, which normally sustained the sheep with a little hay and cereals over the winter months. It was soon apparent that the normal allocated hay for our sheep and livestock was going to be far from adequate, so our hay stock soon started to diminish.

It was so cold that the sheep, even with their thick coat of wool, couldn't stand this intense wind and cold. The wind parted their fleeces and let in this cold wind and soon large losses of sheep occurred as the winter progressed. It was so cold that all the water supplies soon froze solid both to the farm buildings and the big farmhouse. This meant extra work for my father and the farm men. The water for the farmhouse had to be brought in milk churns to the backyard adjacent to the large kitchen door and stored indoors to stop it from freezing solid. The cows had to be released from the cow shed and driven to the nearest small stream some 200yds away from the farm buildings, this all took extra time. Water in the dairy had to be carried from the farmhouse kitchen boiler to wash the various dairy utensils. Actually they didn't require too much washing as it was so cold the fresh milk had little or no chance of going sour.

All the ponds and streams froze solid so we could use them for skating on. Our strong iron clad clogs made good skating shoes, far better than the posh leather boots some of the better-off children had to wear.

The river Ribble froze solid so you could walk from bank to bank without any thought of "Will the ice break?". The ice was at least 6″ thick. My father and mother advised us on where we could play safely on the ice, where the ponds and river were shallow.

The trees in the river valley were laden with ice and crystal formation on their branches. This caused widespread damage when the large branches snapped from the main tree trunk. It was a sight never before seen in the valleys of Bowland.

The bedrooms in our farmhouse were particularly cold so more blankets were stacked on the bed to keep the family warm at night. The frost crusted on the inside of the bedroom windows, so every morning we had to scrape the windows to see what kind of weather was to greet us that day. It was always the same, extra cold. Our clothes were so cold in a morning they were actually quite stiff before our body heat thawed them out.

All this time the wildlife in Bowland was taking a pounding with the cold weather. Each week, food, which was once plentiful began to disappear leaving sparse quantities to support the once independent birds and beasts.

The intense cold continued unabated over many weeks in the early part of 1947, but worse was to come in March. Snow fell in large quantities from the North Easterly direction, blocking all main roads and farm lanes, cutting off almost every farm in the Bowland area and adjacent counties in the North of England.

Our farm was some one and a half miles from the village of Bowland and was totally isolated. There was no help from the local Council or highway department as they had no modern equipment to remove the huge snowdrifts from the main roads in the Bowland and surrounding area.

Snow digging had all to be done by hand, so progress was very very slow. Many times, teams of farmers and farm men opened up the roads one day and found, the next morning, all the digging had been in vain because new snow had fallen and drifted to fill the newly dug out pathway.

We, in Bowland, were classed as lowland farmers where we thought the snow and cold was bad, but it was the farmers on the high moorland farms that got the worst of the storms. In one night of snow and blizzards many farmers lost their entire flock of sheep, buried under snow which had drifted over the high stone walls normally sheltering the sheep from the cold wind. Their sheep were buried under 6ft of snow. This was a far worse disaster than anything we had seen in Bowland. All that these farmers could do was to hope their farm dog could locate the sheep under the deep snowdrifts by its smell. Some dogs had better smelling capabilities than others and were far more successful locating the buried sheep. Many farmers probed the deep drifts with long rods of steel or wood hoping to find the buried sheep. If they were not found within a week of burial by snow, most would die of starvation or malnutrition.

The job for these farmers was also made worse by drifting snow and extra cold temperatures, making it impossible for rescue work to take place. Farmers told of sheep being found alive up to a fortnight after burial by the huge drifts of snow which had formed a cosy igloo, where they had no food or water available to sustain life.

My father had family friends who farmed on just such a moorland farm at a small Yorkshire village of Cowling. They farmed high up on the moor edge, adjacent to the tower that marked the highest point in the area. One day we got an urgent message asking could we get some hay and logs over to them, as they had no coal to heat the house to keep warm. They had felled the last tree for firewood and had only enough hay for a few days, to feed the remaining sheep of their once 200 head now down to below 20.

My father was always a good-hearted fellow and soon loaded an ex-army wagon with logs and hay to help relieve his farmer friends many miles away. This army wagon belonged to a local garage owner who agreed to take logs and hay to this stricken farmer. My father went with the load to show him the way. My mother had also baked a selection of cakes and pastries for my father to take to his friends. How she found the time with all the hard work she had feeding her own large family and staff, I don't know. But she could always find time for anyone in need.

I remember the day my father set off on his rescue mission. The wagon was piled high with urgent requirements with logs in the bottom of the lorry, probably enough for a month's needs. There were also kindling sticks which he took from the store-shed, where I had painstakingly chopped and stacked enough for a few weeks' supply when lighting our own farmhouse fires. There were also a few bags of coal from our coalstore. During winter months we always bought coal by the load so we never ran out during the very cold weather, so a few bags would not be missed.

On top of the wood and coal, hay was piled high similar, to the summer months when we gathered hay for our winterfeed by horse and cart. The wagon was equipped with large knobbly chains that never failed to get the wagon through a deep snowfall and also medium to large drifts. The petrol tank was filled to the brim, water and oil checked to make sure of a safe delivery of all the urgent requirements, also hoping that it would return to our farm in Bowland, with both driver and assistant safe, plus my lambs in good condition.

They arrived at Cowling a good few hours after leaving Bowland, on a journey of a lifetime, passing drifts literally as high as the wagon with stone walls just visible jutting out of six to eight feet drifts. Many houses had snowdrifts to eaves level, denying access to doors that had been used under normal conditions. Once the wagon was empty there was a return load to be loaded, namely the seven young sheep I had been given by the farmer. To get at the seven lambs was quite difficult, as they were approximately 50 yards away from the farmstead.

The small building was the last building before the large, extensive moor that would normally be purple with wild heather, a great sight in autumn. The building, I was told, was almost covered with snow, so, before my small flock could be loaded, a passageway had to be cleared to the building in order to gain access and rescue my lambs. My father could not believe that twenty sheep were huddled into such a small building, but seeing was believing. Normally, on the opposite side of the road was a wooden beer barrel kennel, where one of the farmer's dogs was chained. The purpose of the dog on a long chain at this point was to stop the sheep leaving the moor and straying down into Cowling village or surrounding farms. There was no sign of the barrel as it was many feet below a huge drift. There was also not a sheep in sight, so old Shep, the farmer's loyal sheep dog, was not required on duty. Instead of the residence with a moorland view, the farmer, for the first time ever, allowed Shep to take up residence with him over the long lonely night spent on this moorland farm. Having Shep as a companion probably took his mind off the suffering and loss of his flock of sheep that were still trapped under many feet of snow behind the high, sandstone, dry stone walls, with little or no chance of survival or escape from their tomb below the drifts.

Most farmers relied on their collie dogs for collecting the sheep from the moorland fells and pastures, and in most cases the dogs would work only for one master and be a devoted partnership for the dog's comparatively short life, hence the saying 'one man and his dog'. A farmer would have the same strain of dog on his farm for almost his entire life, with the young puppies seldom needing intensive training because rounding up sheep was literally in their blood.

On returning home this farmer had given my father seven 11-month-old lambs that he said I had to look after and, if they survived, I could have them for myself. I thought this was going to be my golden opportunity to start a thriving farming enterprise for myself. Seven young sheep for a youth of 12 years was unheard of in Bowland. All I had to do was keep them alive. I soon found out the condition of the young lambs when my father lowered the back door of the wagon. Normally they would have jumped out and escaped within seconds of seeing the wide-open space in the yard beyond. Not so with these undernourished, pitiful specimens. One was actually dead on arrival; obviously the poor creature had not been able to withstand the reasonably short journey from Cowling to Bowland. With the assistance of a farm-man, I managed to get the remaining six lambs into a stackshed at the rear of our farm. This, normally, would have been filled to the roof with meadow hay, but, in the spring of 1947, was half-empty and the ideal place to protect and feed the young lambs. Alas, what I thought would have been a fairly simple job of feeding and rebuilding the strength of my remaining 6 lambs proved very difficult.

I decided to feed them from a bottle with milk, which we had in abundance during the big freeze up, when milk could not be collected from the end of the farm lane. At the start, I thought I was going to be successful with my milk diet, but I soon found that their system could not cope with the new food. They seemed to get diarrhoea or scours and then simply died. It was only a matter of a week before the entire, prospective flock was dead. I had envisaged it would be the foundation stock for my future flock. I was upset and very disappointed after the hard work I had put into my project. All I had left was a large pile of corpses, which would have to be buried when the ground became free of frost in a few weeks' time. Normally I would have shed a few tears with the tragic loss of the young sheep, but death on our farm was nothing new in 1947 and we had all got accustomed to it.

As the weeks went by it soon became obvious that the wildlife in Bowland was beginning to suffer from the intense cold and lack of food. Daily we would notice that fewer birds like the blackbird and songthrush would visit our backyard adjacent to the farmhouse kitchen where my mother would throw out bread and large pieces of beef fat, all food for the many different birds, that were once plentiful around the farmstead.

The rabbits died in their hundreds because of the lack of food. They stripped the bark from all the thorn trees to several feet from the ground where the snow had drifted and acted as a ladder for them to stand on. Where my father would shoot a couple of rabbits for a pie, they had starved and become so thin that they weren't worth shooting as there literally wasn't one ounce of meat on them. The Seka Deer also became so hungry they would come to the stack of hay behind our farm and feed, something never seen, or heard of, before.

The fields became a sheet of ice after the days of a slight thaw and then intense frost at night. During all this cold weather my parents insisted that we had to go to school. The only bonus, if you could call it that, was that it was very cold but dry. During the cold winter my Grandma had knitted long woolly knee length stockings, woolly helmets with a narrow hole to see through, long, wide scarves, which went about twice around you and then secured with a large safety pin at the back. She also knitted all the family a pair of mittens. These were stitched to a length of elastic and then threaded through our jacket sleeves, so it was impossible to lose them. We also knew that they were our mittens once threaded into our jacket sleeves, so there was no argument as to which mittens belonged to whom.

During all the extreme cold our family coped reasonably well. We had plenty to eat, which was most important during that period. The food available was mostly the same from week to week and all from the carefully conserved and bulk purchased items prior to the storm. My mother was a good hand at making a nourishing meal out of the least expected ingredients. This, I believe, was knowledge handed down over generations of our farming families.

It was a time when we found out just how vital were the large white pigs we had killed prior to Christmas, as many meals were based on different cuts of meat and offal from pig. There was, obviously, bacon, which was fried for breakfast and mostly fat with a streak of lean in it, just what was needed to keep out the cold. Ham would be roasted, potted pork for stews and pies, the dripping or fat would be spread on toast, the pig trotters had, long since, been eaten, as we had no method of storing them. We did have certain dishes, which had been sealed with a layer of hot fat, and, when set, made a perfect seal for the various meats underneath. A boiled ham shank was a tasty meal when mixed with vegetables and made into a really thick broth.

Two pet rabbits in a pie with a thick crust and plenty of onions, carrots and potatoes was always a very wholesome meal. We, as children, always used to try and find a rabbit egg, which wasn't really an egg at all but the rabbit's kidney. Obviously, we weren't always successful as there was only 4 kidneys in the pie.

There was always plenty of porridge to start the day. This was assured by the amount of oatmeal we had in store. We always bought a 140lb sack of oatmeal, likewise with flour and sugar. Salt was always in big 14lb blocks, syrup in 1 gallon tins, onions by the bag and apples by the case. They were all basic ingredients, nothing fancy, all items from which my mother could make a meal to satisfy farm men and family without much difficulty. A bonus for our family was that, during the very cold spell, none of us suffered from any major, or, in fact, minor illness. I think it was a case of it was far too cold for a common cold or an epidemic of flu or any of the minor ailment children get at school. As the storm continued, being the eldest son, I was kept off school to help on the farm, not so much with the manual work but with the feeding of livestock.

My main job was to feed a small herd of sheep we had at the other side of Bowland Village on a farm we rented from the estate. This was approximately 1.5 miles from the home farm. Each day I was expected to take a large sack of hay to feed and sustain the small flock. This was no easy task under such weather conditions. However, with the necessity to deliver the sack of hay daily we had to improvise a method of transport. My father made a much larger sledge than the ones we normally used on the hills and slopes around the farm. This was to be towed, not by a reindeer, which would have been the most suitable animal under the arctic conditions, but by Molly, our small family pony. To tow a sledge so big, Molly had to be fitted out with a set of harness that in the spring of 1947 had never been thought of, let alone required. It was up to my father to produce a basic set, so the sledge could be pulled with relative comfort by Molly. It was not too difficult for my father to make a useable set of harness, with the many leather straps and buckles he had lying around the farm, that had been used on the large carthorse harness. The completed harness looked far from professional, but it did the job. When driving through the village the local farmers enquired who made the harness and I replied, "My father". They then remarked they thought he had. In fact, the whole sledge, driver and pony was an improvisation.

My clothes were also home made, but did the job keeping out almost all the cold. I suffered badly frostbitten ears that caused large, sore scabs that bled regularly. I remember, it was very painful when I tried to wash them. I had chilblains on almost every toe. These were once again very painful, especially at nights, when we huddled around the large kitchen fire. The cure was 'snowfire' ointment or rubbing with snow. The suggested old-fashioned remedy was to soak them in the jerry. This may have worked, but I never tried it. My small fingers also became very frost bitten and had deep sore cracks, which were the most painful sores of the cold weather.

The villagers soon got to know that I was the only lifeline the small herd of sheep had. They knew more or less the exact time I would pass through the village, sitting on top of the large bag of hay that was tied firmly onto the large wooden sledge. Drawn by Molly, our small family pony, it was a most unlikely and unusual sight, but, unfortunately, no photos ever recorded the unusual method of transporting.

After feeding my small flock of sheep, on returning home, I would have to call at the local Co-op shop in Bowland to collect groceries for the family table. The assistants at the Co-op would put all the family requirements for that day in a strong cardboard box that was secured to the large wooden sledge. This formed a fairly comfortable seat for the remainder of my journey home. Molly soon realised it was time to head back to the farm and needed little or no signal from me to set off at a brisk trot.

My education suffered during the last weeks of the winter of 1947. This didn't bother my parents, as the welfare of the farm livestock was more important. Once the big thaw arrived it soon became obvious the loss and devastation the long cold winter had caused. When walking to school there was not a young rabbit in sight as all had perished through the persistent cold. The once abundant bird song of Bowland had disappeared, with the loss of almost all our birds; the blackbirds and songthrush seemed to have totally disappeared. There were a few of the scavenger type birds such as the rook, carrion crow and magpie, which had more food available with the abundance of dead livestock which had lain unburied during the cold spell.

The fields were a reddy-brown colour, burnt by the intense cold. However, these soon seemed to recover once the spring sunshine arrived with the warmer south west winds and April showers. The River Ribble, once frozen solid, started to thaw, with cracks and bangs as the 6" thick ice disintegrated and started to flow down the river with the spring flood, caused by snow melting on the high ground at the head of the river. The large iceflows caused extensive damage to the many trees adjacent to the riverbank.

The ground soon became soft again after being frozen solid up to 18" deep. This allowed farmers in the Bowland and surrounding areas to bury their dead livestock. This was the time to count the cost of the storm. Dead sheep weren't going to produce the spring lambs the farmers had counted on to pay rent and expenses during the coming summer and autumn.

Many trees had died through cold. Some had been so completely barked by the rabbits and sheep they had to be felled for firewood. The farmyard manure heaps, or middens, soon defrosted so the farmers could get rid of the huge piles which had accumulated at the farmsteads. The small heaps could be spread in the fields that normally would have been spread months ago.

It was late April early May before we expected the return of the migratory birds. True to form, these all arrived back probably unaware of the hard winter and loss of many song bird species. For myself, it was back to full schooling and, for our family, a relief that the cold weather had finished. It was goodbye to scarves, gloves, helmets and leggings. For my parents it must have been a relief from worry and extra work the winter had caused.

Spring soon cancelled out the thoughts and facts of the Great Storm of 1947 for many farmers in Bowland. Even though I was only young at the time, it was an experience I will never forget. Old Tim, the farm dog, and Molly, the family pony, they soon cast their thick winter coats to the much finer summer coat of hair. But alas, the robins that disappeared during the later part of the winter never reappeared. The chestnut trees that lined the village green of Bowland village soon came into full leaf and flower leaving our village one of the prettiest villages in the Ribble Valley.

The cows and horses were released from their winter accommodation to the summer pastures, where they pranced and jumped with ease and joy. The process of reproduction once again started with all the various furry and feathered species pairing up to reproduce their offspring and the next generation of young. These were markedly less than in a normal spring, due to the exceptionally hard winter.

It was also time to have a hair cut, as, during the winter months, it was so cold my father never cut our hair, for obvious reasons. My father was not a good haircutter and his instruments were never sharp. Sometimes he would use the horse shears that were worked by hand. Most times with a pair of blunt scissors the end result was a jagged cut with short top and sides.

Home Cured Bacon

Many townspeople thought that bacon just appeared in the butcher's shop window in various grades and qualities. There would be lean, streaky, smoked, rolled, dry cured and wet cured.

Not many actually thought of the work and skill the farmers and pig breeders put into producing that breakfast time stapel meal. Served with a big basin of porridge, home cured bacon, a freshly laid farm egg, a few slices of thick home baked bread, plastered with fresh farm butter, swilled down with a pot of hot tea, and you were well fed for the strenuous hours of hard work that lay ahead during the day.

It was always reckoned that the breakfast was the most vital meal of the day. When working with livestock and on the land, most of the jobs were manual, hard work that swallowed up the calories. Seldom did you see the farmers and farm men suffering from the problem of overweight. Mostly they were muscular and lean; slimming problems never entered the conversations.

Not every farmer kept pigs. There were always a few in Bowland that were classed as pig breeders. These farmers would keep maybe 3 or 4 sows and a boar. From this stock base, farmers would order a couple of strong 8-week old pigs for their own household consumption. These, when cured or potted, would last the farmer's family and staff a full twelve months in bacon, ham and various preserved products.

There was a set pattern every year when buying these young store pigs. They were always bought from the same farm that you had done for many years previously. The pig breeder always knew just which young pigs would be suitable. They were always large whites that had plenty of growing potential, both to grow in length and width. Seldom did the thought of a thin, lean pig enter our father's head when buying our future twelve months' pork and bacon supply.

On occasions, my father would visit the pig breeder to see the quality of the sows and boars. If we were lucky, one or two of us would be allowed to travel in the horse and cart with him. We were probably just as excited, going to see the sows with six to ten young piglets, as would be our counterparts out of the town. It was quite spectacular, seeing these litters of piglets fighting and squealing for their own individual teat or nipple on the mother sow. For the first few hours after being born each young piglet had its own teat. It was always the case that the strongest, well fed, young piglets sucked the teats nearest to the sow's head, the weakest one was always at the back, which obviously produced less milk.

My father would always request he wanted two good, strong sorts and not them that had been sucking a back teat. He would also make sure that the piglets were spotlessly clean in their bedding and sty. Clean pigs were always thrifty growers and much easier to manage than the ones that fouled their bed areas. The clean pigs, even from an early stage of life never fouled their bed area; this was something no other farm animal would do. They seemed to learn where to do their droppings from the mother sow who would, literally, back up into the farthest corner from the bed, when nature called. These pigs were obviously far easier to keep clean for the farmer than the dirty pigs.

Once satisfied that the pigs were of a good healthy quality my father would arrange for them to be delivered, when they were of a suitable size and age and when we had room in one of the cowsheds, which were empty of cows from the winter period, normally the first week in May. The pig breeder always seemed to know this date as he always came on the same Saturday morning every year.

The mode of transporting these two fine specimens from the pig breeder never varied. It was the same bay, Clydesdale mare, with a broad white blaze, forehead to nose, that had delivered our couple of pigs for many years. The cart also, was the one he had used and was the one he delivered his kits, or churns of milk, to the end of his farm track, where it was collected by the local dairy. The only alteration to the trap type cart, was that he had put the tail door back on its hinges, and a heavy mesh net fixed to the top of the cart, to stop the piglets jumping overboard and escaping. If one of these young pigs did escape it was no mean task trying to catch one, especially if it was a wet morning. In fact at our local Sports and Show there was usually a sideshow where you paid a few bob to catch the slippery pig in a minute. Mostly the pigcatchers lost. The pigcatchers were always the macho type, farmers' sons or farm men who fancied their chances of catching the pig and showing off a bit in public.

Before the pigs were due to arrive the cowshed had to be prepared. The shed would be whitewashed with a lime and water mixture. This helped brighten the place up and also helped keep out flies in the summer months. The sad thing about these two little porkies was that this was going to be their second and last home. Once the whitewash was dry, the old stone pigtrough had to be manually lifted into its proper place in the corner of the pigsty. This trough had been shaped out of a large, solid piece of sandstone to form the shape of a trough. These were far superior to a standard, galvanised, iron trough or bucket. The main reason was that the pig could not get its snout under it and turn it the wrong side up and spill all the pigfeed. Today these troughs are sought after as antique flower containers. They sell for scores of pounds each, representing many weeks' wages for the poor old stonemason who painstakingly shaped the trough with sweat and skill.

All the family waited eagerly for the arrival of the two little grunters. As in previous years, they were unloaded and put in their new home, which they inspected from wall to wall then rustled among the golden straw that formed their new bed. It wasn't long before they decided that it was time for a good long snooze, curling up among the golden straw. They didn't seem to be bothered about parting from their mother and fellow piglets. It was now time for father to bargain the price of these two new arrivals, which was always an interesting time. My father would try to convince the pig farmer that the pigs weren't as good in quality and size as the two he got last year. The pig farmer would reply by saying his pig was much bigger than last year's and that the cost of pig feed was more expensive. However, it was not long before both had agreed the final price and, with a loud slap of hands, the deal was complete, and a large Martin's chequebook was produced by my father for the final payment.

Soon, the horse and pig farmer was leaving the farmstead, probably not to be seen again for another 12 months, when two more piglets would be required for another years' bacon. From then on it was fairly straightforward; all that the pigs were expected to do was to eat all the food required to make them grow into a 20 score pounds bacon pig. Father always fed them just enough food, so that, at every meal all the food was eaten in just ten minutes and none was ever left for the rats, which always visited the pigsty to devour any leftovers.

The piglets soon settled down to their new surroundings, and menu, and soon were growing at a fast pace putting many more rashers of bacon on each day they lived. The growing pigs would not be let out into the lush green pastures for exercise without pig rings being inserted into the rim of the pig's nose, to stop them ploughing up large areas of ground with their strong snouts. It was amazing, the amount of turf the two pigs could upturn in a short period of time.

During the next few months it was mostly a case of eating and sleeping for the two fast growing youngsters. They would always be fed at the same time, within minutes, every day, on almost exactly the same menu. This would consist of all fresh ground cereals of corn maize and barley meal, plus a small amount of fishmeal for extra protein. One very important point was never to feed the pigs too much fishmeal, or it would taint the final product of home cured bacon. There was nothing worse than bacon smelling of fish when frying on the open fire grill. If, however, fishmeal was not available, a compromise would be used in the form of cod liver oil. This was similar to the cod-liver oil issued at schools and doctors' surgeries to supplement the deficiency of protein in the human diet during the war, and just afterwards.

Seldom was there any household waste left over for the pigs, even with such a large family as ours, with eleven in total at every meal. It was the case that, if you didn't eat everything up, you wouldn't get any of the next course. The saying was, "Tha will get nowt else until tha's eaten that".

So the pigs never, or hardly ever, got household scraps. If there were any household scraps these always went to the farm dogs. The months went by and the two porkies became larger. They were now finding it difficult for both to lie down in the same bed and turn around in the confined space of the temporary pigsty. The golden straw had long been discarded for the permanent railway sleepers timber which formed the raised bed area. The timber was always warm laying for the pigs, which was far better than the paved sett areas, which were standard in the cattle shed. Remarkably, the bed was perfectly clean, with not a sign of dung in sight. There were just a few short white pig bristles, or hair, that the pigs shed naturally during their period of residence.

Autumn was fast approaching and the trees were changing from that rich green foliage to the autumn tints, which, in Bowland, were spectacular at that time of the year. There were not the massive plantations of the softwood spruce and larch trees, as in some areas, but a varied selection of hardwoods, which had obviously been planted by the Lords of the manor many scores, or even hundreds, of years previously.

There would be the large beech, oak, ash and chestnut, all adding to that stunning variation of Autumn tints. Also came the fruits of the forest, which had grown and matured from the earlier spring blossoms. We collected these fruits for the household, blackberries, hazelnuts, sloes, crab apples and self seeded plums, damson, rose hips and elderberry.

We also had to collect for the two porkies. This was mainly crab apples and acorns from under the large, mature oaks. We could shake crab apples from the tree branches, then we would load them into the farm barrow. Many barrowfuls could be collected from a single tree, especially if it was a good season for growing fruit. Once collected, we would pile them up in a corner of the farmyard ready for feeding to the large pigs. We found that a bucketful at one meal, was plenty.

These crab apples were far too sour for human consumption, but the two pigs were never bothered by the bitterness of their extra diet. Acorns were always sought after by many wild birds and animals. Among the birds would be rooks, carrion crows and wood pigeon. Small animals would include mice, rats, rabbits and the red squirrels. The squirrel would take acorns for storage and hide them in various places. It might be a hole in a tree, or disused rabbit burrow, or, in most cases, a hole just below the surface, which it had scratched out itself.

There would be many storage sites for the winter's food for the squirrel. How they remembered all the burial sites, months after, was quite remarkable. We would get orders from my father to go and gather acorns for the pigs. A small, farm type, bucket was ideal, which held many hundreds of acorns each. One bucketful was about the correct amount for a single meal for the two, by now, huge pigs. They always seemed to know when a meal of acorns was about to be served. They would be standing on hind legs and peering over the pigsty door, which was a good 3 foot high.

When feeding acorns we never used the old stone pigtrough, because one pig could always eat faster than the other, eating well above its fair share. We simply threw them over the door into the pigsty for them to rummage. This made their tasty meal last much longer than normal. The noise the pig made crunching acorns was quite remarkable. After about ten minutes the noise would cease and there would be not a sign of an acorn; all had been sought out and devoured.

The day of reckoning for these fast growing pigs was rapidly approaching. But first that extra ingredient to their diet had to be added by my father. He always insisted on a pack of oatmeal. This weighed 140lbs, which, he believed, was necessary to put on those extra rashers of fatty bacon before slaughter.

The first pig would be slaughtered in late November to early December. This was when the chill of winter had arrived, and there was likelihood of frost. The reason for this was that the cold weather would help keep the carcass fresh, and all the various dishes that were made when killing a pig. The almost true saying was that the only part wasted when killing a pig was its squeak.

During the war, before you could kill a pig you had to notify the police and the Ministry of Agriculture, Fisheries and Food. This was to ensure that you weren't killing too many pigs for your particular family, as pork and bacon at that period was available only with coupons and a ration book. Many farmers would keep a few extra pigs for the 'black market' and dispose of them for cash to influential customers in town. The local bobbies always did well out of these farmers with eggs, pork and bacon for turning a blind eye to their activities.

As the day for slaughtering the first pig drew closer there was much to prepare. What you must remember was, that there would be in the region of two hundred and fifty pounds of meat to deal with before it went bad. There was no cold storage to help preserve the carcass. My father's first job was to find his butchering knives; these had been stored away in a safe place since killing last years' pigs. They were never allowed to be used for general household carving. He would get out the old sharpening stone and have a razor sharp edge on both knives.

The old set boiler in the corner of the kitchen would be lit. The old steel candlestick had to be found. This was used as a scraper, to remove the bristles from the pig; another of my father's innovations. There was also the washing line type cord to be found; this was used to tie the pig's legs, to stop it escaping, and also its mouth, to stop it biting you.

There was the old oak bench, or stock, on which had been stored bags of cattle feed. This had to be scrubbed and cleaned. A large block of salt had to be purchased and cut up for the curing of the hams and bacon. Empty store jars that were used for potting the pork had to be found and washed in readiness for the huge amount of pork and fat.

Bacon string had to be bought for rolling the large slabs of fatty bacon into rolls. Various herbs, that were home grown, had to be ground for seasoning the sausage, savouries and black puddings. The large ash logs had to be split and ready for the fires to boil the water. Approximately 35 to 70 gallons would be required to scalp the bristles on the pig's carcass. Roasting tins were scoured clean, ready for rendering the excess fat down for baking lard, or the chip-pan. Basins of every shape and size were found, to be used for brawn or potted meat. This was made from the pig's head, neck and tail.

We decided on the day for pig killing to take place. No food would be given to either pig the previous day. This was because a pig was far easier to dress when its stomach wasn't gorged with food. I was only young at this time, but I had to stop off school on father's orders, even at the tender age of ten. There was a job for me on pig killing day and it wasn't very pleasant. My father allocated to me the job of catching blood. I had a three gallon bucket with a small handful of salt in the bottom and a large wooden mixing spoon. Once there was sufficient blood in the bucket I had to take it to the well in the farmyard and stir until it was stone cold. This could take up to an hour by which time my arm was aching and nearly dropping off.

The day finally arrived and there was an extra early rise at the farmstead. Milking was completed early, the dairy was swilled clean, and all signs of dairy utensils removed, as the dairy was the catching and killing area.

Fires were lit early to boil the large amount of water that was required to complete the dressing of the carcass. The first problem was to get this 20 score pounds pig out of its sty and into the dairy. From the word go the pig must have sensed its fate and was reluctant to move an inch without some type of enticement. So a small bucket of pig food had to be offered to this large animal. Being hungry, the pig followed the bucket of bait into the dairy where the door was shut firmly behind it. There was no escaping from now on. The next problem was to tie the pig's mouth in order not to get a very vicious, painful bite.

This was very difficult, because the pig had no intention, at this stage, of co-operating with anybody. My father was fairly skilful at lasso-ing the pig round the nose, and, in no time, had it totally bound so that it could not bite. Next, we had to tie its legs, so it couldn't kick and scratch. This had to be done once the pig was on the bench or stock. This was, probably, the hardest job to do. Remember, the total weight of this large pig was around 400lbs and by this time it was more than uncooperative. Also, by this time, it was quite wet, which made it as slippery as an eel to handle.

Once on the bench, my father performed the final episode in quick time. The pig was soon dead. I had done what I had stopped off school for and caught a good 2.5 gallons of blood and was instructed to take it to the well and stir until it was cold. This took a good hour before I was allowed to stop stirring. By this time the work on the carcass had progressed and many buckets of boiling water had been ferried from the farmhouse kitchen to the dairy to scald the bristles from the carcass. Any sign of dirt on the pig's body was fast diminishing. Soon it was the big pull, this was when the body had to be hoisted from the bench to the roof for final cleaning. This was no mean task with such a huge pig; it took 4 men to hoist it into the correct position. Father soon put the final touch to the carcass with a few buckets of fresh springwater. The carcass was spotlessly clean, and you could now sense the home cured bacon was a step nearer the frying pan.

I had to go into the house to change my clothes as there was lots of blood on my pants and jersey. My father's remarks were that it was all good training and it was best to learn young. In the house the side oven on the old cast iron fireplace was warmed up ready for a session of making black pudding. My mother had made black pudding for many years with, more or less, her own recipe. There was, obviously, pig's blood, which had been sieved through a fine copper wire sieve, boiled barley, small chunks of fat plus various home grown herbs. My mother never used skins for her black pudding, she simply made them in large tin roasting trays usually about 1 1/2 inches deep. When sliced and fried the pudding had a delicious, home made taste.

Black pudding and liver were always the first dishes we ate after killing the pig. There were many more to follow, such as scratching, brawn, savoury duck and pig's trotters. All these dishes were cooked to my mother's recipes which she probably acquired from her parents and, most likely, their parents before them.

The pig's main carcass would be left to hang for two days to get perfectly cold, making it much easier to cut into hams and joints plus all the other by products that came out of the pig's carcass. My father was fairly skilful when cutting up a large carcass into various joints and dishes. Likewise, my mother knew just how to cope with scores of pounds of various parts of the pig. The side oven would be on for many days, cooking all the meat that was not going to be salt cured for hams and bacon.

There were at least 40lbs of pure fat which all had to be cut into small cubes. This was to be rendered down for baking, chip pan and lard. After the rendering you would end up with pork scraps which were very tasty between two thick slices of bread with seasoning. Small bits of pork and liver would be minced, bread and herbs would be added for pate or savoury duck, as it was then called. This we would eat as a main meal with fresh baked bread. There was potted meat or brawn. This was mainly the pig's head and tail which had been cut into sections, boiled, seasoned and all the small bones removed, then poured into moulds or basins and left to cool. This, again, would be eaten for a main meal with mashed potatoes or chips.

One of the tastiest of dishes was the pig's feet or trotters. These my mother would boil in a pan on the open fire for a couple of hours until they literally fell apart. We would have these for supper with plenty of vinegar, salt and pepper. There wasn't a lot of meat on them and you always needed a big plate for the surplus bones of which there were always plenty. It was a slippery, greasy dish and you needed a swill under the kitchen tap afterwards. Small pieces of pork were packed in large 7lb earthenware jars, then boiled until cooked in the side oven. Once cooked, warm pork fat would be poured on top of the pork. This was to preserve pork for many months until required.

Fried liver and kidneys was the meal of the day. This we would eat until all was used up quickly, as no method of preservation was available. For many days it was pig meat products for breakfast, dinner, tea and supper. We often said by the time we had eaten through this pile of pig meat we would all be grunting.

The work on the pig's carcass was still far from complete. Curing of the bacon was still to do. The large stone bench slabs in the lower pantry had to be cleaned to make way for the large slabs of bacon. The slab, or sides, were a good 4 feet long x 2 feet wide x 3 inches deep. These my father laid out flat ready to cover in salt which had been previously sliced and crushed from the large cobs of salt bought purposely for the curing process.

Hams would be laid on top of the slabs of bacon, then salt would be piled on top of the mass of bacon and ham. Finally the pig's cheek would be laid on top of the pile of meat and salted. The cheek was always the first bacon ready for eating; this was after 14 days in salt. After salting all the bacon and hams many hours of work had to be done on them. First, the pig's cheek would be washed clean of salt and a piece of bacon string would be inserted into the lip of the cheek to be used as a method of hanging to suspend it from the old oak beam in the kitchen ceiling. After a period of 14 days the pig cheek would be ready for eating. The cheek was reasonably lean, compared with the last year's rolls of bacon which, by now, were all finished.

The sides of bacon were always left in the salt for about 3 weeks before being removed and washed ready for rolling. There was plenty of hard work in making a large flat slab of bacon into a roll. My father had acquired this skill over many years. He had his own ideas and methods on how to create a perfect roll and there were no specific tools for this job. He used his own personal leather belt which was a good 1 1/2 inches wide with a big brass buckle. The only difference was that he had made extra holes in it to make it small enough to be tightened around the roll.

He would take the stirrup leathers for the hunting or riding saddle and utilise them for the tensioning of the roll. He would get a lightweight wooden mall, or hammer, from the farm workshop to pound these extra thick sides of bacon into a roll, leaving no air space in the centre of the roll. There would be a roll of bacon twine, or cord, which would be firmly tied round the roll to avoid any risk of air, or foreign bodies, entering the roll. It would be a full night's work, rolling the bacon.

After rolling, it would be hung on the hooks in the coldest part of the house to dry or until a roll was required. The best place was up the staircase leading to the bedrooms. These were always a long way from the steps and very difficult to hang that huge roll of bacon so high from the floor.

It was a rewarding sight looking up at two huge rolls of bacon and two large hams thinking that, at least, we will have enough bacon for the next 6 months. You never thought of the poor little porky that arrived by horse and cart 6 months previously. Being farmers of livestock you never got too attached to any particular farm animal, because you could never afford to keep it as a pet. It was the farmer's job to feed the nation in those years when food was scarce, and also your own family. After drying out for a few weeks the bacon would be ready for eating. It was always interesting when tasting the new season's bacon, would it be salty or not salty enough, would it be lean or too fatty? The answer to the last question was simple, the rolls contained very little lean. The pack of oatmeal had made sure that the percentage of lean to fat was in favour of fat. It was just what my father required. He believed in plenty of fat to keep out the cold and grease your inside or bowel. There was no doubt your bowel was going to get well greased with the new season's bacon.

The bacon was always kept for a long time so the rind on the roll was rock hard. Also, the fat was by now going a little rancid. This didn't improve the taste, but we had it to eat. Some summers would be very thundery and warm. This always increased the problem of bluebottles, that, no matter how careful you were, sometimes got into the area where the rolls of bacon or hams were stored. They would lay their eggs, unnoticed, on the roll of bacon. The first thing you would know about such happenings was when going up to bed at night and finding the odd maggot or two meeting you on the stairs. It was then time to lift the affected roll down and open it up and cut out the affected part, leaving the rest for consumption, be it boiled or fried. There was never a hint that the maggots had been present at breakfast time when having bacon and egg, or at teatime, when having a cold bacon sandwich or salad.

Was all the hard work worth it? I believe it was, when eating our own home cured bacon.

The twelve months had soon passed and the two new porkies had arrived once more. These were doomed to the same fate, ending on the kitchen table.

That's what farming is all about!

Brown Rat

Over the centuries vermin and disease have plagued both town dwellers and farmers. The diseases can be transmitted in many different ways; by birds, by the wind or by small animals like the fox, badger, magpie, starling or carrion crow. But by far the biggest carrier, as far as we farmers were concerned, was the brown rat, which could always be found wherever food was available. The brown rat is a versatile creature, able to live in either cold or warm climates. To cope with the cold, it simply grows more hair or fur, less where it is warm.

Its habitat varies immensely. The rat is at home in a multitude of surroundings. It can make its nest under a poultry cabin, in an embankment, in a stone wall or a riverbank, in a haystack or in bags of grain. It could even house itself in farm buildings, the farmhouse, the pigsty, or anywhere where there is a readily available supply of food and he is not much interested in whether the venue is dirty or not. He will do untold damage gaining access to the food store, by chewing holes in the hessian sacks and letting all the grain run out onto the floor, or by chewing through timber bins, water pipes, floor boards and under doors. There is no place he cannot penetrate.

I have experience of rats on the farm, acquired, at an early age from my parents and the farm men. I was always taught to respect the rat and warned never to get close enough to be bitten as they had sharp dentures which were, in most cases, poisonous or were carrying some disease. For all of us, it was a case of once bitten twice shy, and when we came in contact with rats we made sure we were well armed and at arm's length.

My memories of the rats remain vivid. The farmhouse roof was their place of residence. When I was young, I was easily frightened by the antics they performed above the bedroom ceiling. Generally, they slept during the day unless they were unwell or had taken poison, then they would be seen during daylight hours, but they were often dopey and not so alert. We could dispose of them fairly easily, either by shooting them with the old Webley Scott air rifle or clobbering them with a stout hazel stick from the hedgerow. Sometimes the farm dog would put an end to the rat's suffering with a sharp firm bite and a flick of the neck, throwing the rat well clear to avoid being bitten.

The healthy rat, however, was shrewder and would come out after dark. In my experience they came out when I was in bed. Quite often they made their nests in the farmhouse's random built stone walls and could circulate to any part of the house by a series of tunnels and holes. Some had set up home in the farmhouse roof, which was an ideal place, because it was nice and warm. They seemed to rise about 8 p.m. and I think this must have been the time they flexed their muscles over our bedroom, at a height of about six foot above the bed. I think they thought it was a racetrack. They appeared to run to and fro at great speed, squeaking as they went. I always felt that at any moment the roof would come falling in.

One of the most frightening experiences was when the rat ventured into my bedroom. The first things I missed were my socks which I always threw on the floor when I took them off. At first I accused my brother of stealing them, which he flatly denied. He let me look in his drawers and other possible hiding places, but after a thorough search there was no sign of my socks. I was still not convinced that he didn't know where they were and the next night, as I got undressed, I left all my clothes in a heap. On this night it was a new pair of stockings my grandma had knitted that went missing. I didn't often get new socks, mine were generally hand-downs, so I needed to find them.

It was very cold in the long room where we all slept in winter. No heating, no double glazing, just sheets, army blankets and an eiderdown. The window, in the morning, had a crisp coating of frost on the inside, which we used to scrape off so we could look out to see what the weather was like outside. Once I got warm, and the rats above the ceiling had finished training and settled down to hunting for their breakfast or first meal of their day, I slept well, soundly and long. Each morning we were woken, not by the ring of the alarm clock, but by a good bellow from my father. I had no fancy pyjamas; I slept in a vest and shirt, so I only had trousers, socks and a waistcoat to put on in the morning. My trousers, I remember, were exceptionally cold. They crackled and were very cold to the skin and bum -underpants were unheard of in our house. There was no electric light, so finding my socks was more of a search by hand than a visual scan. This particular morning there was no sign of my new socks. I asked my brother, but he assured me that he hadn't taken them and I didn't challenge his words. It was a case of waiting until it became a bit lighter, then searching the bedroom - not a pleasant thought on such a cold morning. The oilcloth on the bedroom floor was slippery and exceptionally cold to the feet.

At last, light dawned and we were able to make a thorough search, but, although we checked in every corner and under the bed, we drew a blank. I was very annoyed and, although I only had a small vocabulary, I found words suitable to describe my feelings. The only other place I could think of looking was in the fireplace. "What the hell is the use of looking in the fireplace; it's over the other end of the bedroom", my brother said. But it was our last chance.

The fireplace was an old cast iron black-leaded one, which had probably been there since the house was built. It had a low fender and a surround decorated with half moon shapes with a brass ring in the middle. There was no ash pan, just the sandstone flags to form the base, so the fire was only ever lit when someone was ill. We pulled the half-moon surround away and it revealed one of my new pair of socks, but the other was nowhere to be seen. I immediately accused my brother of hiding it there, but again he denied all knowledge of it. On further inspection we found a hole about three inches in diameter. It didn't take us long to realise that this was not a mouse hole, but a rat hole. It must have been a large rat to need a hole so large. The normal way of persuading the creatures out of their dwelling was to break bottles and stuff them in the hole, but as this rat was obviously so big, we decided that the glass would be more likely to be scratched out by the rat.

A trap was the answer. There were two kinds; a box trap or a gin trap. We decided not to use the box trap as the rat had to be tempted into it with food, and if not tempted, would be likely to roam the bedroom - not a nice thought, particularly if it made use of the bed. No, a gin trap would be the best. There was one in the workshop, somewhere amongst the saws, axes, hay forks, muck forks, cart harness and chains. Eventually we found it and took it back to the bedroom.

The gin trap is similar to, but smaller than, the original mantraps and very powerful and it was a skilled job to set it. We depressed the spring and set the pressure plate very lightly, so that at the slightest touch the trap would be released. We slid it into position in the fireplace, placing a couple of bricks either side of it so as to make a passage way for the rat. We retired early to bed, but there was no chance of us sleeping. Waiting for the rat was a bit like waiting for Father Christmas, ears cocked and one eye always open; ready for any sound or sighting.

An hour later and we were in total darkness. Suddenly there was one hell of a shriek, followed by the rat-trap banging down. My sock thief had got his just deserts. We had taken candles in the bedroom just in case the rat came back for the other sock. Opening up the fireplace we encountered the biggest brown rat you can imagine; trapped, but not yet dead and still able and angry enough to use his large teeth to bite us with if we got too close. The question now was what did we do with our unwelcome foe at this hour of the night? The poker was handy and thus our only weapon. We had to put the rat out of its misery and did so by administering a powerful blow to its head. As a temporary measure, we filled the rat hole with a stone, just in case there were more of them. Having lost one of my new socks, I wasn't prepared to lose the other and I would now have to make do with my old ones. That night we slept well and the next day we repaired the fireplace wall and had, we hoped, put an end to our late night bedroom visitor once and for all.

It was not the end of rats, however; they were always there. The young rats infested the farm buildings, poultry cabins and hedgerows, for here they had comparatively safe access to food and water. As children we often passed our time catching the young ones, particularly those which lived in the stone walls of the pigsty where their mother had scratched out the plaster and burrowed into the inner cavity to build her nest. She was no fool; the hiding place was safe, with food and water in close proximity - a good location to rear her young.

The young rats were always born totally blind and would probably be so for about fourteen days, and then it would be another fourteen before they started to move around within the nesting area. After that it was not long before they ventured out of the nest to look for their own food. They always came out in semi-daylight and always into the pigsty; it was at this point that we young rat catchers came into our own. We had no fancy traps for this work, no air guns or dogs, just a homemade drop trap. To make this we used a relatively heavy picture frame there was always one to be found in the loft above the coal and wood shed. We took the glass out and stapled some fine wire netting onto the frame. To complete the device we needed a long length of binding twine or string and a piece of wood about a foot long. It was important that we sited the trap in the right position and that we also placed ourselves in the best vantage point from which to see the young rats. But firstly, and more importantly, we had to remove the pigs from their sty. This was not as difficult a problem as you would expect. First we made sure all the farmyard gates were shut, then opened the sty door. Within seconds, Porky was pounding across the farmyard and heading for a roll in the nearest mucky puddle or in the midden. In less than a minute, instead of being a large white, the pig was a large black and smelling strongly of cow muck.

Silently, so as not to forewarn the rats, we would enter the pigsty to set the trap close to the hole from which the young ones would appear. We needed to be able to see both the young rats and the trap, and the best place was in the granary loft overlooking the pigsty. Our excitement was growing. With luck, it wouldn't be long before our first catch. To set the trap, we propped up one end with the twelve-inch long piece of wood we had attached to one end of the length of binding twine. The other end we fed to our hiding place. Leaving the pigsty, we made sure its door was firmly closed to prevent Porky coming back in to wreck our sport, then ran round the outside of the barn, through the big door and up the granary steps to our vantage point. Checking the binding twine was tight enough, we sat and waited, relishing the thought we were only a tug away from success. We waited about half an hour, not daring to utter a word, in case we warned the rats of our presence.

The light was beginning to fade and the catching area was becoming less visible. Suddenly, a young rat appeared, slightly larger than a mouse. It ran around, keeping about a foot away from the hole, then disappeared into its hiding place again. I decided that this was probably the messenger rat, surveying the ground, then returning to report its findings. It was several minutes before it reappeared, but this time accompanied by three playmates. Soon one of them strayed away from the others to sample the pig food. It was completely unaware of the trap, so we had to decide whether to pull the string now and catch the one rat, and thereby warn the others, or whether we wait to try and trap all four. We decided to be greedy and to wait to try to catch all four. This proved more difficult than we thought, but more exciting.

The rats were curious and soon we had two under the trap, then three. But as the fourth approached, two of them decided to retreat, leaving only one. Eventually we agreed that we were probably not going to get all four at once and that three would be our aim. When the required number was in the trap, we would pull the string to release the peg and thereby drop the frame over the rats.

Whether they were full of food, tired, or whether they had become aware of our presence I'm not sure, but they began to return to the trap less frequently, and then only one at a time. It soon became obvious that we were not going to get all four at once, so we reverted to our original plan. We would pull the string as soon as there was a rat in the trap, even if there was only one. It didn't take long, and we soon had a rat caught in the trap.

We dropped our end of the twine, ran down the granary steps, through the barn, out into the yard and into the pigsty. We went over to the trap, to wonder at our first capture. There was no sign of our first victim. We looked at each other, disappointed at our lack of success. We had been so sure that we had caught the little blighter. Disgruntled at not having a live young rat, we decided to abandon our sporting activities for the day and remove the trap until we were ready to use it again. We lifted the heavy picture frame and there, to our glee, was the rat's body. It had obviously been killed instantly when the trap had dropped. At least it hadn't suffered and there was now one less rat to breed and feed.

It had been a great afternoon's sport, my mother had spent a restful afternoon without us under her feet and we had a rat to add to our record, with the possibility of many more to come. Over the next few nights we returned from school to our rat catching activities and by the end of the week we had notched up another six. We were pleased with ourselves, as we had helped out on the farm by keeping the rat population down. Also, it kept us out of mischief, and to us it was cheap entertainment and quite different from the other, more ordinary children's activities.

During the winter months rats infested the poultry cabins which were usually located well away from the farm in the middle of the fields, but close to water where the hens could drink. During the colder months, the rats left the banks and woodland for better protection from the weather and a plentiful and more easily obtainable supply of food. They lived on the mixed poultry food and, on occasions, the eggs, which they maneuvered out of the nest and down the rat hole. There were many theories about how they achieved this feat; some said there were always two rats, one acting as horse and the other as the cart. The method they employed, it was thought, was that one rat laid on its back grasping the egg between all four legs whilst the other grasped his friend's tail between his teeth and dragged it to the hole with the egg. A nice thought, I feel, but improbable. It is more likely that they rolled the eggs. Either way they were able to transport them quite long distances.

Like the others, these rats provided our recreation. When we were older, we set about to make the sport of rat catching a little more exciting. We now had a ferret (polecat), a white and brown animal, ideal for bolting or disturbing the rats from their burrows under the hen cabins. We always believed in giving our rats a sporting chance of escape - and with the cabins located in the middle of the field, their chances were rated at about 50:1. Our method of approach was different from before. This time we had no traps or guns, just our friendly brown polecat and our stout hazel sticks. It was most important that we planned our strategy.

The plan had three components for discussion. The first was where to stand to give the rat a chance to get into open ground and for us to be ready for whichever line of escape he chose. The second was to decide who would let the ferret loose and the third was who would hold onto the dog, to be released only if the rat turned out to be an Olympic runner. After that, the chase and victory depended on who was the best runner, the rat or us. Once our strategy had been agreed and we were in position, we were ready to release the ferret.

It was seconds before our first rat appeared. He headed at a speed of knots towards the bank some distance from the poultry cabin. The idea was to let him get as far away as possible from the cabin before we attacked. This particular rat was a larger specimen, no youngster, but very athletic. We needed to cut him off, both from the bank and the cabins. We ran, swiping at him with the young hazel saplings. The rat was far too fast for us, able to turn a complete circle at a fantastic rate and we missed him every time. There was no doubt we were losing the battle, so the time had come to release Tim, the farm dog. Within seconds, he had seized the rat and with a sharp snap of the jaws and flick of the head, the rat was three feet in the air and stone dead. In the meantime, our polecat, unaware of the activities out in the field, was still bolting rats from under the cabin. Within ten minutes we had six big ones.

The most frightening experience I had with a farm rat happened in midwinter when they had left their summer habitat to return to the warmth of the barn. It was general practice, when feeding the cows during the winter months, not to use hay from one side of the barn all at once, but to cut it into sections. In this way the hay was kept nice and fresh and crisp, but also the good hay was not used up. It was the custom to feed different standards of hay to different stock and in most cases the good hay was fed to the milk cows and the not so good to the young stock.

The tool used to cut the hay was one of two types. The first, a large heart shaped knife about a foot wide, sharpened on both sides. The large handle allowed the user to yield maximum pressure when cutting the hay. The other was a long narrow knife and with this the farmer would kneel on the hay and slice off the amount required.

This particular day my cousin, who worked on the farm, was kneeling down to slice the hay when he disturbed a rat, a fully grown male, who in search of a safe haven, promptly ran up the inside of his trouser leg. Out of sight it might have been, but as far as my cousin was concerned it wasn't out of mind, because he could feel it edging up the trouser leg. It had an easy run because there were no long underpants to impede its journey. It passed the knee and was soon heading for a more sensitive area. My cousin sat still not moving a muscle. If the rat found it a warm place to settle, my cousin wasn't about to put it under any more stress or make it any more agitated than it already was. To his relief the rat moved higher and eventually became trapped at the trouser belt which prevented continued ascent. My cousin, motionless, felt around with his hands until he located the animal. He needed to know where the head was, so that when he administered the death squeeze, it did not bite him. Once located, he squeezed hard with both hands, holding on for some five minutes before he felt sure that he could release his pressure on the animal. Assured that the rat was now dead he dropped his trousers and saw, for the first time, the size of his adversary. It was huge. It was a different way of killing a rat and I can't say that many ended their lives under such circumstances. From that moment on my cousin tied string below the knees of his trousers, as he wasn't prepared to go through that experience again.

Rats were a menace in the spring when the chicks were born. Reproducing laying stock was laborious and demanded care and patience. First you needed a broody hen and, as they were not always available, you had to enquire around the other farms until you found one. In the meantime we prepared a slatted wooden orange box, formed a nest out of turf and dead grass, and placed it on a sheltered wall. The broody hen was placed in it with pot eggs, which remained for the first twenty-four hours to make sure the hen was, in fact, broody. This was easy to determine, you simply ventured your hand close to the hen and if she ruffled her feathers, squawked, and attempted to give a vicious peck to prevent you from removing the eggs, then she was broody. Once we were sure, we would place twelve eggs under her. These would be of uniform size with good thick shells, and, hopefully, fertile. This, of course, depended on the old red rooster and how active and virile he was. After just twenty-one days the chicks would hatch.

But before then there was plenty of work to do. The hen had to be fed and watered. At first she was tethered at the leg by a piece of string attached to a fifty-six pound weight. She remained like this until she had her bearings and knew to return to the nest - this usually took about a week, after which the hen was allowed to run loose from the nest. Sometimes, if more than one broody hen was running free, they would return to the same nest, leaving a clutch of eggs to become cold; so it was important to check them every twenty to thirty minutes. If this happened, we'd confine the errant hen to the nest by placing a sandstone slate infont of the box, propping it ajar with a broken wooden post or stone to give some light and air.

We were always curious to find out how fertile the eggs were, so we candled them at about ten days. A candle was placed under the egg; if it was infertile the light passed through, but if fertile the light wouldn't penetrate. Sometimes there might be three or four infertile eggs in a batch of twelve, and they would, by this time, be quite explosive. When carefully aimed at speed at the nearest wall, they burst with a thunderous bang and gave off an almost unbearable stench. This smell, it had to he said, was often out-done by the broody hen which had been sitting and as a result constipated for a week or more. Once she had a bowel movement, the smell was appalling and we quickly retreated to a good distance away.

At the end of the twenty-one days, there could be nine or more new chicks; loud, chirping balls of yellow fluff which in no time at all would be running to and fro from the broody hen to gather food. The food, always fresh, consisted of hard-boiled egg, chopped finely and mixed with oatmeal. It was mouth watering, and quite often the chickens didn't get to eat the whole lot.

Eventually, it was time to put the new arrivals out to open ground. But before that we had to make a chicken coop, a small waterproof unit with bars on the front to stop the broody hen getting out and taking the young chicks to their death. This could happen in bad weather if the young birds became cold and wet. Seven days on and the nine sturdy young chicks had survived, thanks to all the hard work. Every night the coop was closed to stop the young birds straying in the early morning, when the carrion crow and the magpie were out and about, looking for a tasty morsel for breakfast. The chicks would have been easy prey had we gone to bed without closing up the coops.

We were duly proud of our young chicks and felt sure that our egg requirements for the next twelve months were in hand. Unfortunately, I was proven wrong. The chicks were only ten days old when they were visited by the brown rat, who got in by burrowing under the side of the coop and worried and removed all nine of my prospective egg producers without trace. They were probably dragged down into the rat's warren and become a regular meal for the rat family over the next few days. So much for the old saying, never count your chickens before they are hatched. In this case they were hatched, but fell foul of that villain, the brown rat.

It was not all bad though, for there was often an income to be made on the local farms or estates where the owner would offer the staff a reward of three pence per tail for every one they handed in at the estate office. The workers knew that it didn't matter where it came from, a rat's tail from anywhere was eligible for cash. Drovers and horsemen would find a rat, look at it and say, "I'm sure I've seen you up at Bowland Hall", then cut off its tail and collect their three pence, even though they might be some five miles away from the estate.

During the early forties, farmers were forced to grow grain to ensure food for Britain, and in August the harvest commenced with the old green standard Fordson tractor and binder arriving to that field of golden corn. Within a few days all sheaves were stored in pyramid stacks to allow them to dry and ripen. After that period of time elapsed, they would be taken by horse and cart to the homestead, where the huge circular stack was constructed to a high standard so as not to allow the rain to penetrate. Finally they were thatched against the winter storms.

They remained like this until a few months later when the threshing machine was driven round to the stack. By this time the brown rat would have moved from the hedgerow and made itself a cosy nest, well inside the stack of corn. And why not? He was well insulated against the weather and there was a readily available stock of food, and outside he had access to water.

The rat always left the farmer two clues that he had taken up residence. First, he would make a straight-line track in the grass between the stack and the local watering hole, and secondly there would be the telltale droppings. These forewarned the farmer and the thresher that rats were present. We looked forward to the arrival of the thresher, in the anticipation of some good sport. The thresher was pulled into position and the powerful tractor maneuvered close to it, then connected with huge canvas belts to propel the threshing machine.

Wire netting barriers were erected round the stack and soon the threshing was in progress. The farm dog and the terrier stood by, waiting to pounce on the first rat that left the safety of the stack. I held my stout hazel stick, my father his twelve-bore hammer gun, ready and waiting in case some of them escaped the first line of troops - which wasn't often.

There was little activity during the first hours of threshing the large stack of corn sheaves. The rats seemed to move towards the base of the stack as the stack size decreased. It was only when the stack got 1 foot off the ground that the rats began to leave their cosy, and, what they thought, secure haven. Once one rat left, I think it was a signal to abandon home for the rest. There were rats poking from all sides; our small terrier dog and farm dog seemed to sense from which hole the rats were going to bolt. It was extremely fascinating seeing these two dogs at work, or maybe pleasure. They would snap and bite the moving rat at lightning speed, shake it and then throw them 3 foot in the air. This was to avoid receiving a nasty bite from the rat. I never saw a rat escape once bitten by either dog.

At the end of a day threshing there would be rows of rats, from the very large male to the small rat that had just left the mother's nest. On a good day, forty to fifty rats would have been killed, drastically reducing the rat population on our farm.

Holidays

Holidays on most Bowland farms were seldom heard of and certainly never took place on our farm. I could never remember my parents ever taking a holiday together.

Farming was unlike industry, where there were annual July holidays, or wakes weeks, where every factory and shop closed and everyone left for a seaside holiday at Blackpool in the many boarding houses and small hotels. Some families stayed with the same landlady for every holiday almost all their working lives. Their budget for these family holidays would be exceptionally tight, leaving just enough money to purchase the family food on returning home.

Most would travel to these seaside resorts by chara banc or by train which serviced the cotton towns of North East Lancashire well. With a station in each small town and regular, almost hourly, services, holiday time was the time for the enterprising young lads who wanted to earn that extra spending money, by transporting the holiday portmanteaus and cases from home to station. The mode of transport could be a 2-wheeled truck, mother's old pram or simply the garden barrow. It didn't matter, they gave the service and earned a bob or two.

We were always envious of our schoolmates after the summer holidays when they told us where they had been on their summer break. Little did we realise the idyllic countryside where we lived was much envied by our counterparts in the cotton towns of East Lancashire. The towering mill chimneys belched black acrid smoke 24 hours a day and where almost every household burnt coal on their living room fire to keep warm. The air in the Ribble Valley was pure and clean not blighted by the toxic smells of industrial pollution.

July was always a bad month for holidays as far as most farmers were concerned, because it was the time to make hay for feeding cows and sheep during the oncoming winter months. So there was no chance of holidays in July or August. If we ever did have a holiday it was to relations, mostly grandparents or aunts. These were mainly within walking distance of the family farm. My first holidays were always at my Grandma's cottage, on the same estate, a good half mile across the fields from our homestead. I was probably no more than five years old when I set off alone to cover the short distance across the fields. As it was over a small hill my parents could watch me arrive at the top of the hill and then my Grandma would be waiting for me at her small cottage. The best part of going to stay with my Grandma was that she always let me do what I wanted. This was a big difference from back at home. I could stop up that much longer at night and I also had my own single bed, quite a change from the three in a bed situation at home.

The meals were different; she would give an option for breakfast. At home, I had to eat what was available at the time so it was a change from oatmeal porridge. My Grandma always had Welgar Shredded Wheat. This we never had at home, basically because they were too expensive for a large family. My grandma also made many unusual dishes and cakes that we never got at home, because it was too time consuming for my mother to make or bake for so many mouths. My favourite was her gingerbread and biscuits that were always stored in her small pantry, in circular cake tins. I knew exactly which tins, and on many occasions got the kitchen stool to stand on to reach the shelf where the biscuit tins were stored. I never told my grandma about my many visits to the pantry, although she did remark many times that the biscuits had disappeared fast and she would have to bake more. Even at that early age I tended to twist my grandma's arm for those extra little tit bits I could never have at home.

I bet she knew where her biscuits were going and who was taking them but during her final years she was not bothered as she always looked forward to her grandchildren's visits. Most would think that, for a five year old, staying with grandma might be a dismal and boring experience, but it was not so. I believe my Grandma knew just how to make it enjoyable, both for her and myself, on the few visits I made to her small isolated country cottage.

She was a big radio fan and enjoyed many programmes that I never heard at home. The radio I remember was a small H.M.V. which stood for 'His Masters Voice'. The trademark on the radio was a small dog with ears cocked listening to a megaphone record player. The dog's name I believe was Nipper. The programmes we listened to were varied, but our favourites were; 'Dick Barton Special Agent', Wilfred Pickles in 'Have a Go' where Barney had to 'give them the money'; Tommy Handley in 'Itma' and many more that had not to be missed. All these made the night pass much more quickly before I went to bed, which was always a good hour and a half later than at home. She would have all sorts of games, such as Snakes and Ladders, Ludo or Dominos. Maybe she would play Snap or simply Patience which she played when she was by herself. Before going to bed I could have a cup of Ovaltine or Horlicks made with milk. These were very tasty drinks that I never got chance of at home. My grandma was the one who used to knit stockings for part of the family. When I was on holiday there she would get me to hold the hanks of red and black wool so she could wind them into bobbins, or balls, before knitting began.

She would also peg all the rugs we had back at home. This was a very skilful job and she would use basic materials such as old clothing. These were washed before being cut into $3/4$ inch wide strips, then cut again into 4 inch long strips. This is when I came in handy. It was a job I didn't like, but I always knew she would reward me at the end, maybe with sixpence, or just some of her special home made treacle toffee which she kept in her old oak corner cupboard. During the day she would send me on various errands, maybe to the adjacent farm for milk and eggs, or, if it was warm wet weather, to the local fields to pick fresh mushrooms. She always seemed to know just where and when to find the tasty fungi.

Also, occasionally, I had other holidays, mainly to my aunt's farm at a town called Bacup. This, once again, was an industrial town where the main product production was cloth and shoes. All my cousins worked in the slipper factories. Bacup was by no means a holiday resort, in fact it was exactly the opposite. There were large weaving sheds with red brick or stone chimneys towering into the sky. Trams and buses were the main means of transport in that area along with push bikes. The River Irwell, I believe, was the most polluted river in England. This was where everything from the heavily industrialised area finished up. There were dyes and detergents all mixed with the already irony water pouring from the rugged terrain of Rossendale to make a potent solution where no fish could survive.

Why did I like Bacup? There were many reasons:

There was something to see and do whereas at home there was nothing. At night there were always the picture houses to visit if you could get a seat; this was something Bowland didn't have. There were fish and chip shops that we visited after the pictures.

There were the swimming baths I could visit most days, where the water was always nice and warm, a far cry from the River Ribble back at home, which was either in flood or ice cold. There were the shops where I could spend my holiday money on toffees, or on a present for my mother. There were also streetlights, something else that Bowland had never heard of.

This type of holiday would not suit many young lads, but I was not one for bright lights at the seaside with donkey rides, Blackpool rock, crowds of people and boarding houses. My type of holiday had to be interesting, but, most of all, low cost; I probably only had a couple of pounds to spend.

During my teens I did have just two more holidays. The first was when my brother and I decided to tour Scotland in the family car. This was a 1935 Austin 12, 4-door model. The idea was to load the back of the car with tent and cooking utensils, plus almost all the food we would require. My mother made sure we would not go hungry. She baked some bread and cakes, home made jam and packed eggs in rolled up newspapers to avoid any breakages. There was bacon, potatoes and everything we might need. There was never any beer or drink as the family was teetotal, so all we had to buy was petrol and oil for the car. It was late August before we could spare time to leave the farm. This was when haytime was finished, and we were all ready for a rest after long, strenuous days raking and forking hay. This was to be stored in the large, stone slated barn, for winter consumption by our large herd of cattle and sheep.

From the start of our holiday venture to Scotland most things went wrong. On our first day of travel we had a puncture on the front wheel of the car. It was only a minor hiccup, but it slowed down progress on our Highland fling. We had to find a garage to repair the puncture; this we found quite a problem in the remote country areas.

On the second day it rained cats and dogs, there was water everywhere. It got into the distributor of the car so it just stopped the engine dead. It was no mean task trying to dry out the distributor in a Scottish downpour. There was so much water around that day that we couldn't find a dry place to pitch the tent so night accommodation was in the car. We decided to sleep in the driver and passenger seats. This was alright for the first hour or so until cramp and cold took over, and, with no reclining seats in the car we had to attempt to sleep upright. The steering wheel and gear lever were in the way if you moved to try to get a more comfortable position. We slept in our daytime clothing which we soon found was not adequate for the long, cold Scottish nights. We had no sleeping bags, only the odd woolly blanket which didn't cover us both adequately, so it was a case of a bit for you and a bit for me.

On the third day I fell ill with a type of flu, or heavy cold, so my brother was doctor and driver combined. We transferred the camping and cooking equipment into the front passenger seat, and I was well and truly wrapped up on the backseat. I must have had some type of fever, because I was just sweating like a bull and wringing wet. I was so bad we decided to forget about Scotland and return home. I didn't remember too much about the scenery that we had set out to observe, as I was still very feverish and cold wrapped up in the back seat of the car. My brother drove all that night, heading South back to Bowland. We came over Shap Fell, a notoriously bad road for heavy wagons passing the English Lake District. By this time I was feeling much better and more like eating some of the food my mother had packed for our Scottish expedition. By the time we arrived at the farm we had travelled around six hundred miles and neither of us had enjoyed the Scottish Highlands. My fever had passed and I felt perfectly well. The food that was left in the car soon got devoured. A poor consolation prize was that we had spent hardly any money. The holiday was only four long days instead of 7 to 10 days and we didn't get the extra days as holidays because, when back on the farm, we had to work.

On the next and last holiday I had from the family farm we took a southerly route. This holiday was not in a car or motor cycle, but a cattle wagon. We had just purchased this cattle wagon. It was brand new, so it was ideal for holiday purposes. It had not been used or fouled by cow dung or urine. It was in mint condition and all we had to do was fit out the back into kitchen and sleeping accommodation. We used the sheep decks to support the straw mattress borrowed from our regular bed. The sheep deck was about 3'6" off the floor so getting into bed was not so easy. The other problem was that it was a long drop if you fell out of bed. There was plenty of room for a table and two chairs, cooking stove and a couple of milk kits of water for washing up. The toilet section was non existent, but we were more than capable of coping with this as it was an every day situation when working in the fields back at home. There were plenty of secluded areas where we could stop and answer the call of nature out of sight of the public eye and being in a cattle wagon, nobody bothered to care. We used lush grass as toilet paper. My father had a saying, which he always adhered to, which was, "What man taketh from the land must be returned to the land and that's what farming is about". He was probably right.

This holiday was from the start, much better than our Scottish escapade. The wagon was new, so there were no breakdowns, and we could see far more, being seated higher in the cab than in the car. The climate in the south was better and much warmer. It was a totally different type of farming not so many sheep and cows, more grain and root crops, also, lots of fruit that we could buy at the roadside stalls. There were small thatched cottages bounded by large estates, no smoking mill chimneys or cobbled streets or Lancashire clogs.

It was a different way of life, just what we needed to see. The farthest place we visited was Torquay where, for the first time, we encountered lots of holidaymakers. Probably, some would be from our local towns. I doubted that there were many, because they appeared to be much better dressed and looked a little more affluent, and not from a weaving or farming background. Their speech sounded much more refined than ours. My brother and I were fairly broad 'Yorkshire spoken' and in fact I had difficulty in understanding what they said. They sounded very much like the gentry who lived on the large estates back at home.

We attempted to find a park for our cattle wagon in Torquay centre and almost every time we were asked to move on. We told one car park attendant that it was a holiday van but he didn't believe us, so finally, we lowered the cattle-loading ramp at the back so he could inspect our holiday home. It created lots of interest with the many holidaymakers. I was convinced it was unique, with side loading gates, slatted loading ramp, sheep deck raised bedroom complete with chairs and kitchen table, but minus toilet facilities. Some questioned our toilet facilities and we replied they were just outside the bedroom door, which was almost correct!

We stopped a full day in Torquay looking round the shops and tourist attractions. To date, we had not sent a card home so they had no idea where we were on holiday. I was the worst writer of cards possible, so I left the job to my brother. There was a wide selection of cards from the scenic to the saucy. We were more interested in the saucy ones and selecting which we dare send to whom. There was a card suitable for everybody we had in mind. The selection took up a fair lot of time. We probably sent a dozen cards back to relations and friends in Bowland. We also sent one to a cantankerous farming family in Bowland village. The lady in charge of this household I will call Mrs D, who had two unmarried daughters in their thirties to forties. We found just the card for these two spinsters. It was the picture of a spindly middle aged woman making a single bed, and when leaning over, tucking in the sheet at the far side of the bed, she could see her own feet. On seeing a pair of feet under the bed she remarked "Ah hah, a man at last, I can see his feet". This was the card we must send to Mrs D's daughters; it was to be one of the many joke cards we sent not signed, only by a ? mark.

It must have been at least a month after returning home to Bowland village before I saw Mrs D. I was sitting on the tractor seat, having an ice cream that I had just purchased from the local pub, when she came marching up the village from the co-op shop. It was a glorious day, I remember, and unwittingly I remarked "It's a lovely day, Mrs D", forgetting all about the card we sent to her daughters. Her reply was not so pleasant as the day. She said, don't you lovely day me you cheeky young bugger. I know who sent that postcard to my daughters. I can tell the Bowland school writing anywhere". Her language didn't improve; in fact I heard new words, even to my own ears. It was a good job I was perched high on the tractor seat and out of range of her frantically waving arms. What would have happened if she had had a stick I dread to think. I doubt it did her blood pressure much good. The villagers wondered what all the shouting and hullabaloo was about. When I told them of the card they thought it was a suitable card for Mrs D and family. It was a good job we only took holidays on rare occasions.

All our holidays on the farm were on the cheap, either at relations or in makeshift holiday vehicle, cattle wagon, etc. We never had the chance to go on a seaside holiday like many of my school companions or the lads from more wealthy farming families.

I also went on short holidays to relatives with my Auntie Henriette who lived with my grandma before she died. These holidays were normally for two or three days' duration and within a few miles of our homestead.

I remember one holiday at my Aunt's smallholding that we

visited for a long weekend. There was no extra accommodation at this small bungalow, so it was always makeshift. On this occasion I had to sleep with my cousin in a loft over the pig and poultry shed, where the coal was stored, along with many other useful farm implements and tools. I remember the rickety stone steps to this shed that were called the stone erection, and the old iron bedstead that was only used when visitors came. There was no oilcloth or carpet, no electricity or toilet, we used to have competitions on who could wee the farthest from the top of the stone steps, sometimes I won.

My cousin was slightly older, so he had different hobbies. He would fish in the local stream for small fish that I found easy to catch, so most of my holiday was taken up fishing. I used to get sodden wet through on our fishing escapades and, on returning, I would get a good telling off from my auntie and be made to take my pants off to dry, as I only had one pair with me on holiday. I had to wear a large pair of my cousin's pants which were far too big for me.

I also remember he had a Webley air pistol. This we used for shooting starlings and sparrows which fed with the small flock of hens kept for both eggs and roast chicken. Once, I loaded the air pistol with coal dust from the pile of coal in the bedroom, not knowing the effect if it was shot. I aimed it at my cousin from about six-foot range when he was bent down with his bare backside facing me. There was a hell of a scream from him and he truly thought I had a lead slug in the pistol. It left a nasty red pattern on his bottom that I don't think was permanent.

I also went to another aunt in a town some miles from home. I travelled by bus, which was totally new to me. I was put on the main bus to be collected at the other end of the journey by my aunt. But, just in case I got lost, a label with the address on was fastened around my neck with a piece of string. Fortunately, I never got lost.

My aunt's husband worked on the co-operative farm in the town. His job was to deliver milk around the streets with horse and cart, totally different from back at home, where ours was sold in large kits to the local dairy. I couldn't wait to go on the milk round that was always early morning. So, if I wanted to go, I had to get up at around 6am. I was only very young at this stage so I had to be well wrapped up against the early morning cold. I was thrilled at being allowed to ride in a milk cart with my Uncle. He placed me behind the large kits from which he dispensed the milk by pint measure into various kitchen pots and jugs supplied by the customers. There was no escape from this secure position in front of the milk cart. My uncle was far too busy delivering and dispensing milk to think about my natural welfare and never offered to stop to let me answer the call of nature. I was too scared to ask him to let me out of the cart, so I had no alternative but to wee in the cart. I thought my uncle would never know, but I forgot that the cart was leaning backwards. It was only seconds after I had relieved myself that a telltale torrent of wee ran out of the back of the cart, in full sight of my uncle, nearly ending up in his boots. He smiled and said, "Well young lad, it's better than in thee breeches".

This aunt and uncle had not had any family of their own, so it was a case of everything had to be done according to the book. I had to be washed and in bed for seven, not like my grandma's, when most times I never got washed at nights and also stopped up late. I had to clean my teeth twice a day, something I had never done before in my life. The bath was a proper bath, not an old tin one in front of the fire, and there was carpet on the floor, so I had to make sure to wipe my feet before entering the house. There was a roll of toilet paper, not a recycled newspaper as at home, and I definitely had to wash my hands after going to the toilet. We also had a prayer before each meal, as she was a religious woman and a true Methodist. She was not my favourite aunt but I enjoyed my few days' stay with her. How she would have coped with seven kids and two farm men I couldn't imagine. One thing for sure, her over hygienic habits would definitely have had to change!

I enjoyed all my holidays. They didn't cost my family much compared with my schoolmates who had been to London or Blackpool, with all the hustle and bustle of trams, buses and people.

Farmers Story:
Farmers seldom took a holiday during their working life. Once a retired, farmer decided to take his wife Maggie to Rome for a weeks' holiday. Maggie was fairly deaf so she was always asking for most conversations to be repeated.

The couple arrived at Rome airport and booked a taxi to take them to their hotel in the city. Whilst travelling in the taxi, the driver asked, "Which part of the world do you come from?" Her husband replied, "England". Maggie then asked, "What did he say?" and the husband replied, "He asked me which part of the world we came from, I told him England". After a couple of minutes, the taxi driver asked, "Which part of England do you live in?" and the husband replied, "Near Manchester". The taxi driver said, "I once had an affair with an ugly woman in Manchester". Maggie then asked, "What did he say?" and the husband replied, "He says he knows you".

Walking Livestock

Walking cows and calves:

In the mid forties transportation of farm livestock was difficult as there were few cattle wagons to carry them from farm to market and vice versa. This is where my father found me very useful and cheap, and appointed me as driver of his cows and calves. Distances the cows were required to be driven could vary from a single field or meadow length, to nine or ten miles. The single field case could be where you were changing cows from field to field or from one farm to another. Cows, you must remember, always liked a change of pasture or meadow, as the herbs and texture of grass varied from each field, so it was a fairly common job moving cows around the farm. One of my jobs was bringing home the newborn calves if they were born in our meadow adjacent to the buildings. The cow would always find the furthest corner to give birth. My father would say, 'Take that barrow and bring that calf and cow home'. This was no mean task and one I used to hate. For starters, the barrow would be dirty so I would have to swill it clean with water from the farm trough, then a small bucket of sawdust from the circular saw bench would be sprinkled in the wet barrow.

The barrow was a large specimen, made by our village joiner, with a large wooden spoke wheel with iron rim, by no means the easiest barrow in the world to wheel for a young lad. The meadow, I remember, was long and narrow, and called the long meadow, a full 400 yards long. So, by the time I had wheeled the barrow to where the cow and calf were, I was totally shattered. Still, I had more problems of how to get the calf into the barrow. I had my own method, where I laid the barrow on its side, and pushed the slithery newborn calf in and then tried to upright the barrow. This could fail many times if the calf was not willing to co-operate with me. In that case I would tie the calf's legs with a piece of string, which a farmer was always supposed to carry in his pocket, along with a pocketknife and a nail.

My language, in such instances when nothing went right, was best heard from the far corner of the meadow. Once you had got the calf settled in the barrow, you were heading for home, yet there was still the problem of: 'would the silly bloody cow follow you and the barrow?' Not always! I had often arrived at the farmstead when the cow decided to turn tag and dash back to the top of the meadow to find it's calf.

My father was a cattle dealer and was away visiting farms and cattle markets and buying more cows. All the cows were in calf, in their latter stage of pregnancy, and would soon be producing an offspring. The idea was to take these cows to our second farm at the other side of the village and, as they approached the due date to calve, we would walk them home. This didn't always work out and often the calf would be born away from home at the other farm. This farm was a good 2 miles away, so the calf had to be left there sometimes, until it was strong enough to walk that distance or, at least, that was the idea. Sometimes you would have difficulty locating the newborn calf, as the mother might have abandoned the calf in a patch of thistles or nettles, maybe, two fields away. The mother always knew where her calf was, but was always reluctant to disclose its whereabouts. Once you had found the young calf it would lie low and pretend not to be noticed, rather like a young fawn or deer. Once you aroused the young calf it would set off bawling for its mother who, in seconds, arrived to give protection to its offspring. This was sometimes the time you wished you were in the next field, or you had a good stout hazel stick handy to ward off the very irate mother that always had a pair of very sharp horns.

There were many funny sides to walking cows and calves. One stands out above them all. On this day in mid summer I was walking cow and calf home through Bowland village. The cow was a fairly alert, Ayrshire type cow, and, unfortunately, a refined lady who lived in a charming cottage had left the gate open to her garden, and the door open to her house. She was also the owner of a little, yapping, terrier dog that was obviously not familiar with a newly calved cow and her offspring and, upon seeing the cow, decided to fly down the garden path and into the road where the cow was more than prepared for it. It was worse that waving a red flag at a bull. There was a huge bellow from the cow and soon the dog was withdrawing at great speed back to the safe haven of this lady's cosy cottage, or so it thought. There was urine and muck deposited en route to the house where the cow continued to pursue the, by now, howling dog. There was a crashing of pots and glass, breaking of wood, and screams of terror from this fine, once well spoken, lady. Her vocabulary at last had been stretched to the limit. The cow soon exited the cottage none the worse. I didn't go in to observe the damage, all I told her was to keep her dog under control and shut her garden gate. It turned out to be a talking point for the village over the following few days.

On many occasions I would be kept off school to go to the cattle market with my father. Once again, I was the cattle driver at the tender age of only nine years old. The cattle market was in Gisburn some 3.5 miles from home. We we would rise early on market day, which was Thursday, to arrive at the cattle market in good time, in the hope of purchasing a bargain. Sometimes, you would catch a farmer half asleep and get him to sell you his cow for pounds below market value. On the odd occasion you would stop at the market all day and buy nothing. I would get bored to tears with this situation and go and sit on the railway bridge at Gisburn watching the huge L.M.S. trains. In the mid forties the trains were often used for cattle transportation, from as far afield as Perth and Oban in Scotland to Holyhead and Stranraer, where all the Irish cattle were shipped. There were special cattle transport trucks that held up to 20 cows each.

On this day I was off school, waiting for my father to purchase cows. This was late May 1944 and, instead of watching the trains, I watched the army on the move. I sat on the Auction Market wall all day from 9am to 4.30pm taking note of the various hardware. There was thousands of troop carriers and men, tanks, bren gun carriers, motorbikes and sidecars, radio wagons, ambulances, etc, they were all there. Little did I realise what was happening at that young age. I later found out it was the start of the transfer of troops to the D.Day landings in France. How many of those young army lads never returned I cannot tell. After that full day my father bought just a single cow to drive home. I also had another cow to drive home for another farmer who always paid sixpence per cow for the driving service.

During those years there were very few cars on the roads and most farmers shut their farm gates, making life much easier for the drive. What you always had to do was think one step ahead of the cow, and anticipate what it was going to do next. My father always told me, 'It is no use running, lad, when the bloody cow has gone'.

In the early spring, my father visited farms on the outskirts of the cotton towns of East Lancashire, Nelson, Colne and Burnley. He visited these every year to buy their surplus cows after they had milked all winter, supplying fresh milk to the mill workers and families. He would call on, maybe, ten farms during the day and at every farm bartering would take place. It didn't matter if the farmer's price was low my father always wanted to buy for less. It could be two or three pounds, or merely shillings. He always said, if he got the cow for £3 less with ten minutes bartering who would pay him that sort of money for that time spent working.

Once all the cows had been forward bought, it was a matter of arranging collection from the farms. With most of these cows collection would not take place for at least a month. So, diaries were filled in with dates and times, on each individual farm, to be strictly adhered to, as there were no telephones to help you communicate. You would start collection at the farthest farm away from home at, say, 8.30am, and the remaining farmers with cattle would join the train of cattle at the end of each farm road until all purchases had been collected. There could be as many as forty cattle in one drove and the distance we had to cover was some 11 or 12 miles. By the end of the day both cows and drovers were well tired.

The secret of a good drover was never to treat your cattle badly. Seldom did you use a stick to upset or frighten the animal. The less nervous, and quieter you kept your drove, the better it was to control. On long walks of 10 or more miles, you would have to allow time for the cattle to drink. In some cases, there were stone troughs by the roadside where the heavy carthorses stopped to drink and rest. Many public houses were named after the troughs and watering places for horses and cattle, e.g. Stone Trough. There were also secrets that you, as a young drover, had to keep strictly to yourself. The one I used was a horseshoe nail, for emergencies only. It always seemed to happen, when I was driving cow and calf through Bowland village, that the calf decided to lie down. You daren't use your stick on such an innocent, tired, young animal when villagers and hikers were looking on. My method was to conceal the horseshoe nail in the palm of my hand and, at the precise time it decided to lie down, give it a sharp prod with this nail. It always worked, and nobody ever saw the nail. If, however, the calf was too tired to walk, I would simply open the local farmer's gate and put cow and calf in the neighbours' field overnight, and collect the following day, which most farmers never objected to. You would also get the really tight farmers who wouldn't pay sixpence for the drover's services, so you put that cow in the neighbourís field and let him get it home himself, or your forgot on purpose to collect it from the cattle market.

Driving cows was also a very trashy job, and dirty. If it was wet, I had no modern protective clothing. In my early years, it was clogs and long stockings, which, normally, had slipped down to the top of my clogs, a pair of short pants above the knee and a woolly jumper. I don't remember having a good jacket, or even a waterproof jacket. Frequently I would return home from driving cows soaked to the skin, scratched with brambles and stung with nettles. I always had to wear a big neb cap like the old farmers wore, five times my age. The farmers often remarked, 'Did ta get weighed or measured for they cap?'. I never used a dog when driving cows, probably because I was no good at whistling, and also because my father's dogs were totally useless, so I thought they were best left at home. At least they didn't upset my cattle drove.

I found sheep much easier to drive than cattle, as I always drove them in a flock. A single sheep would have been totally impossible to drive, where a single cow was possible. The most awkward thing to drive was a newborn sheep, or lambs. It was easier carrying the lambs when they were newborn than trying to drive them, simply because the mother was so protective, you couldn't get her to move forward. You also had to be careful, when driving or handling new born lambs, that your farm dog didn't follow up behind you, as the protective mother could literally knock you to the ground when trying to ward off the dog. It was especially painful if the mother was a hill type sheep with a pair of large, sharp horns.

I seldom drove pigs as we only occasionally kept a sow for breeding purposes. Then the only time I had to drive it was when I was taking it across the field to the neighbour's male pig or boar pig. The old sow seemed to know where I was taking her and never tried once to stray off line. She seemed to sense that her visit to the boar was going to be the high spot of the year. Once I arrived at the neighbour's farm and got close to the pigsty the old sow would refuse to move until mating had taken place. Once the old boar had finished his proceedings, the sow was ready to return to our farmstead with a satisfied smile on her face.

So much for droving cows and stock. I could have made a small fortune, but once again, I failed. I can say, for sure, I was a professional cattle drover with no certificate of recognition for my skills.

The Farmhouse Kitchen & Pantry

Farmhouses in Bowland were, in most cases, built in local stone that had been quarried within a few miles of the actual house. Many of the houses were built in blue limestone, a very hard type of rock that wasn't easy to dress into individual or standard sized walling stone. Therefore, most were built randomly which meant stones of every shape and size bonded together with a blue mortar, a very strong type of local cement made from lime ashes and sand.

The roofs could be clad in many different types and colours of slate. There was slate from the English Lake District that had a green/grey tint. These were never of a standard size or shape. They could vary from 4 foot x 3 foot to 1 foot x 6 inches and all had a square bottom edge and, in most cases, a round top edge rather like a loaf of bread. There was also Welsh slate that was all of a uniform size and thickness, and looked far better on the farmhouse roof. This was also much easier for the slater to fix and nail into a permanent position on the roof. The finest roofs on Bowland farms were the heavy sandstone ones. This slate was from Lancashire slate quarries and, once again, the slate varied in size and shape but was mostly around 1inch thick. So together, the blue limestone building and the sandstone roofs made all these farmhouses more picturesque.

The interiors of these farmhouses varied considerably from one to another. I suppose, going back in history, the interior design of the farmhouse dwelling depended on the type of family and its financial circumstances. If there were large families, more small rooms would be the feature, and if there were small wealthy families, large rooms would have been the desire and design of the day.

Our farmhouse was, I would say, a halfway house with rooms not too big and not too small. The room I remember well was the kitchen. This was because most of the other rooms were out of bounds and only used on special occasions. The parlour, I remember, was for the special days like Christmas and New Year, birthdays, Christenings and special family occasions. The other room which we used more often was the 'house part'. Why it was called that I will never know, today it would be called the sitting room. This room was filled with old oak furniture. The chairs, I remember, looked nice but were damned uncomfortable to sit on for any length of time. There was also a window seat that, once again, was very uncomfortable and cold, especially in winter. My father used to say, "It's a poor arse that can't adjust to the shape of the chair". He always had the best and most comfortable chair. My mother seldom sat down, as she was always busy in the kitchen.

The kitchen, I remember, was of a reasonable size. It had to be, to seat our large family for every meal. There was no such thing as carpets or oilcloth on the floor; it was just bare sandstone flags. Only in front of the kitchen fire was a large pegged rug that my Grandmother had taken pride in making, from worn out overcoats and clothing, with cattle feed sacks for lining. The kitchen floor was always scrubbed, swilled, and mopped clean everyday by my mother. The flags just inside the door, along with the doorstep, were worn hollow by the continuous wear and tear of clogs worn by so many bodies. When the back door was shut there was a good 2 inch gap between floor and door, good for ventilation in summer but damned draughty and cold in winter. It also left easy access for rats and mice. The draught stopper in winter was a cattle feed sack, formed like a Swiss roll, tied with string, and pushed up to the door to fill the gapeing hole. It worked well.

The door was large, thick and very heavily built and was, most probably, the original one, since the house was built many hundreds of years ago. The hinges were heavy, gate type hinges, similar to those on the barn and cowsheds. To support his heavy door, gudgeon type hinges were leaded into the huge sandstone door pillars that were definitely original. These were probably made by the local blacksmith in Bowland village who didn't believe in flimsy, weak fittings. These, once again, were similar to those used on the farm building in both design and strength. There was no way a burglar was going to open the door once the huge bolt was in place; it would have been easier to break in through the walls.

The ceiling in the farm kitchen was a maze of oak beams. There were two large support beams running from wall to wall. They supported smaller oak beams at intervals of about 18 inches which, in turn, supported small timber laths that were used to support and bond the plaster to form the ceiling. These laths had all been split from solid timber logs into sizes 1 1/2 inch wide by 1/4 inch thick, then nailed onto the oak beams at regular intervals. The beams had a multitude of uses. They did not just support the bedroom floor, they were also used for supporting the clothes drying lines. Into the sides of these beams large staples had been driven at intervals of about 1 foot. Through the staples a cotton rope was threaded from side to side, forming a ready made drying rack at ceiling level. This was always full of clothes, in various colours and sizes, belonging to the family and farm men.

The front line nearest the fire had yet another use. This was draped with oatmeal cakes that had to be left to dry and go hard before use. The oatcakes formed part of a traditional dish, in the Yorkshire/Lancashire border area of 'stew and hard'. These oatmeal cakes didn't have much taste, but once covered with a good thick coat of fresh salted farmhouse butter and a good helping of stew it was a meal to be remembered.

Farthest away from the kitchen fire, the beams had yet another use, with large steel hooks nailed onto the beams with extra thick nails. Onto these hooks rolls of bacon and hams were hung to dry. They would hang there for a few months until it was decided they were dry enough to move to a less warm area, which was usually on a beam going up the stairs to the large landing leading to the bedrooms. These large hams and rolls had to last the family twelve months, until the next years' pigs had been reared, killed and cured. During that period there were the summer months to contend with, and on the farm there was always plenty of flies and bluebottles. Even though the hams and rolls were dry, and protected in a muslin bag, a bluebottle always managed to find a place to lay its eggs. My father, once again, brought out his guarded butchering knives and soon cut off the infested section and parts. He never believed in throwing anything away, so the bacon or ham was soon back on the breakfast plate, or put in a stew.

The fireplace was yet, I believe, an original from when the house was built. This was a huge cast iron one with side oven, where my mother did all the baking. With eleven mouths to feed it was rather like a production line for bread, cakes and buns.

The oven was almost always on the right hand side of the fireplace and the side boiler on the left. The side boiler would hold about twelve gallons, which wasn't a lot when washing and bath nights took place. The side boiler was also cast iron and therefore the water always had a rusty appearance. In the centre of the chimney was a large hook where the kettle was permanently hung ready for regular, unexpected brews that were frequently needed. There were yet more fixtures on the fireplace, one was a heavy, gate type bar, which hinged down to be used as a support for the many pans when dinner was being cooked. Often the potatoes and vegetables tasted of smoke when cooked on the open fire. My mother took particular pride cleaning the fireplace; all the chrome parts were polished and the rest black-leaded weekly. The chrome parts were polished with Shineo, until you could see your face in it. The large brass fender, tongs, poker and shovel had also to be polished to perfection.

Wood was the main fuel for the kitchen fire; this was plentiful around the farm. It had to be, because it took so much to cook and heat water. Coal would be used more in the evening when all the family was present. There were many of us, so we had to sit well away from the fire to gain more heat. It was my job, after tea, to get all the firewood into the wood box by the back door, in order to keep the fire burning for the next day. Two large buckets of coal were required daily to keep the kitchen fire burning. These buckets were large cattle buckets which, when I was nine or ten years old, really took a lot of carrying. I also had to chop the kindling sticks. These were small thin pieces of timber, used with paper every morning when lighting the kitchen fire.

Over the fireplace was a large mantelpiece where two brass candlesticks stood. These had a dual purpose. The first was decorative and added that little refinement to a drab, down to earth, well-used kitchen. Their other use was that they propped up the incoming post until my father decided to side it away onto a long wire, which was hanging on a nail in the far corner of the kitchen. This was the only filing system we had for house and farm. Also, on the fireplace was a large clock that was the only timepiece we had in the house. Above the clock was a large painting called 'shoeing the bay mare'. This picture had been handed down through a generation of our family. I don't think it was worth anything, it had only sentimental value.

In one corner near the fireplace was the old oak corner cupboard. This was the medicine cupboard and contained all the medicinal cures of the day. Just a few that I remember were, Fennings Fever Cure; this was used for most ailments. Also used was Germolene, for cuts and sores. Camphorated oil was used for coughs and sore throats, and rubbed onto both back and chest. Aspirins, in a large bottle containing 100, were always kept on the top of the cupboard, well out of reach of the abundance of children. Syrup of figs was another standard bottle always present in the medicine portfolio. Worm cakes my mother always had in stock, and she frequently made us take them as it seemed we always had worms. A large bottle of liquid paraffin was always present and this she used to rub on our hair to remove scurf. There was also a tin of Keetings' powder that she was always putting on our head, to remove head lice. There was a small toothcomb that was a special comb used to remove headlice, or just to comb our hair to see if we had any headlice, or nits, as they were commonly called. The cupboard also had a good side to it as on the top shelf she kept the toffees. These were out of bounds for most of the family and she always knew if the older members of the family had taken any. They were the only ones who could reach to the top shelf of the cupboard.

Below this old corner cupboard was an ancient oak longsettle. This had definitely not been made by any well know furniture maker such as 'Waring and Gillow', more probably by my great grandad with axe and saw. It was very robust, but rough. The tenon joints were so loose the longsettle was almost dual purpose, providing a rocking longsettle. The old oak timber was well worn and worm eaten, resembling a well-used dartboard. The boarded back of this longsettle had long since lost it horse hair filling and leather covering. The seat covering had been patched many times and resembled a patchwork quilt.

Next to the longsettle was a large sandstone slab of stone that was used for a work surface. It must have been 6 foot x 3 foot wide x 2 inches thick. This was where all the baking and meal preparations took place. Behind the work surface was a pinewood pot rail, where all the everyday crockery was stored. The rail was quite a size as it was the only place to keep pots and plates. The plates were stored in racks and the pots on individual hooks. We all had our own individual hooks and we all had our individual pot and plate. This plate we had to use for both meat, vegetables and puddings. What this taught you was to clean your plate off as best you could, after the first course, before you got the rice pudding or whatever was on offer for dessert. If not, it was a bit like when the tide went out, on the outside edge of the plate, gravy and potatoes, with rice pudding in the middle. My dad used to remark "It will do thee no harm, it all gets mixed up once tha's getton it down". It was the same at breakfast time, no clean cup for tea, the large porridge basin used for porridge had to be used for tea, saving my mother washing up and also hot water.   The basins were always quite big, so when you were drinking your tea your head almost disappeared inside the basin.

Another main feature in the kitchen was the large sandstone slopstone or sink. This was a good 4 feet long x 2 feet wide with only a 3 inch lip surround so you always had to use a large vessel when either washing pots or washing yourself. There was no tiling surround to the sink, only rendered concrete painted a drab dark green to match the kitchen door. On the left hand side of the sink, was a large piston type pump with a large wheel and handle. You had to wind this to pump water from the spring some distance away from the farm. I seldom remember that pump working properly, so other water had to be used. When it was bath night we used water from a big tank by the kitchen door, which had been collected from the farmhouse roof. This was always a soft water, unlike the hard limestone water that had channelled through the ground. Quality of water varied a lot on the farm. If it was very wet, the water would turn a rich brown colour and always had to be boiled. In the spring, when we spread farmyard manure on the meadows adjacent to the water storage tank, the water would go extra brown and smell heavens high of farmyard manure. It was totally unusable, either for baths or drinking. This only happened when there was very heavy rain immediately after the heaps of manure had been hand spread.

The centrepiece in the kitchen was the huge wood table that had to seat ten at most meals, seven children, my father and two farm men. My mother seldom sat down at mealtimes with the family, as she was occupied sorting out and serving food. The table was one into which you inserted extra leaves to make it the size to suit the family. Ours, I remember, had two of these extra sections. There was no tablecloth, just a type of light oilcloth that was wiped down with the dishcloth after every meal. This was the only suitable way, as at most meals spilling and slopping occurred. The table legs were stained and polished. They were the circular type turned on a lathe to form a pretty shape. My mother protected them with her old cast-off woolly stockings. This, she believed, protected them from the many pairs of clogs that scraped on them daily at meal times. They looked a bit like a concertina.

There were no chairs round the table at mealtimes. Instead were two long forms, or benches, down each side of the table, and four legged stools at each end. The stools were always put under the table after each meal and the benches taken away down the long passage leading to the pantries. The benches were very rough and had been made by my father from rough sawn timber from the estate. The boards had not been planed or sanded to make them smooth and comfortable to sit on. Therefore, if you sat on them, as we did many times with no pants on, you had a fair chance of finishing up with a wood spell in your bottom, or with a rough wooden timber pattern on it.

In one corner nearest the slopstone, or sink, was a large circular set boiler. This was used only four or five times a year. Once was to supply hot water when we killed a pig, for scalding the pig hair or bristle from the carcass, cleaning it perfectly before the final dressing took place. The other times we used the set boiler was in spring and autumn, when sheep dipping took place. The hot water was used to take the chill off the large dip tub of stone cold water. Also, it helped to melt the full buckets of paste type dip used on these dipping days. We had to make sure ample coal and wood was available, as the side and set boiler could burn barrowfuls in a day when lots of hot water was required.

Also dotted around the kitchen walls were various sized nails, used to hang various items. One was used to hang a thick leather strap that, fortunately, my mother rarely used, although it was always handy if required. This was a good deterrent. Once you had been on the receiving end you never forgot. Another nail supported the hairbrush box and mirror. This was where the shaving took place and general sprucing up. My mother seldom used the mirror when doing her hair as she always sat on the longsettle and combed her hair, then tied it in a bun at the back. Another nail supported the paper rack. This was used mainly for local papers and an odd National Farmer's paper. There were no daily papers in Bowland as I remember, or if there were, we never took them. The papers were always kept well folded and clean. They had a dual purpose; as toilet paper, they would be cut into suitable sized squares, then threaded onto a wire and hung from a nail on the toilet wall. It was not the best of toilet paper, being rather coarse, but it had to do the job, as there was nothing else. In another corner was a small table which held the main source of news. This was the wireless, or radio. The one we had was a large H.M.V. that stood for 'His Master's Voice'. This kept us up to date with time, also National news, and was literally the only source of entertainment in the evenings. It also kept us informed on how the war was progressing, important to our family as quite a few relations were involved, in the services.

There was always a large calendar that displayed all the relevant information my father required. There were farm sale dates, auction market dates and dates of functions in the village; no birthday dates, or days we were setting off for a pleasure outing. There would also be pencilled in the day the ram was turned to the ewes, and the day the lambing time starts, Irishman hiring day, village June sports, harvest festival date and many more.

The farmhouse kitchen had yet another use, and this was as a wash house. Every Monday, without fail, washing took place. The first requirement on washing day was hot water, so, from first rise the kitchen fire had to be piled high with wood and coal, to produce as much hot water as possible. Once there was plenty of hot water the two galvanised dolly tubs would be filled with the required amount of water. One dolly tub would be used for washing and the other for rinsing. There were no fancy detergents or soap powders just soap flakes which we got in large bags from the local Co-op shop in Bowland village. The method of washing the clothes was by a posser or dolly posser. There were two types of possers; one was wood, with six prongs at one end set in a circular piece of timber, with a handle on top, which was used to gyrate the clothes. The other was a copper type dome with holes in it, that you propelled up and down through the submerged clothes until they were reasonably clean.

Once washed and rinsed the clothes had to be mangled. The mangle we had was a heavy cast iron framed type with wood rollers, and this used to stand out in the back yard. The rollers were hand operated via a large hand-wheel with a cog type gear action. Hence, it took a strong person to wind it when in use. The wood rollers on the mangle had seen better days and were well worn in the centre. The wear had been compensated for by nailing muslin cloth onto the roller where wear had taken place, this saved buying new rollers.

Once washed, rinsed, and mangled dry, the clothes would be hung out to dry on a long clothes line strung between apple trees in the orchard adjacent to the house. The small washed items would be hung on the gooseberry and blackcurrant trees. This saved a lot of time pegging out on the rope and wire clothes lines for my mother. It was much easier on washing days if it was fine and dry, but in Bowland this seldom happened. Being set among the Pennine Hills it always seemed to be raining.

The kitchen was always used as the ironing room. This took place on a Tuesday when all the clothes were, hopefully, dry. Once again, no mod-cons, we had a couple of the old cast iron type irons into which you inserted a red hot cast block which, in turn, had been heated in the kitchen fire; not the most efficient of irons, but all that was available in the early forties.

The clothes for washing in that period was fairly scant; we didn't make a lot each week. The farm men and my father would change shirt, vest, pants and socks only once a week. There was no such thing as underpants used in our family so all this cut down on washing. My father, in winter, wore woolly long johns to help keep out the cold, and my mother woollen combs. These, she would always carefully hand wash to avoid shrinking.

It was surprising how clean my mother's washing was kept, with the scant washing utensils she had to hand. A good farmer's wife was always judged by neighbours and villagers on how clean her washing was, and on the appearance of the children when visiting important functions in the villages of Bowland.

The farmhouse kitchen had yet another function. This was the bathroom. I would say very few farmhouses had separate bathrooms, because the water supply tanks were not set high enough above the farmhouse to supply water to the upstairs rooms. Also, there was not the technology for hot water supplies in those days. Our bathing routine was simple; number one, we had to have plenty of hot water. So plenty of wood and coal would be put on the fire then the big tin bath would be brought out of the far pantry, where it was stored when not in use. We had two types of baths, one was oval shaped with a high back and was used for the youngest members of the family. The other was a kidney shaped long one that was used for the older members of the family, and Mum and Dad. I can say with certainty, I never saw them bathing in this bath at any time. If they did, it must have been when all the family was hard and fast asleep. The farm men, I believe, used to bath or wash down in the dairy during winter months, and in the River Ribble in the summer. There was also a belief that, if you washed too regularly, you opened the skin pores and let in cold and germs. There may have been some truth in this theory, as the dirtiest children at school were never off sick whereas the spotless, pampered children were always off sick.

Once the small bath was brought up from the pantry the pegged rug would be removed from in front of the kitchen fire. This was to avoid it getting soaked with bath water. It was particularly nice having a bath in front of the roasting hot kitchen fire with the two candlesticks lighted on the mantelpiece, and the old paraffin globe lamp burning on the kitchen table. This was far better than standing up on the slopstone holding onto the large water pump or having a large sponge down, daily wash.

During these bath nights there was no change of water, so a set boiler full of water had to wash at least four or five. It always got a bit grimy towards the end of each session. After four or five had bathed my father would take his clogs and socks off and give his feet a good soak and wash. My father never suffered from sweaty feet, and after a week his socks were always fresh.

There were not many labour saving gadgets in our farmhouse kitchen as I remember. There was a large knife and fork box where the entire cutlery was stored. These varied a lot. My father always used a genuine bone handled knife and fork and he also liked the knife to have plenty of spring, as he used it rather like a scraper, to clean off his plate. Before the second course, his plate would be so clean after scraping that you could not tell it hadn't been washed. We, as kids, would be given half a slice of dry bread to mop up gravy and surplus food before the second course.

There was a large wire toasting fork that always hung from the mantelpiece ready for use. It was a fair task toasting for our family as by the time the last member had got a slice the first served was ready for the second slice. To make the best toast, a good coal fire was best. What we had to do was rake out the burnt embers of wood and coal from the bars in front of the fire exposing the maximum heat for toasting. Once this had been done it was surprising just how fast fresh toast could be made. Toast was a regular supper time meal and tasted especially good with the varied assortment of home made jams, always preceded by a generous coat of fresh farmhouse butter.

There was also a large glazed earthenware bowl where all the various mixing took place, for cakes, scones, pies or bread. The mixing was always done by hand and it was always made to look so simple by my mother, although a fair degree of skill was required to be 100% successful every time. The other standard gadget, used frequently in the farmhouse kitchen, was the egg whisk. This was used for scrambled egg, custards, whipped cream and mixing various everyday mixes. We used to fight over who could lick it clean when it had been used for whipped cream, cake mix or icing sugar.

There were no electric gadgets to save work, as, at that period, we had no electricity on the farm at all. There were the normal simple aids like a large set of weighing scales with a lot of individual round cast weights. These, when not in use, we used for building bricks. There was a wooden, paddle type churn. This was not automated in any way and it was sheer hard work winding the churn for maybe half an hour before the cream turned into butter. One churn full of cream would produce 7 to 10lbs of butter. Once the butter was made, wooden butter pats would be used to help remove the buttermilk from the butter. Some of these pats would be carved, or embossed with a trademark or farm name, when butter was sold from the farm.

The waste buttermilk would be fed to the pigs. In summer my mother used buttermilk as a sunburn lotion. It was free and it worked well, although the smell of the buttermilk was none too pleasant, especially when you got warm in bed.

The farmhouse kitchen was also a coat and clog store. Behind the large kitchen door, nails had been driven into the strong cross-timbers. These were used to hang the farm mens' jackets and coats on, and also my parent's everyday coats. These were well patched and well-worn garments, which had all come from jumble sales in the village, quite good enough for every day use around the farm.

Under the large oak longsettle were rows of clogs and shoes varying from very small to large. All were matched in pairs, and always in black. My parents believed in our shoes being kept polished at all times. This helped preserve them and the wearers looked so much smarter with well-polished shoes. It was a job I was designated to do once or twice a week, which I didn't like doing, but had to get used to. The clogs never got polished, these were always oiled, dubbined or greased. The grease was from the Christmas goose that could produce at least two pints of grease if it was a fat bird. Oil would be bought from the local clogger if they were heavy working boots. Dubbin would be used. This was much more expensive, but gave better protection.

The décor of the kitchen was not very exciting. There was no fancy patterned wallpaper or paintwork, just the basic whitewash exactly the same as the cowsheds. The only difference was that a lot more care had been taken when the whitewashing took place and it was more of a professional job. I suppose it was all that was available, or all that could be afforded.

The kitchen had yet another use and that was as a hairdresser's shop. My father never paid out money to have our hair cut. He believed his cutting and styling was good enough for the family. He used a large comb and the kitchen scissors most times.

Occasionally, when he had a few of our family's' hair to cut, he would use the old Lister hand wind horse shears. These were always blunt and most painful on hair and head. My father used to laugh and say, "Ay lad, I can't feel owt". The finished haircut was always a jagged mess and the donkey fringe at the front never level. My mother's hair was always quite long and she tied it in a bun at the back. I often saw her washing her hair in the sink but I never saw her cutting it. I suppose she only trimmed the long tails herself and it probably didn't need to be so perfect, as she seldom left the farmstead.

Outside the kitchen window was a large stone slab. This had no particular use that I remember. Its only occupant over many years was old Tim, the farm dog. Tim occupied the slab in all weathers, be it mid summer or mid winter. He was our early warning system when postman or visitors came to the farm.

The kitchen also had yet another use. This was a sewing room that was mostly for darning or repairing damaged clothing. The darning was almost a nightly occurrence with so many socks being in use. Even though my mother only had one eye, she could do a perfect darn on the many pairs of various sized socks and stockings. Her darning was so fine you had great difficulty in detecting it from the original knitting. The tool for the darning was a wooden mushroom, which you used to expand and support the area around the hole, plus a medium sized darning needle.

We had a sewing machine that was always used by my Aunt when making the various sizes and types of clothes for our family. The sewing machine was a foot operated type, manufactured by Singer. I can't say my mother used the sewing machine. I believe she could not see well enough to use a machine that could sew so fast.

On most farms, large or small, the most important room in the house was the pantry. This was where both fresh and preserved food was stored.

In the early forties there were no refrigerators, so storing fresh meat and fish was literally impossible. Therefore once you had purchased fresh food or grown it in your large kitchen garden, you had to eat it as soon as possible, which wasn't too difficult in our household.

During the season, stocks in the farmhouse pantry varied from enough for a week to enough for a month, so a large pantry was required. On our farm there were two pantries, one was the near pantry and the other was the far pantry. The near pantry was for everyday food such as milk and eggs that we produced on the farm, also for salt, fat, lard, currants, raisins, oatmeal, flour, etc.

I remember the first pantry well. This was at the end of a long passage leading from the kitchen down a single step. Both pantries had large, smooth sandstone flag floors that I suppose had become smooth with the constant scrubbing and washing. Also, with the constant wear from the daily trips to and from the kitchen by the many pairs of lightweight clogs which our family used to wear.

In the first pantry there were two large slab sandstone flags on adjacent walls. These flags were around six feet long by four feet wide and a good three inches thick and probably weighed around five hundred weight each. The first slab had three holes in the centre of the slab drilled or cut at equal distances apart. This, I was told, was where the metal cheese vats were positioned so the drainage pipes went through holes in the slab, into buckets. When cheese curds had been produced the surplus milky water was called whey, and was used to feed pigs or for mixing into the poultry feed. Alas, I never saw cheese being made on our farm. I did, however, see the metal vats in use on the farm when we cured our bacon and hams from our own pigs.

I heard many tales about the cheese carts and their drivers who bought the cheese from the local farms and sold it on the markets of Nelson, some dozen miles away from Bowland. These hardy strains of dealers were noted for their drink and would call at all the pubs on the return route from Nelson home. They always made the excuse that their horses required a rest and a drink. It was common knowledge that on most occasions the horse brought the driver home, on its own accord, from the last pub.

These large stone slabs were also used as storage benches, well out of the way of vermin, rats and mice, etc. There would also be stone jars and pots containing a varied selection of potted pork, lard that was used for pies and pastry, also fat for the chip pan. There was always a 3-gallon bucket of milk on the slab ready for a multitude of different uses.

There were also large tins of rice, semolina, sago, tapioca and sticks of macaroni ready to make the large pans full of puddings required to feed the many young mouths. There would be a bucketful of new laid eggs, maybe three or four dozen, also a large earthenware tub where cream was stored to make the many pounds of butter the family used every week.

On a corner there was a large wooden meatsafe, which, in simple terms, was a wooden cupboard clad in perforated zinc. This was where we kept fresh and cooked meat to protect it from flies and bluebottles. The meatsafe also allowed the fresh air to circulate around the stored meat, giving it that extra shelf life.

Also on the sandstone slab was a stone jar containing crushed salt which was purchased in large fourteen-pound blocks. Crushing the salt was yet again one of my many unpaid jobs. What I had to do was slice the salt from the slab, then crush it with my mother's large wooden rolling pin which she used to roll out all

her pastry when baking. Rolling salt was probably a once a month or every six weeks job. The salt I rolled was no good for a standard salt pot because it was far too coarse, so it was always put on the dinner table in a small pot basin from which you would take a pinch to season your meal.

Under the slab was a huge stone pot that was used during winter months to store or pickle the surplus farm eggs laid during late summer and autumn. This we did in waterglass, which I have no idea what it consisted of. During the long dark and cold winter months the hens almost completely gave up laying. Seldom did you have any eggs to collect, maybe only once or twice a week. There was a true saying that was, "Not to worry, they will always lay again when the crows lay", which was late March or early April. This we always found to be true.

On the flagged floor in one corner, stood an extra large earthenware pot that was more or less sealed with a loose fitting wooden lid. This pot was used to store the many loaves of bread, either that my mother baked in the old side oven in the kitchen fireplace, or loaves bought at the Co-op shop in the village of Bowland.

There was also a large pine cupboard in the first pantry. This was used to store baking tins, large meat plates, potted meats, bottled fruit and many varieties of home preserved jam. There were also large oak beams that supported the bedroom floor; these had a dual purpose. There was an abundance of various hooks and nails that all had a use and from which hung dried herbs, mint, strings of shallots and onions, also the filed bills and receipts for many previous years' accounts on the farm, all gathering dust on the unique filing system.

The far pantry was yet another Alladin's cave with so many different items, some used regularly and others just gathered dust. There were the end over end churn which you could make, possibly, 20lbs of butter at one churning, also an old Lister cream separator which would have been used daily to separate the cream from the milk. The cream would be used totally to produce butter. The skimmed milk would be used to feed calves and pigs, hens and farm dogs. The old incubator that was used during early spring to hatch the chickens for our future egg supplies was also stored in this far pantry. There were yet again many hooks and nails that were used to hang the many sets of harness used on our donkey, ponies or horses when out hunting or with the pony club.

There was also a range of shelves which were used for many items, candles, shoe cleaning brushes and cloths, saddle soap, chrome cleaner, the old flat cast irons which were used to do the family ironing, empty fruit bottling jars, jam jars, various paint tins and brushes. You name it, we had it, stored in the near and far pantry. During the autumn months my father would buy a few boxes of Bramley apples to store for winter. These were also stored in the far pantry. We, as children, always tended to pinch a few of these apples; they were darned sour and only supposed to be used for cooking purposes. We always tried to rearrange the apples so that my mother didn't know any had been taken from the box. This we did very well, but she always seemed to find the cores we had deposited out of the bedroom window into the orchard. We didn't get into serious trouble for eating her sour cooking apples.

The far pantry was also the game cellar, where we would hang any game that we had shot on the farm. During and after the war there was no gamekeeper on the estate, so there was no hand reared game such as pheasants, partridge or duck, all were wild. Frequently hanging from the nails in the old oak beams there would be a brace of rabbits, or a single wild hare. Hares were always a darker flesh than the rabbit with being game and it was not so popular with our family because of its strong game taste.

There was sometimes a brace of pheasant hanging for seven to ten days to mature and tenderize. Most game required hanging because of their muscular lean flesh. If not allowed to hang, it was mostly very tough and unchewable. On just a few occasions we would have the haunches of venison hung from the oak beams. This we would shoot on rare occasions when a large stag wandered close to the farm in range to shoot. The stag was always Seka, a breed popular in Ribblesdale. Mostly they would be very mature, six to ten years old and exceptionally strong and tough. With this type of venison you would hang in winter months, three to four weeks at least, before it was tender enough to eat.

I remember one occasion when my cousin had shot a large Seka stag which was many years old. A family friend, Tom, visited our farm and requested some, straight from the freshly killed carcass, to take back to Oldham, where meat was very scarce and on ration. We cut him a piece from the stag's neck, which was the only part of the body where we could get a decent piece, until we decided to totally carve up the body into joints. We warned him that the meat would be tough, but to no avail, he definitely must have some venison to take home. It was five weeks later when he visited again, complaining that he had literally broken his false teeth, and that the only way it was ever going to be edible was to mince it and make it into a pie. It was the same weekend my Mother had decided to cook a haunch that had hung a good 4 weeks to tenderise. First, Tom totally refused a sliced Venison sandwich, on the ground that he didn't want to break his false teeth again. Eventually we convinced him to try a venison sandwich and he could not believe the difference in the tenderness, after it had hung that extra four weeks in the pantry of our farmhouse.

Even though both pantries had flagged floors, plastered and whitewashed walls which you thought were fairly proof against mice and rats there always seemed to be times when you had visits from one or the other. During the summer months there was no problem with mice as they lived outdoors in the banks and under hedgerows with ample food. During the winter months there was little or no food outdoors, so they moved to the barn or to the farmhouse. There were a few methods of catching the mouse. The most popular was the little nipper trap. You put a small piece of cheese onto a spike on a hinged flap which, when depressed, released a strong sprung wire, which clobbered the mouse on the head, killing it instantly. There was also another product that was exceptionally successful called Dak. This was an extra sticky, in fact, bloody sticky paste, which we plastered onto a board and placed it onto the area most frequented by the mice. The mice simply walked or ran onto the Dak and had no chance of escape. We always had to burn the area where the mouse was stuck. There was no hope of removing the dead mouse and re-using the Dak. Seldom did we get a rat in the pantry. If we did, there was always a large hole that the rat would have scratched out from the inside of the wall. These holes we filled with broken bottles and, once cemented up, stopped the rats re-entering.

There was one utensil or kitchen gadget that was always hanging from a nail in the near pantry which my Mother used most days in the kitchen. This was a large galvanised metal ladle that had happy memories. It was when I was, maybe, twelve or thirteen years old that I decided, with the few bob I had saved over the year, to buy my deserving mother something that would be sturdy and last her for many years. At this juncture of my life I was at school not far from the main shopping area. During dinner time or lunch hour I had time to visit the shops. I had great difficulty finding a worthy present that would last with the meagre amount of money I had to spend. I looked at various shops but all the items I thought she may like, and I knew she hadn't got, were beyond my pocket.

My last resort was the main ironmonger's shop in the town. I looked around for quite a while and, finally, saw this large galvanised ladle which would definitely hold half a pint. Dare I buy this for my mothers' Christmas present, would she appreciate my choice? Would she hit me on the head with it? I decided to part with my hard-earned income and purchase the ladle. I got it separately wrapped in Christmas paper. The ironmonger remarked it was the first time he had ever wrapped a ladle in Christmas paper and said it definitely was a most unusual present. I paid the twenty-two shilling and nine pence gross, as he wouldn't give me any discount, as I requested. I took it home and hid it in the barn until Christmas morning. On Christmas morning I gave the present to my mother not knowing what response I would get for my unusual present. To my surprise, she was over the moon with my selection. Within minutes it was in use ladling the hot, bubbling porridge into the many large basins at breakfast time that Christmas morning on the farm.

She remarked it was the most useful present she had received for years. I felt very proud that I had made the right choice. The ladle was still being used when I got married some 10 years later, ladling milk from the three gallon bucket, broth from the large cast pan on the kitchen fire, and jam when in season from the large brass jam-pan.

The Local Hunt

The village of Bolton-By-Bowland was part of the Ribble Valley or Ribblesdale approximately 30 miles from the Ribble estuary and a similar distance from the source at Ribblehead in the Pennine range of hills.

This particular part of the river Ribble was flanked by large woods, rising from both sides with adjoining meadow and pasture land. Our farm was rented from the Bolton Hall Estate which owned quite a large area of land, also fishing rights on the river Ribble. This estate had probably suffered, like many others, estates during and after the war from shortage of both manpower and money. Therefore, it had reached a run down condition, compared with the early years of the century, when nearly all of the villagers worked on the estate, in various capacities, for the landlord or Lord of the Manor, a Major Wright.

Even though the estate workers and gamekeepers had been serving in Her Majesty forces, the wildlife in Bowland and on the estates in Ribblesdale flourished in all its variety. The brown rabbit, in particular, was plentiful in the hedgerows and on the wooded slopes leading down to the river. The Seka deer was fairly common on our Estate. This deer, I believe, originated from Japan, and had been introduced to our area by the late Lord Ribblesdale. There were hares, fox, badger and, on the river, otter.

There was also quite a selection of game birds including pheasant, partridge, wild duck, woodcock, snipe, wood pigeon besides the less popular vermin such as magpie, carrion crow, jay, stoat, weasel and fox, the latter all helping to depopulate the area of songbirds and game. With such a selection of wild birds and game, vermin had to be reduced to a minimum to allow these species to breed and flourish, so most farmers would have guns at their disposal to keep down the magpie and carrion crow. These two birds alone could cause extensive losses to both wild songbirds and farm stock. Both the magpie and carrion crow caused severe, and expensive, damage to the farmers around Bowland in lambing time by pecking out the eyes of newly born, and sometimes part born, lambs. The magpies would pillage the songbird nests for both eggs and young, besides pheasant, partridge and wild duck. It was fairly common to find a nest of eggs totally sucked dry by magpie or carrion crow. The telltale sign was a single hole through the shell where the offender pushed its beak to extract the contents.

The fox was the worst villain of all. It was commonplace to find the remains of a wild duck nest, with feathers and bones from the carcass, where the duck had been brooding a nest of 12 to 14 eggs. This was a total loss of wildlife for a few years, with neither young nor adult female duck to lay and reproduce next year.

The red grouse, in particular, was very susceptible to fox damage, even though the grouse nested on heather moor land where there was vast acreage. The fox had an exceptionally good capacity for smelling and hearing, so tracking the red grouse was not too difficult for him.

Where foxes were present on moorland the farmer had a better opportunity to control them than the lowland farmer. Because the moor was less wooded, and during the winter months there was heavy snow, so the fox could be easily tracked to its lair and then destroyed by terrier dogs, or just by simply digging out the lair.

The worst fox damage occurred if you had forgotten to fasten your poultry in the cabin before dark. Once dark, the fox would visit your poultry cabin every night, to check for that easy meal. The trouble with the fox was that he killed for lust, and would worry every hen, nearly always removing the head in such instances.

During lambing time on the farms, which was from March to early April, the fox was the farmer's worst enemy. Many times during lambing time, a farmer would go round his sheep to check for new arrivals or, maybe, a difficult birth, only to find a ewe with no lamb, or a single, small lamb. This was a sure sign of fox trouble. A fox with a large litter of cubs needed a substantial amount of meat each day, and two or three lambs could be easily devoured to sustain their growth and appetite. So, drastic action had to be taken to eliminate the culprit before the lamb crop had been devastated. The new born lamb crop was one of the main sources of income for many Bowland farmers and families. Once the fox had taken lambs, the farmers had two problems. The first was that he had kept and fed the ewe for almost 12 months, hoping that the ewe would produce one or two offspring. When the fox had taken the lambs there was no income from that ewe, in fact, a huge loss would be incurred when there were no lambs. The second problem was that a spare or kade lamb had to be found. This was usually easy when lambing time was in full swing on the Bowland farms. To find the spare lambs, mostly, it was word of mouth around the farming community, or simply a notice in the village paper shop window. The local farmers would organise a shoot day, when everybody in the village who had a gun would turn out, plus many villagers, as beaters, to drive the fox from the thick wooded slopes on the river banks. Not every shoot yielded success in catching the cunning fox, and in such cases the local hunt would be called in to locate, and hopefully kill, the fox or simply flush the fox from the wood to be shot by the farmers.

Many outsiders did not understand the hunt. They thought of it as sport for the wealthy mill owners and landed gentry, also as a killing machine. They were totally wrong. The hunt was part of country life that helped keep the villagers in work. Not many people realised just how many jobs, which were very scarce in Bowland, were created because of the hunt in those days.

In Bowland village alone, there were blacksmiths that made heavy shoes for the carthorses, and a lightweight range of shoes for the hunting horses and ponies. There were grooms and families living adjacent to the large country houses, in the stable cottages, with all their family attending the village schools, creating jobs for teaching staff, caretakers, etc.

There was kennel staff to look after huntsmen's horses and hounds, in all, probably, four or five men. The wives of most of these hunt servants would work in the surrounding large houses. There were different jobs for these kennel men to do, varying from grooming and exercising the horses to training, cleaning, and feeding the hounds. The hunt kennels in Bowland would keep around 20 couples of hounds of all varying colours. The type they kept were Harriers, which were mainly used to hunt the wild hares of the Bowland and Craven Valleys.

The worst job for the kennel men was skinning and dressing the dead carcasses, collected or delivered from the farms adjacent to the kennels. Removing the dead carcasses from the local farms relieved the farmers of a lot of work burying the livestock. It also made keeping the large number of hounds less expensive. Burying a large cow or horse was a major job for any farmer in those days, when all the mechanisation available was a pick and shovel plus brute force. The stink these men had to put up with was horrific, especially in the summer months, when it only took hours for the carcasses to rot. Passing the kennels on a hot day was a once in a lifetime experience for the town people who used to walk the road from Gisburn to Bowland. They, most likely, had never smelt anything like it before, and never wanted to smell anything like it again. Next to the road were barrels of dog muck. This, I was told, went to the dyeing factories for dyeing the khaki colours in different types of clothing. This all created more jobs indirectly for the town people of North East Lancashire.

With almost every horse that went out hunting with the Bowland hounds, most of the horses would finish up at the hunt kennels, as food for the hounds, when their hunting days were over.

In my father's case our horses never ended there, not unless they died on the farm. My father always sold them on to a horse slaughterer or a horse dealer so he could actually receive a few pounds for the horse. Most farm horses would go for human consumption instead of feeding the hounds. It was also common knowledge that, when the kennels got a young horse in for feeding to the hounds, the kennel staff lived exceptionally well on young horse steaks.

Sometimes we would take a horse to the annual horse sale or market. These were not horses for killing, or aged horses, but schooled to work on family farms, or even milk rounds in the cities or towns.

There were many hundreds of jobs created nationally, producing all the harnesses for the hunt followers, large and small. All the special clothing had to be made. This kept weavers, dyers and finishers in jobs; the jodhpur boot and shoe makers, harness makers, saddlers, jump builders and repairers. After every hunt most jumps had been flattened to the ground, so needed repairing.

It was always quite interesting to watch the hunt. With various types of jumps the faint hearted riders and horses that refused, or couldn't jump, they always waited until last, hoping that the jump had been levelled to the ground so they could just walk over it.

The kennel men and workers from the large estates also had the job of building the jumps for the point to point races for our local hunt, the Pendle Forest and Craven Harriers. They would mostly have to make a brushwood type of fence. These were always made from young silver birch trees that grew wild in the vast and various estate woods. It took weeks, in the spring of the year, to prepare for the local point to point.

Many townspeople did not realise just how much work went into preparing for a point to point race day. People flocked in their thousands from the local cotton towns and villages to gamble that 10 bob or a pound, in the hope of making a bob or two from the many book makers on the big race day.

It was always a very interesting day out at the point to point races, seeing the fashions and different vehicles the punters had arrived in. There would always be the slick Rolls Royce cars, Bentley, Jaguars and many sports cars. Buses would arrive from scores of miles away. People would come on the train to Gisburn station, on the extra trains laid on for the races. There were not so many small private cars, as only the businessmen and, probably, mill managers could afford to buy them. It was always interesting, walking along the rows where the huntsmen and hunt patrons parked, overlooking the final section of the race course and paddock area.

Our farm was about 3 miles away, as the crow flies, across the river Ribble. So, if the river was in low water, we used to take off our boots and stockings and paddle across to save walking miles round by the road.

I don't know whether the purpose was a day at the races, or who could put on the best packed lunch and bar. There would be champagne and whisky flowing freely, salmon, chicken leg and breast, ham and pies to eat, in fact, anything you care to mention. However, at best, I had a paper bag with a couple of jam butties, a couple of rock buns and a small bottle of diluted orange juice to sustain me for the day.

There was always a beer tent at the races, where many punters spent all day, and never backed a horse or saw a race. I never visited these tents as our family was, and always had been, teetotal.

The races were always a gathering point for the eligible young ladies and gentlemen, from both local estates and big houses from farther afield. Many would be very wealthy, and others would be putting on the wealthy image in the hope of meeting a future husband or wife. Also, many farmers' daughters and sons would meet, and romance would eventually blossom from a single meeting at the races.

I felt I had no chance with any of these well spoken young ladies with my humble background, as in those days we did not have a car. If I had been brave enough to ask any of them for a date, my mode of transport would have been my old Raleigh bike, or the local Bowland bus service, which would have been a total let down for these well groomed young ladies, or so I thought.

There was always scandal surrounding these estate owners and their sons and daughters, which opened the eyes of many of the Bowland village dwellers. The theory was that the young ladies didn't work, so they had to use their energy on other activities, and sex was a common method. Many were notorious for this type of relaxation with grooms and farm staff, unbeknown to their husbands and wives, or mother and father. Many of them thought these affairs were a secret, but in Bowlands' tight-knit community there were no secrets, especially where they were having 'a bit on the side'. It soon got round, what was going on.

The hunt would meet at various villages in the Ribblesdale and Craven area and the followers would come from the surrounding towns and villages and also from the other hunts further afield. This was also where romance started among the young eligibles. They were probably the best riders with the best horses and jumpers, but always seemed to lag behind and get broken away from the main hunt. These couples must have found more pleasure in a different type of hunting, not for a fox or hare, but for a partner.

There were lots of stories from the tenant farmers about the ones that lagged behind, and got lost in their out-barn building. Many times the farmer would report seeing these riders warming their hands down their partner's jodhpur breeches or pants whilst riding side by side. One old farmer called Jimmy Dinsdale told of the time when he surprised a riding couple fondling each other when he popped up from behind the hedge and raised his cap, and said, "Good afternoon". Both were well known to him, and married. When he saw this lady some time later, he remarked to her what a good way it was to warm one's hands and that his hands sometimes got cold.

Our family were keen hunt followers, but alas, we didn't have any fancy horses and ponies. We hunted on the horses that did all the work on our farm. They were not the fine-legged thoroughbreds, but half-bred heavy Clydesdale carthorses, with large hoofs and a fair amount of feather or hair next to the hoof, far more powerful horses than the normal hunting type due to working on the farm.

We seldom exercised our horses as they were always doing the heavy farm work. This made them exceedingly strong and exceptional jumpers when out hunting. They were envied by many who had paid hundreds of guineas for a useless jumper. My father followed the hounds almost every Saturday, if the weather was suitable. In winter the hunt would be postponed on many occasions because of snow, frost, or simply waterlogged ground.

We, as farmers, never paid to hunt with the Pendle Forest Hounds, this was because, on certain days, the hunt would go over our land in pursuit of the hare, or deer, which was always plentiful in the Bowland area. Also, we let all our dead cows and sheep go to the kennels to feed the hounds, which saved the hunt money.

When the hunt hounds went into Bowland area and picked up a deer's scent, it was not long before the deer had totally out-paced the hounds. The deer would be many fields and woods away, so the hounds never caught the superbly fit and agile animals. They could cover long distances in minutes, negotiating the treacherous wooded and rock faced banks and thick woodland. They even swam the river, when it was in full spate, with the greatest of ease.

I went hunting on many occasions myself but was never very enthusiastic over it. The only thing I ever caught when out hunting was cold, as it was always raining or freezing cold at that time of the year. Most of the regular hunting people carried hip flasks full of whisky or rum to help keep out the cold. But in our household there was no choice, as drink was seldom available.

There was a lot of unseen work when your family hunted with hounds, as no matter how wealthy or poor you were you had always to be dressed well and your horse to be presented, on the hunt day, well groomed. At our house this had to be done to the highest standard. First, the harness had to be cleaned and saddle soaped, and polished, if it was a special occasion. The stirrups and bits would have to be scrubbed and polished with chrome cleaner. Jodhpur boots or boots and leather leggings would have to be polished literally until you could see your face in the polished parts. Breeches and jodhpurs would have to be perfectly clean. This was all extra work for my mother with washing and ironing, which always took place on a Friday night, in front of the kitchen fire, so there was no chance of relaxing after a hard day's work.

On every hunt morning it was an early rise at about six o'clock. First it was the washing of the hoofs and tail of the horse or pony to get rid of any manure stain which the horse had gathered, whilst laying down to rest the previous night. If the pony or horse was grey, these stains really did take a lot of removing.

There was also the plaiting of the horse's mane and sometimes the tail. All this was to enhance the look of your horse on the hunt day. Often you would find that the best turned-out horse was from the least wealthy owners and householders.

These horse owners felt very proud of their grooming when hunting with the Pendle hounds. I believe that these rider owners decided to spend their limited resources on the pleasure of riding in the country, following hounds, whereas their neighbours would decide to spend their money on holidays, in pubs, gambling, cinemas, etc. It was all down to individual choice.

During the hunting season the future racehorses that would take part in the point to point races had to hunt with hounds on a certain number of occasions. This made them eligible to take part in the races. Then, at the end of the point to point season, these same horses, if proved to a certain standard, would be eligible to take part in the Grand National at Aintree, Liverpool.

Prior to the hunting season there was a lot of unseen work done at the local kennels. It was no coincidence that, when the hounds began to hunt, they all obeyed the huntsman or whipper-in. They had all been trained to this very high standard over many months. Firstly, they were trained for road sense and obedience. How to follow behind the huntsman in an orderly manor, also to respond to the sound of the huntsman's horn and what each sound stood for. They were trained not to chase sheep or worry hens and geese, also to return to the huntsman when ordered to do so.

If they did not obey these orders, the huntsman would give them a stern verbal warning. If that was insufficient there was his last resort, his long tailed whip, which he would crack around the backside of the offending hound. Seldom did he actually hit the hound to bring it to hand. Probably, when he had them in training, out of sight of the public eye, they felt the full force of the long tailed whip and never forgot how it hurt. You seldom heard of a hound doing harm to a farmer's livestock, but on a few occasions there would be hens worried by hounds. The offending hound would always be destroyed, because once a dog tasted warm flesh and blood it would return to worry, be it a chicken or a sheep.

As with every other farm animal, hounds always grew old, so replacements had to be bred, and new puppies had to be trained. It was not just simply putting a male hound with a female hound and taking pot-luck. The huntsmen would observe the best male or female hounds over the hunting season. This was not always taken as crucial, but the confirmation of the hounds had to be studied as well.

The male and female hound would not necessarily be from the local hunt but from hunts in counties far from Bowland. This idea was to introduce a new blood strain to the hounds to, hopefully, enhance the hunting capabilities and stamina of the future puppies. It was always a very interesting time of the year to see the new puppies playing out in the pens, adjacent to the main Bowland to Gisburn Road, before being sent out to the farms and large estate owners to be reared. Often, the villagers who never hunted would rear a puppy for the local hunt, once their puppy had been returned to the kennels. These people would follow the hunt to observe their hounds. The hound would always recognise these people on hunt days, and sometimes were reluctant to return to the pack. The people who walked or reared the hounds were always rewarded for their hard work. The occasion was the puppy walk. This was the day of reckoning when all the hounds that had been successfully reared were judged for size, quality and sense. The puppy walk was usually held at the residence of one of the huntsmen, not far from the kennels. The most popular residence I remembered was Gisburn Park, the home of my favourite huntsman, J R Hindley. He was a wealthy land-owner, but I never found him a snob. He always had time to pass the time of day with any member of our family, unlike some of the hunting people who would walk past you with their nose in the air and just ignore you.

On these puppy walk days you either dressed for the occasion or made the best of what you had. The latter was our family situation. We were more concerned about the condition and appearance of our hounds than ourselves. I must say, my Mother always turned the family out in spotlessly clean and ironed clothes that had probably cost very little compared with some of the other puppy walkers' outfits. There would usually be a large tent, where there was a lavish provision of food of all kinds, something we had never seen before, let alone had a chance to eat.

A solid silver tea spoon was given for every hound returned to the kennels alive. Not every puppy placed with a puppy walker in the spring survived the rearing period. There were large silver cups, for every class, that must be returned for the next puppywalk day, and always an expensive prize which was for keeps. All this led to a more competitive approach by the puppy walkers.

Our puppies were always well looked after on the farm, because they could roam and enjoy the countryside, and they soon got their own ideas on hunting without the attention of huntsmen. Mainly, they would hunt together. I don't know whether they ever caught much but they certainly made lots of noise when in full cry after prey. This always gave them a head start compared with the hounds that had just been reared and mostly confined to kennels. We were always sorry to let these hounds go back to the kennels after the months on our farm.

Even though we lived but a few miles from the kennels our hounds never returned or strayed back to the farm. They always recognised any member of our family on hunting days and would always acknowledge our presence by a tailwag or a lick. The huntsmen often remarked they wished all the hounds could hunt like the ones we had reared and walked. They seldom needed to learn the scent of whatever they were hunting on any particular day, because they had had so much experience back at home on our farm unattended.

My mother always attended the puppy walk day. I suppose she felt that she had done most of the work rearing the puppies. She had done it and it was a reward for all the hard work. She always went up for the prizes if we were lucky enough to win. I can't remember a puppy walk when we didn't go home with a prize of some sort. For my mother it must have been a break from the every day chores back on the farm. It was also an opportunity to meet, if only annually, the neighbouring farmers and their families, also the hunt servants whom she had not seen since the last puppy walk. She felt highly honoured when the huntsman and his wife stopped to catch up with the latest family news, and the happenings in Bowland and the surrounding countryside.

Another major annual occasion, that everybody connected with the hunt looked forward to, was the Hunt Ball. This took place in the largest ballroom in the area and many hundreds would attend. It was quite an occasion, especially for the display of fashion, both for male and female. All the best clothes would be on show at the ball of the year. Most of the ladies would be in evening dress, some must have been very expensive from fashion houses in Manchester and London. The huntsmens' wives and big business owners' wives, wore these dresses, perhaps just once, for that occasion. The men wore dress suits at these large gatherings. The senior members of the hunt would wear hunting pink jackets.

I wore my best suit at these balls. It was not from any famous fashion house, but from a man who travelled and stood at the local cattle market selling shirts, pants, boots, shoes or simply clog laces. This man, I believe, was a good gents' outfitter, starting in business on a shoestring, selling these items by the least expensive method. I remember, when I first had a suit from him, he had a large suitcase that held all his wares and he travelled by train to the local auction markets. When having my suit fitted I had to change in the scant auction toilets and appear with a half finished suit in the auction yard.

My parents' ball outfits were nearly always the last year's models, preserved since last years ball by an abundance of moth balls in the chest of drawers or wardrobe. I remember most farmers' wives always looked exceptionally smart and trim. The answer to the trim was Spirella corsets, which they laced tightly around their bodies, to pull in the 'spare tyre' parts of which there were plenty on many farmers' wives in Bowland.

Otter Hunting

The river Ribble was reasonably clean. There were a few farms, adjacent to the river, that emptied their liquid manure store into it and some farmers drained the sheep dip, after summer and winter dipping, into the adjacent stream, but these were the exceptions.

When the river was so unpolluted, it was the ideal habitat for a wide range of freshwater fish. There was an abundance of brown and sea trout, grayling eel, chub, and, of course, the salmon which was plentiful, depending on the season and water levels of the river. If it was too dry and the water level was too low, no salmon would reach the salmon pools in the Ribble valley around Bowland.

As the river was always well stocked with fish there was demand from predators, both legal and illegal. There was the fisherman who was a member of a local angling club and who paid hefty annual fees for the privilege of fishing in such an idyllic setting, and relaxing surroundings. He took the occasional salmon or, more often, a good-sized sea trout or brown trout.

There were also local farmers living adjacent to the river who would catch the occasional salmon, or trout, by fair means or foul, maybe with a net, as a last resort, his bare hands. The most professional fisher in the river was the wild otter. These were very seldom seen wandering about in daylight as they hunted at night on most occasions. The only way you knew otters were present was the sight of footprints left on sandy or muddy areas on the riverbank, or on the entry to their lair or burrow.

In Bowland there were three known sites where otters could be found. One was the otter's cave, which was a large opening into a limestone rock face. It was a good 15 feet x 15 feet, with a more or less circular, entrance. This led to two smaller openings where the otters obviously lived. Often you could find the remains of a large salmon or trout and lots of otter footprints. This cave was about 30 yards from the river, in the blue limestone rock.

There was also the otter's well, about 400 yards from the cave, upstream. This was, again, a small blue limestone rock face, where water emerged from the ground. There was no visible cavity where a dog or terrier could enter, as the only way to the area beyond the entrance was by diving under water. This, obviously, was no problem to the otter, as otters can remain submerged for long periods of time without taking in air.

Also, along the riverbank were lots of large, mature trees, namely sycamore, beech, oak, etc. The roots of these trees made ideal cover for both otter and rabbit. This was because, over the years, the underside of the tree had been swilled with floodwater, washing out sand and soil, leaving a ready made, safe haven for the otter, adjacent to the river, where fish was plentiful.

After the war there was quite an interest in otter hunting. This, I suppose, was done to keep a balance of otters to fish. In other words, too many otters = no fish, or just enough otters meant fish for both fisherman, and otters, and farmers' sons like myself.

Otter hunting took place possibly only once, or a maximum of twice, a year, depending on how many otters were caught on the first hunt day. I only ever heard of them catching the single otter, or, if it was an exceptional day, maybe two. Before a hunt was arranged there would be a site survey to see if there was much damage being caused by otters. This would be done by water bailiffs or the actual fishermen themselves.

The otter, I believe, preferred the cave as a home, rather than the burrow on the bank, or under the large sycamore tree roots adjacent to the river itself. The cave would be a better, and safer place to have young as well. The cave was, in most cases, totally safe, where hounds, terrier dogs or even man had no chance of catching them.

Prior to hunting the next day, the cave and well entrances had to be blocked, so that, once the otter was out of the cave, hunting or fishing, it could not return to its safe haven. This was where I could earn a couple of pounds for services rendered. At approximately midnight, in total darkness, I would have to go down to the river, which was about half a mile from the farmhouse and block the entrances to both cave and well. I used to throw large boulders into the water. That soon blocked off the entrance to the well denying the otters access. As to the cave, there was a permanent wire mesh barrier that I could use to completely block off the cave entrance. I had to do all this work with the assistance of an old paraffin lamp that we used around the farm buildings. The well and cave were, obviously, in the most inaccessible section of the river bank, with steep slopes down to the river and deep swirling water below. This was dangerous, even for me, who knew well that part of the river, and the steep, wooded slopes.

I remember on the occasion of the last hunt, the paraffin lamp went out and I had literally to return home, negotiating the rocky terrain, on my hands and knees. My mother would always be waiting patiently for my safe arrival home, even at that late hour of the day, or next day.

The otter hounds were not the same hounds that were used to hunt wild hare, fox or deer, but hounds bred and kept especially for that type of hunting. They were big, rough types of hound, much bigger than the local hounds, some with quite long hair. Possibly, this was to protect them from the cold, fresh water. Always, on hunt days there were small, wire haired terriers. These dogs were rugged, vicious little devils, much more savage than the large otter hounds. The terriers used to bolt and catch the otters under the tree roots and shallow burrows.

The otter hounds were not kept locally, as they were used during the hunting or culling season to hunt on rivers within a 50-mile radius of Bowland. I believe these particular hounds came from Cumbria some 30 miles away. Otter hunting was always carried out on foot, by both sexes, and on most days between 20 and 30 would follow the hounds. The terrain was far more difficult than that covered by the local hunt, the followers having to negotiate slippery rocks, deep roots of fallen trees and steep wooded banks. The huntsman, on hunt days, always wore blue hunting attire consisting of long jacket, plus-four, baggy type breeches, with red stockings and strong boots. He always had a very strong, thumb type stick, for extra support on slippery stones and precipitous banks.

Otter hunting people were seldom young, but mainly senior followers of hounds in their forties to sixties. I never heard of much romancing when out otter hunting. I suppose it was the least likely location when you had wet feet and, most likely, wet breeches up to the backside, and it was usually a cold day. On such days the old solid silver hip flask came in very handy. In fact, I think it was part of the standard attire for otter hunters when filled with a good brand of scotch.

The last otter hunt I can remember was on the Coronation day of Queen Elizabeth, June 1953, when the wagon and hounds, plus followers, arrived in our farmyard for the day hunt. My father knew quite a lot of the locals. One in particular, was a retired Colonel Robinson, who was about 65 years of age, and had followed otter hounds for many years. At that time we had just installed our first television on the farm and my father mentioned to him that the Coronation was on, so he decided to stand inside the house and watch the Coronation celebrations.

However, it was not long before he said, "I think I would prefer to forget about hunting otter, Jack, (that was my father's name), and let those silly buggers get soaking wet through and tired out. We can manage this whisky between us". He stopped all day, had his dinner at the kitchen table and left long after the otter hunt had finished.

As far as I can remember, that was the last otter hunt held in Bowland. Maybe it was the end for the pack of otter hounds, which were probably 'put down', in hunting terms, or simply shot. It was the end of yet another country sporting activity where there was no gain. There was no increase in the number of otters, in fact, they seemed to decline rapidly. You did not see the telltale signs of otters, the footprints in the sand, or the fish bones and footprints in the cave.

The wire fence remains to this day. I was most certainly the last person to make the treacherous journey at midnight to the otters' cave and erect the wire fence. There was more pollution in the lower reaches of the Ribble, Hodder and Calder where chemicals from heavy industry were leaked or were illegally dumped.

There were, also, more nets on the Ribble estuary which caught the salmon before they could make the journey up to the river where they were born many years before. There was no better sight, on a summer night, than when the salmon were jumping in the big pool below our farm.

The Pony Club

The pony club was part of the Pendle Forest Hunt, run by senior members to benefit the young riders of tomorrow who, hopefully, would hunt with the hounds when they had gained experience and confidence.

Hunting was not simply learning how to ride and jump. Every hunt day presented its own challenge, with wide variation in landscape. The land could be totally flat, or very hilly, and the jumps were most certainly different. There would be stone walls and thorn hedges, but mostly post and rails. On some estates the landlord who was a keen hunter or, follower of hounds, would get his estate workers to build special, very sturdy jumps, that seldom got smashed or broken. However, they did cause many spills and thrills on almost every hunt day.

The first lesson you had to learn in the pony club was how to walk your pony or horse in the correct manner, then trot, and finally gallop. I could never bother with all the fancy styles, and positions, as requested by the tutor of the day. There was also the teaching of aids, which was communication between horse and rider. The type of horse, or pony, I was used to riding, back on the farm, for my father, was the newly trained or broken horse. Sometimes, a horse that some other rider had not been able to ride, basically because it was half wild, or it was a wise horse, that knew its owner was afraid of it and did exactly what it wanted to do.

The normal communication I had with such horses was a whip. First, I had to show them, in no uncertain way, who was the boss. Some horses I was expected to ride were, literally, bucking broncos, similar to the Wild West cowboy horses. They would simply buck and buck until they, hopefully, threw you to the ground. I had my own method of riding these initially by holding the reigns slack and sticking to the back and front of the saddle. My father's words, before mounting these types of ponies or horses were, "It looks a bit wild, lad tha will have to stick on for dear life".

I was never frightened of such horses, but many times I was thrown off and left badly bruised. I suppose, being only young at that time, I bounced better than the older more professional riders. Often I would be asked to ride one of these spoilt ponies, or horses, by owners and members of the pony club. I soon showed these owners how high these ponies could jump without a refusal, and how fast they could gallop, when all they could persuade the pony to do themselves, was a lazy trot.

The pony club members from the more wealthy families went to boarding school miles away, in the South of England, so there was very little activity when the teenage riders were at school. When they were at home for summer holidays there were summer camps and many gymkhana events. These were always in the Ribblesdale and Craven area, not so far from our farm in Bowland. This was fairly important for our family, because the only mode of transportation was to ride by horse to these events. Probably the farthest distance we would travel in a day was twelve to fifteen miles.

The best-supported event was the hunter trials at our own farm in Bowland. This, my father made with assistance from family and neighbours. The type of jumps we made were reasonably large, with great variation. We mostly called the jumps after the Grand National jumps such as Beecher's Brook, the chair, water jump, etc. The water jump was not too wide, but quite deep. We made these specially by damming up the small stream to form a deep section adjacent to the jump. It gave me and my friends great pleasure to see a pony approach at speed, then stop dead, depositing the rider over the fence and into the water. We doubled up with laughter when this happened.

On the hunter trial occasions, at pony club and at senior level, the farmers in Bowland offered very stiff opposition to the other members and competitors. Our farm type horses and very agile ponies always out performed the normal hunter-type horse. Many times we would literally win all the prizes at these events. There were seldom money prizes, but good, useful items both for rider and horse.

The pony club was a meeting point for the various young eligibles, both male and female, and you could say they were a fairly randy lot. I don't know for sure, but it was fairly common knowledge that there was many romances started, and lots of hearts broken, in the pony club of Ribblesdale.

The theory was that the young virile lads and lasses had been penned up at boarding school for months, then let loose two or three times a year. Also, the fresh air and wide open spaces. I believed it was a little of everything, but it all made for a good time for both sexes.

As a teenage lad, I was always being asked to do the rough and unpleasant jobs many pony club members didn't want to do, or just couldn't do, such as getting the straw for bedding down the horses, or climbing the ladder to get hay from a part of the barn were it was always stored for the winter months. I used to get the help of the willing lasses up on the haystack, some of these lasses were more helpful than others, and one or two in particular were very helpful.

The hay gathering used to start with throwing hay at one another and usually finished up with me stuffing the young ladies riding breeches with hay. One girl, I remember, used to say, don't, don't, stop it". I always took it she meant don't stop and I didn't. They would shout up from the barn floor, "Are you coming?" Some five minutes later I would throw down the required amount of hay, then descend down the ladder a bit flushed and ruffled, especially the lass, and we would complain that the hay knife was very blunt and the hay was very difficult to cut.

There were certain girls who really looked forward to helping me gather hay from the barn, in fact, I always had plenty of volunteers, mainly from the more refined teenage girls that mummy and daddy thought were little angels.

I always found the true country girls to be more knowledgeable about the birds and the bees, as the normal everyday happening on and around the farms.

We seldom bought a horse on our family farm. We always bred from one of the working mares that were normally dual purpose horses, with exceptional strength and durability, plus good conformation and temperament.

We would cross these mares with a thoroughbred stallion, as used in flat and point to point type races. The offspring would always make more powerful and better jumpers, both at hunter trials, show jumping, and when hunting with hounds.

When these horses were fully trained my father never sold them to the genteel hunting class. Perhaps he never asked enough money for them, or he never talked in guineas, or they didn't want to tell their friends that they had bought a carthorse-type hunter. They may have thought that I had trained the horse, and it might be a bit of a tyrant, or slightly unruly.

One of the many social events of the pony club was the annual Pony Club Ball. This was held, normally, in late summer, during the holiday period for the boarding schools, where most, if not all, of the pony club members attended. The Pony Club Ball, along with most pony club activities, had to be organised during a holiday period.

I had never attended the Pony Club Ball, mainly because it was regarded as a 'posh do', where all the girls were wearing evening dresses and the young lads were all in dress suits, or monkey suits, as they were called locally. I had been asked many times to come to the Pony Club Ball, but without the proper attire I would have looked out of place, so I never attended.

My only suit at that particular time was a lightish blue, totally the wrong colour for such a prestigous event. The jacket and pants were a sloppy fit, because we always expected the suit to last many years before outgrowing it, or wearing it out. I often had my leg pulled about my oversize suit with extra wide trouser slops and broad waistline. The local farmer, Percey Geldard remarked, jokingly, that my pants reminded him of a poultry cabin. When I asked why, he remarked, "There is plenty of room for the cock to stand!"

It was probably in my later teens when my sister and I decided to go to the Pony Club Ball, after much persuasion. It meant buying a completely new outfit; dress shirt, new suit, socks and shoes, plus a dicky bow tie. My sister, likewise, had to buy a new long dress and shoes.

I didn't have much money as I hadn't caught any rabbits during the summer. My only other income had been muck spreading and hay making for the local farmers during spring and summer. I decided the best place to purchase my dress suit was at my personal gents' outfitters at the cattle market. I knew he could make a good suit, but had no idea if he was capable of making a classy evening dress suit. The only way to find out was to visit his stand at the cattle market. He now had a motorbike and sidecar, an update on when he came on the train, with just a single large suitcase containing his wares.

I enquired about the suit, which was no problem for him to make. He had a fair selection of styles in his small brochure, consisting of pages taken from a well-known high street gents' outfitter. He had cut, trimmed, and cut the names from, the many pages which would have disclosed the high street designer. My only consolation was that I knew he would be at least half the price for the same suit, basically because he had no shop, no wages, no overheads; only the odd gallon of petrol for his B.S.A. motorbike and sidecar.

It was a dry day, so there was no need to stand inside the cattle market to get measured for my dress suit. He carefully measured and booked down every measurement required to make a perfectly fitting suit. Whilst being measured I was watched by the many farmers who were at market to buy and sell their livestock.

He requested that I should be at the market in three weeks' time to have a final fitting. This I did, as time was getting short to obtain the full attire for the Pony Club Ball. On fitting day, I had a pair of trousers temporarily tacked together with white cotton, and a jacket with only one sleeve attached. It was an unusual fitting, with may onlookers passing remarks about my new suit. One farmer I know remarked, "It looks a bit expensive to go muck spreading in".

The day of the big event soon arrived. I looked a real bobby-dazzler in my monkey suit, new shoes and dicky bow tie. My sister had been down to Bowland village to have her hair washed and set. Once she had her ball gown on, plus new shoes, she looked a million dollars. In fact, we could both have passed off as the offspring of the country squire. The only difference was that our ball expenses had literally left us both skint.

I had washed and disinfected the family car, or livestock transporter, for which it was mainly used at home, so it didn't smell too strongly of calf muck or urine. I could have been a little embarrassed if I had got fixed up at the ball with one of these fine spoken, well groomed, young debutantes and offered to take her home in my unusual smelling passion wagon. Once at the ball we both had quite a shock. I found that many of the revellers who I thought I knew quite well, who I competed against at pony club events, totally ignored us. In fact, they were darned right ignorant. They walked past my sister and I with their noses in the air, as if there was a foul smell. I thought, "It can't be the car, because I made such a good job of cleaning it". They were totally ignorant young snobs. It was a different story when the huntsmen and many of the parents, walked past. They did stop to enquire about our parents, and how all the horses were back at home.

What we didn't realise, until, maybe, half an hour after arrival, was that we weren't with a particular party so we were left standing a little bit like stuffed dummies, with nowhere to sit. However, it was not long before one of the well-known, respected, hunt servants came and asked us both to join their table. This we did and found their company and hospitality very enjoyable. There was whisky and wine and every kind of drink, in abundance. Both my sister and I didn't drink alcohol, so we didn't take advantage of the situation.

As the night progressed, the snobbery continued. My sister was hardly asked for a single dance. I asked many young ladies for the next dance but got put off with the answer, "I have already been asked", only to find, afterwards, that they never left their party table.

The Pony Club Ball was, most certainly, an experience where we found out who were our true friends, and who were not total snobs. I will certainly remember who they were the next time they want me to ride their pony for them. I may even take advantage of them when getting hay and straw for the horses from the hayloft!

Rabbits Of Ribblesdale

From the estuary of the river Ribble to its source, some 60 miles up stream, at Horton in Ribblesdale, there were idyllic habitats for the rabbits to breed and thrive. At the estuary of the river there were sandy riverbanks and hedgerows that divided the large, flat fields where grain and root crops grew prolifically. This was where most of the fresh vegetables grew, to supply the cities and towns of the North of England. The rabbits of these areas had a more difficult environment in which to survive than other parts of the Ribble Valley. This was because the farmers had a far more expensive and intensive crop to grow than did farmers upstream. Rabbits could destroy large tracts of grain or cabbage type crops that grew here. A few rabbits could devastate a field of young cabbage or carrots, during the first few weeks of growth, so the farmer had no mercy when seeing a rabbit among these crops. He simply took his rifle or shotgun and shot them dead.

As the Ribble Valley got nearer to the source, the terrain completely changed from the large, flat, arable fields to the small hill and dale pasture land, where no grain or root crops were grown. Only cattle and sheep were kept in these areas, to produce the fresh milk, cream and beef, also mutton and lamb for the family's Sunday dinner.

In these areas the rabbit had a much better chance of survival because of the extra cover that was available. There were densely wooded slopes leading down to the river's edge, where large trees lined the river bank, ideal for the wild rabbit to breed and prosper. Also, there were small quarries, where stone had been blasted out to build the many picturesque villages along the river and adjacent countryside. These were ideal places for the rabbit to breed and thrive and where it was very difficult for the farmer and landlord to reach the pests.

In these areas, well away from the river, there were also vast areas of woodland, planted by the many landlords to supply their estates with timber for both housing and stock fencing. These woodland areas were dual purpose; pheasant was reared for shooting during winter months by the landlord and his business guests or friends.

On the outskirts of these woods there were many varieties of low growing bushes and brambles, providing cover for the pheasants, during their rearing period, until days when they were driven out of the woods to the guns, waiting to take a pot shot, 200yds. away from the woods' edge. These woods make the most perfect place to give maximum protection for the young rabbits when they have left their birthplace burrow, or nest, and become independent, and having to fend for themselves.

Nearer the source of the river, the habitat of the wild rabbit changed considerably, yet again. This was because of the height above sea level. At the estuary it was sea level, whilst upstream maybe 250ft. above sea level rising at the source to maybe, 500 to 1000ft. above sea level. At the higher level it was relatively tree less and there were very few woodland areas as on the lower reaches of the river.

This higher level, however, was no deterrent for the wild rabbit; the large woodland areas were replaced by vast areas of limestone outcrop, where the natural cracks, faults and crevices in the rock provided a very safe environment for the rabbit. These cracks could go many hundreds of feet into the rock surface where there was no chance of catching a rabbit with nets or ferrets.

There were also scores of miles of dry stone walls which gave warm and dry shelter for the rabbits during the heavy rains and snows which were far more prevalent than in those areas some sixty miles down the river, nearer the sea. The fields were vast, often many hundreds of acres in size, also, very hilly, where the only livestock farmed was a rugged, special breed of sheep which could survive on the high pastures, mostly Swaledale.

The rabbit population in all these areas, could vary drastically from year to year, depending on the breeding season and winter months. If it was too wet in the breeding season, tens of thousands of young, new born rabbits would drown and perish. If there was an exceptionally cold winter, with hard frost and heavy snow falls, the rabbit population could be, literally, wiped out. The latter was the case in the winter of 1947, one of the worst winters on record for the rabbits and the many species of wildlife that lived during the winter months in Ribblesdale. The wild rabbit was an exceptional reproduction machine and far outpaced any other wild animal in the Ribble Valley in the 'rapid breeder' field.

Without natural losses and predators the statistics of the reproduction cycle of the rabbit are outstanding. For a mature female rabbit, from conception to giving birth is 31 days, producing six to ten young. A few days after giving birth, the rabbit will again conceive , and produce another litter within 31 days. In the meantime the first litter of young will have opened their eyes and left the nest or burrow. They will be self-supporting, eating only grass and herbs from the adjacent meadow or pasture or if on the lower reaches of the river, young cabbage plants or the early shoots of wheat or corn.

This first born young rabbit would also mate and conceive within a few months. It is a truly mind boggling thought that from, say, twenty mature female rabbits in March, how many thousands of rabbits there would be to eat the farmer's valuable and necessary crops, to sustain both humans and farm animals over the following winter months.

The wild rabbits never used an existing burrow to have their young. This, I suppose, was because there was multi occupancy of the large burrows, where ten plus rabbits could live permanently. The expectant doe, or female rabbit, would usually scratch out its own maternal burrow, normally in a field or meadow, maybe two to three hundred yards from the main burrow. This short burrow would be a maximum of 6 feet long and maybe 6 inches to 12 inches deep.

Before giving birth, the female rabbit would almost completely pluck all the fur from its belly, or underside, to line the maternal home creating an exceptionally warm and cosy nest. Plucking its belly also exposed the very small nipples where the many young took the mother's milk, to promote exceptionally rapid growth, during the first few weeks of life.

Immediately after birth the female rabbit would leave the young for long periods at a time. Whilst the female rabbit was away from the maternal burrow, the entrance would be completely sealed daily. This was to prevent predators from accessing the burrow and killing the young rabbits.

When the young rabbits were newly born they were a rich pink colour, with not a trace of fur. They also had their eyes closed for the first few days of life. The female rabbit's milk must be exceptionally rich in both vitamins and protein to nourish the babies at such an exceptionally fast rate. Within a few weeks the rabbit would be literally self-supporting, eating grass and not requiring milk from the mother. The maternal burrow was always completely closed for the first week to ten days. After ten days the burrow entrance would be opened to allow the young rabbits to exercise and graze the fresh new grass, or crop, adjacent to the burrow.

It was always very easy to recognise a maternal rabbit's burrow where the young had survived the critical first few weeks after birth. The ground close to the burrow would be padded flat and the grass would have been eaten bare. There were also the tell tale droppings of the small rabbits, in abundance, around the burrow's entrance. A sure sign of an unsuccessful rearing of a clutch, or nest, of young rabbits was if the burrow was open, with all the fur scattered around. Also, there were similar signs if the nest had been dug out by a dog, or cat, from the local farm, or maybe the cunning wild fox, badger or stoat, and there would be no padding of the ground or young rabbit droppings around the nest.

The young rabbits of Ribblesdale had to endure many predators and climatic conditions during the first few months of life, and even as mature rabbits. There was always some animal or human ready to take advantage of the prolific amount of food made available by the vast numbers of wild rabbits. When the rabbits were very young, they really had a high risk of perishing.

There were so many different birds or animals that could make a meal of a very young rabbit. When the nest was first opened the young rabbits were very small and totally unaware of the danger to their lives, once they left the nest. There was the barn or tawny owl that could pick up a small, young rabbit, quite easily when in flight during late evening, or even in total darkness. This was a swift and silent death for lots of young rabbits and field mice. There were also the semi wild cats and farm cats that would take young rabbits from the nest or even half-grown young rabbits.

The cats had great difficulty carrying the rabbits back to their young at the farm. It was interesting, seeing a cat, with a large rabbit in its mouth, dragging a carcass many hundreds of yards back to its young.

The farm dog would seldom catch a half grown or mature rabbit because it was by no means as good a stalker, or hunter, as the farm cat. The dog usually took the young rabbits from the nest by excavating the burrow and gaining access to the young.

The badger would always take the young rabbit direct from the nest because he was more cumbersome and far less agile than the farm cat or fox. The badger had no difficulty in digging out the burrow with its powerful front legs and feet, or simply digging up the burrow with its strong, pig-like nose.

The fox was probably the best of all the wild animals at catching the wild rabbit. Even from the young to the mature rabbit the fox always had the upper hand. The fox would scratch out the nest or simply play the waiting game and grab the young rabbit when it was leaving the nest or burrow. It would also lay and wait in the semi-long grass, positioned as close to the burrow as possible, so that the rabbit was taken totally by surprise, unaware of the fox's presence. The fox could easily out run a rabbit over the first few yards, and take a relatively easy meal for a family of fox cubs which could eat lots of meat, before being capable of hunting for themselves.

The stoat was another wild animal in Ribblesdale that reduced the population of wild rabbits. The stoat never, or seldom, ate the carcass of the rabbit, it normally only sucked the blood and caused death to the rabbit in that way.

You would often see a rabbit, during the daytime, running across a field or even through the farmyard being pursued by a stoat. The rabbit would eventually stop in a mesmerised state and not be exhausted at all. It would then allow the stoat to bite it on the back of the head, just behind the ears, where it would literally penetrate the main artery, and suck all the blood from the rabbit until death took place.

The rabbit normally squealed during those last few minutes of life. This sometimes attracted the farm cat or dog and, if it was in a large wood, even the fox. The fox had exceptionally large ears, capable of receiving, over a long distance, such distress sounds of a dying rabbit. It was a sure sign that stoats were around, if you found a dead rabbit with a mutilated small area at the back of the head, where blood had been sucked.

The stoat had no permanent burrow or home. It normally lived in stone walls, farm drains of the old stone type, or disused rabbit burrows. The stoat was quite small compared to a large fully-grown rabbit. It was smaller than the average ferret, maybe from head to tail 15 inches long with a white blaze down its chest and a black tip to it's tail. In winter, many stoats would change from brown to totally white, making themselves less conspicuous, and giving an advantage when catching prey.

The golden eagle or buzzard would take fully-grown rabbit in flight to feed their offspring. Although a common sight in Scotland, alas, there were no eagles or buzzards in Ribblesdale to lessen the rabbit population.

As children, on our family farm we had loads of pleasure with the wild rabbits. We would take two young rabbits from the nest and try to rear them ourselves. We were rarely successful. The young rabbit always seemed to fear our presence and be totally afraid when we fed them and changed the hay from their nest-box hutch. They died mostly of stress within a week. The mother rabbit, somehow, at their very early stage of life, made them fully aware that man was no friend of theirs. The odd two or three young rabbits we took and lost made very little difference to the vast quantities of rabbits in the Ribble Valley.

As I grew older the rabbit was a prime source of income, or, should I say, my only source of income. We would catch rabbits for sale only when there was a letter R in the month, that is, from September to April. There were so many different ways to catch wild rabbit. The most popular method we had was the ferret. These we used to breed in a similar type of hutch to the rabbits, a two-compartment hutch with separate nesting facilities.

The ferreting method of catching rabbits I used from ten years old up to my early twenties. The price we could obtain for a large, fully-grown rabbit in the village was three shillings and sixpence, a lot of money in the mid forties and early fifties. As I got older, I obtained my own small shotgun, a .410 bore, ideal for shooting rabbits when at close range. The .410 was an ideal small gun when bolting rabbits from their burrows on an open embankment or wooded slope. When a rabbit was bolting from the burrow it was fairly difficult to shoot, but, as with many sports, you only improved with practice, and on our farm we had plenty of practice when the rabbit was in season.

When catching rabbits it was always best on a cold, dry day in late Autumn or Winter. We seldom tried to catch rabbits in rain or snow. Another very popular method of catching rabbits was by snares. We used to buy these from the sports shop or agricultural merchant in the local town. They were professionally made from twisted copper wire with a flexible cord that you attached to a large peg that held the rabbit when it got caught.

Selecting and setting the snare was a fairly professional job. You had to make sure to place it on the run where the rabbits left the wood to graze the adjacent meadow or pasture. Some of these rabbit runs started at the boundary fence adjacent to the wood and continued, maybe, one hundred to two hundred yards up the field. Why the rabbit used to stick so rigidly to the same path to make a significant run, one may never know.

The best site to set the snare was close to the wood fence, or 30 to 50 yards out in the field. Two pegs would be required; a large peg to secure the snare in the ground and a fine, sharp peg with split top to set the snare upright and at the correct height from the ground. The latter fixing position was very important if you were to be a successful snarer of the wild Ribblesdale rabbit. When setting snares you always had to remember how many you had set and exactly where in the fence or field you had set them.

I had an Uncle who tried to snare rabbits without much success. He always decided to set his snares in the centre of the field, on the best-used runs where he should have been very successful. His problem was that he couldn't see very far at his ripe old age of 75. Therefore, his method was to collect or pull the large feathers from the White Leghorn cockerel and stick them in the ground alongside the newly set rabbit snare so that he could easily find them. This, I believe, scared the rabbit from the snare, so my Uncle was no threat to the rabbits on our home farm.

You could always demand a slightly higher price for a snared or ferreted rabbit than one that had been shot. The reason was no lead pellets or damage to the flesh. The wild predators and also human predators, like myself, with snares and ferrets, only made a small dent into the vast amounts of rabbits on our farm and neighbouring farms. There were simply just too many rabbits.

In my mid to late teens, with my cousins and neighbouring farmer's sons, we decided to make a long net in which we could, hopefully, catch large numbers of rabbits at once. We taught ourselves how to knit a rabbit net with string. We spent long nights and weekends making this net by hand. The finished product was 50yds. long and was only a fraction of the total nets we anticipated using to catch the rabbits.

After our first trial nights of netting, using our new net, we found out that the type of string we had used was too thick, and a grey/white colour that the rabbits would not go near, let alone get entangled in. Once wet, the net was too heavy to carry for long distances and proved to be a total flop and no use whatsoever. Our next nets were found advertised in a national farming paper and were made in Shrewsbury. These were quite expensive to buy, especially when all the money I had was saved from either spreading manure heaps for local farmers, or selling the occasional rabbit in the village of Bowland.

Five of our local syndicate clubbed together to buy the nets, a total of 250yds. in length. We really believed we could earn some spare cash catching the rabbits with our long nets. What we did before going out early evening in darkness was to practice running out the nets in daylight. This we did after lunch, early evenings, and Saturday afternoons or Sundays. After a dozen or so practice runs we found that within three to five minutes we could run out the net and pegged it down perfectly, vital when catching the wild rabbit by the long netting method. With long netting you had always to select the correct wind and weather. The perfect night was slightly moonlit, dry, and with a medium wind. You always had to net into the wind. If the wind was blowing from the west you always faced the wind. This was because the wild rabbit had a very sensitive smell, and, if it picked up the human scent, it would immediately warn its fellow rabbits of imminent danger. The wild rabbit did this by stamping the ground extremely hard with its hind legs, creating a large thud type bang which could be heard over a fair distance by its fellow rabbits, causing them to retreat quickly to the more secure areas of woodland or burrow.

By September the rabbits were mostly fully grown and in prime condition for the winter. They had, by this time of the year caused severe damage and nuisance to the many farmers in the Bowland area. They had totally eaten the grass in pastures and meadows along the length of the River Ribble in our area. They had also fouled the area with urine and droppings, so the livestock refused to graze any grass that was left.

Many farmers would ask us to catch their rabbits urgently, so they could have winter feed left for their sheep. So it was all go for the 'bunny boys' as we were soon called. The first night that we decided to try out our new skills, of semi-professional rabbit catchers, was fairly successful. With a bag of seventy rabbits, this was a lot of rabbits for our new team of long netters. Not only had we to carry them at least a mile, they had to be fastened on a short rope and divided between the three of us, with a fourth man carrying all the nets. This was a very tiring night, but well worth our hard, enjoyable night's sport.

There were many hundreds, if not thousands, of rabbits on the other side of the river Ribble close to our farm. The owners of the land always requested that we helped reduce their rabbits early in September, or as soon as the rabbits came in season. Those on the far bank of the river always caused us a problem. The main problem was the water level. If it was too high there was no way we could cross the river, and it was far too long a distance to travel around to the rabbit fields by road bridge. Therefore, we just could not catch the rabbits until the water level on the river dropped to low, or average, summer levels.

The method, when we did cross, was to remove our clogs and stockings and wade barefoot, that 30 to 40 yards. We did not believe in having wet feet all night just for the sake of a little cold and pain from the icy cold water and rough gravel bed of the river.

I well remember one particular night when catching, or attempting to catch, rabbits for one farmer, who had requested our services for many weeks. It was a perfect night, fairly windy, semi moonlit and crispy dry. The night had all the signs of being a record bag for the 'bunny boys.'

We knew the rabbits were extra well fed because there was a field of turnips and kale, ideal for fattening the many hundreds of rabbits in the immediate area of the field. We took four of our best nets, a total of two hundred yards, also enough short lengths of rope to fasten the rabbits together to carry them back to the farm after a successful netting operation.

All went extremely well. We crossed the river easily without falling in or getting wet. The water was extremely cold as there was a slight frost. We arrived at the field in high spirits and within a few minutes had run out and pegged the two hundred yards of net perfectly, all ready for the flush of rabbits from the turnips and kale. Normally one man stopped with the nets to kill and remove the rabbits from the net in order to allow more rabbits to be caught, and also to prevent the netted rabbit from chewing the string mesh, leaving large holes where the rabbits could easily escape. It was only seconds before the net vibrated with the shock of a rabbit hitting the net at speed, a signal for the net attendant to go and remove the rabbit as soon as possible making room for the expected stampede of rabbits scampering from the turnip field.

All of a sudden there was a thundering sound, just like a large animal was heading for the net, something we had never heard before. It was only seconds before the nets were ripped out of the ground, the supporting cords snapped, and large holes appeared in the net and no rabbits. We soon decided that the culprit was a badger that was at least ten times the weight of a rabbit, exceptionally strong, with sharp teeth that caused extensive damage to our nets, rendering them useless that particular night. I don't know just how fast a frightened badger can run down a steep field but it seemed to be in excess of 20 miles an hour. There was no way we had any chance of netting a badger that night. We learnt afterwards that there was a couple of badger setts in the wood adjacent to the turnip field. We returned home via the river with only seven well nourished rabbits in the bag. We didn't need the short lengths of rope to transport our catch home that night.

There were many hours of net repairing to be done before we could resume our netting enterprise. I suppose it was a good example of don't count your rabbits before they're caught'.

My father would always look into the rabbit store first thing the next morning to count how many we had caught and remark there would be a lot more grass for the sheep with so many less. In the few months we caught rabbits in the Ribble Valley, a conservative estimate of the total bag would be in excess of 2,000. This obviously drastically reduced the rabbit population in our area. It also boosted our spending money considerably. Most of these rabbits were transported to a small town butcher, where he could have sold twice as many if we could have supplied.

Even with all the various predators and human methods we had of reducing the rabbit population, many farmers would call in the Ministry of Agricultures' pest control officers to gas the remaining strongholds of rabbits. They would use cyanide gas in the burrows while the rabbits were resident during the hours of daylight. They did this by blocking up the many entrances to the burrows and finally pumped in the cyanide gas, killing all the occupants.

By the early fifties the rabbit population was more or less out of control with rabbits once again in the thousands. In summer, as we walked along the meadows and fields adjacent to the river, the fields literally seemed to move with so many wild rabbits scampering to safety back in the wood. Then, out of the blue, came the final solution to the many thousands of rabbits, Myxomatosis, a disease originated, supposedly, by a chemist in Australia. Within 2 months the disease had really taken its toll, there was literally not a single uninfected rabbit left. They could be found totally blind around the farm buildings and fields, but still eating grass as though there was nothing wrong with them. Their eyes and ears would be very swollen and red, oozing pus. Also their abdomens were very enlarged. This disease was sexually transmitted, so it was no wonder it spread so rapidly.

By mid September the pools along the banks of the river Ribble were polluted with hundreds of rotting rabbits' carcasses making swimming or paddling for our family and friends unsafe. We all waited for the thunderstorms and heavy rains to literally flush the thousands of carcasses away. Heavy rains did at last oblige and flush all the stinking carcasses from the pools on the Ribble. But there were lots more rotting carcasses left around our farm. These soon got cleansed of the rotting meat by the blue bottle flies, which laid their eggs on the carcasses. These, within a short period of time turned into maggots and soon devoured the rotting flesh.

The farmers of Ribblesdale were glad to see the end of the rabbit infestation. Their meadows and fields could now grow grass to feed their livestock. There were no longer the rabbit runs from the many large woods or areas of grass polluted with urine from the many rabbits.

We missed our rabbit pies, also, the spending money we received during the winter months from catching the Ribblesdale rabbits. Our long nets we burnt, the snares were no longer required and the ferrets we had to destroy. Our net making skills we would never again require. The young rabbits we used to take home and hope to rear, were gone. It was, finally, the end for me of a truly interesting era of my life in Bowland.

Once the rabbit population had been devastated to, literally, a single rabbit, the wild hares then returned to the meadows and pastures on the farms in Bowland. They didn't return in significant numbers, just, maybe, one or two to a hundred acres. This was partly because hares were territorial and could be seen boxing and fighting on many occasions, protecting their territory and partner.

The hare was totally different from the rabbit in that it always lived above ground, and never burrowed like the rabbits. The hare never stopped in the same place for long, you could see it on a warm, sunny day, squat, basking in the sun in the middle of a meadow or field, with no camouflage on any side. This was probably a good defensive idea as the hare could see if danger was approaching from all four sides and was forewarned of imminent danger.

During the winter months the hare would tend to live more in the large woods amongst the dead bracken and brambles. These were warm areas in the winter and good cover and camouflage for the hare. If there were no woods, the hare would simply scratch a suitable temporary shelter out of a small clump of wild rushes. This was ideal camouflage and a good, sheltered windbreak.

When the hare gave birth to the young leverets, or baby hares, the nest was quick and simple, unlike the rabbits that dug a short shallow burrow. The hare simply selected a clump of rushes or overgrown dead grass and in a short period of time scratched out a cosy sheltered nest for its young. The hare was once again different from the rabbit in that it only produced 2 or 3 young, instead of the rabbits 6 to 10. The young leveret was born with a full coat or fur and unike the rabbit it was also capable of running at speed within a few days of birth.

After two to three weeks the young hares would leave their nest and split up, each going its own way, still to be watched over and fed by the female hare, until strong enough to graze grass and be self supporting without milk from their mother.

The hare population in Bowland was never a problem to the many farmers simply because the hares only gave birth to two or three young at once and most only had one litter of young per year. I can say, I never liked to eat hare simply because it was of a strong game taste, and red flesh, unlike the wild rabbit which was mild and light fleshed. Also if you had hare you always got a few lead pellets to chew and spit out because you mostly had to shoot a hare to kill it, unlike the rabbit which you could ferret out of its burrow, and net, causing no damage to the carcass and flesh.

Fair Maids Of The Land

During and after the war, staff on most Bowland farms was in short supply. Extra staff were very difficult to find to help cope with the demand by the Government to grow more food.

The only answer was work hands from outside the villages. Therefore, the Government recruited a workforce of teenage to mid twenties girls, who were, appropriately, called the Women's Land Army. These girls' statistics varied considerably, from the slim petite young lass to the 16 stone buxom brunettes, with bust and backside of similar proportions.

In Bowland there was a variety of names for this newly recruited army of fair lasses. It could be the W.L.A. or the 'Women's Layking Army', plus many other slang names not suitable for printing. The farmers were notorious for not mincing words and speaking what they thought. Our landgirl, called Dorothy Simpson, was one of the latter statistical types, with an appetite like a horse. Her calories must have been counted in thousands and not hundreds. Her nickname was Dot, which under described this 16 stone damsel, standing a good 5'10" high. Whatever their age or statistics they certainly filled the gap left by the exit of young farm men conscripted to serve in Her Majesty's forces for military service. These fair young maidens came from towns and cities many miles from the scenic Bowland. They had a big shock when they found out about country living on remote farms and villages

They couldn't understand why there wasn't a town within 8 miles, why the nearest shop was 1.5 miles away and why the bus didn't pass every 15 minutes. Also, no newspapers, no chip shop, no pubs, no clubs and no football teams. There were so many things they took for granted back home, that they had a major shock on the Bowland farms. Many left to return to the town and city life because they were so homesick. They also missed the red telephone box where they could ring back home or to their friends.

Many had no idea what farming was about and where farm produce came from, or how. Some thought milk came out of a bottle, butter out of a packet, beefsteak out of a tin, oxtail was invariably always covered in cow muck (just to add to the flavour). Eggs were almost certainly always in a basket. They soon began to understand the fact that a farmer was a producer of live animals, which were eventually sold for slaughter, to stock the shelves in the town and city stores. Most of the food produced on farms during the war was on ration, with coupons allocated for almost everything but vegetables.

There were various jobs for the landgirls on and around the farms. The main work for many of the local landgirls was tractor driving. This was for cultivating, ploughing, seeding and harvesting the extra food farmers had been compelled to grow to help stock the larder with food for the nation. There was a depot at Gisburn, our next local village. There were many different tractors, from the Fordson standard, to the huge Case and International supplied to England under 'Marshall Aid' from the United States of America, to help in food production because of the shortage of imported cereals from Canada and the U.S.A. Most of the tractors ran on T.V.O., which was short for tractor vapourising oil, and a far cheaper fuel than petrol during that period of war. It was also a time before diesel engines were available to the agricultural tractor and most commercial vehicles. The tractor would not start solely on tractor vapourising oil, as this fuel had to be pre-heated before it would ignite. All tractors had to be started on petrol until the engine was warm enough to be changed over to T.V.O. If the engine was changed over too soon before it was warm enough, there would be more smoke on the unburnt vapour belching from the exhaust than the flying scotsman train. The exhaust fumes from T.V.O. was quite pleasant to smell compared with petrol or diesel and seemed to have an effect on the landgirls complexion, leaving them with a mild suntan. To be fair, this could have been a mix of Bowland air as well. Driving tractors and working on farms during the early forties, and all types of weather, was a rough job. There were no tractor cabs to protect these fair lasses or even adequate clothing.

It was a lovely job on a midsummers day, but darned cold sat on top of a tractor in mid winter, with pouring rain and a stiff north easterly wind blowing. The landgirl soon lost that mild white office complexion for a rugged outdoor wind swept coarse headed; acclimatised; country lass.

Many crops which the Bowland farmer were required to grow were totally wrong for that part of the country. Root crops such as turnips and mangols which was very succulent and only used to feed livestock.

There were many implements at the Gisburn depot, never seen before by many Bowland farmers. There were drag ploughs, hydraulic ploughs, disc harrows, cultivators and Massey Harris binders used to cut the corn, barley and wheat into sheaves. There were also the huge Marshall threshing machines, stationary balers that used a fine steel wire to securely tie the bales of straw.

There was no power steering on any of these tractors to help the fair town maidens steer them. It was a heavy job for a man, but somehow they coped. Their soft, silky hands soon became cracked and rough and, no matter how they tried, the hard work took its toll. So, they accepted the situation that their job was manual and not office work that most had been used to. Some of the girls soon learnt to plough a near perfect straight furrow, with little or no grass showing on top. Others were absolutely useless and never learnt, or didn't want to learn. None of these tractors had electronic starters on them so all needed winding, or swinging by hand, to start them. This, once again, was a man's job, but most landgirls soon found out how to start them by winding. Many times the landgirl would come down to the farmstead, requesting a hand to start that obstinate tractor on that cold spring morning.

On the stock rearing and dairy farm they were expected to do various jobs. Their first obstacle, when arriving on any of these farms, was to get approved by the farmer's wife. Many farmers' wives would not entertain a live-in landgirl, as they were sure that it could cause rivalry within the household, matrimonially. So, the husband was left to struggle on, trying to cope with the extra work himself. When a landgirl had been employed on some farms the rivalry actually worked well for the farmer. His wife would try and do that little bit more for him, and generally be a bit more loving, cooperative, and more interested in what was going on outside with stock, and on the land.

In a few cases there was a total breakdown of the marriage when the farmer was caught by his wife in a compromising position with the landgirl. Or, it was a case of the landgirl packed her bags and left immediately, or the wife would walk out. The farm was an ideal place for the farmer to have a bit of 'fresh', or a change of partner with the landgirl. There were so many idyllic places around the farm, from the haystack in winter to under the old oak tree along the hedgerow or woodland glade. It was very romantic and scenic on the farm in spring and summer. Today, in Bowland, there are a few farmers who married landgirls who have been very successful together. Many found the landgirls handy with their office and commerce experience doing their farm accounts. Most farmers were very good at looking after animals and livestock, but useless with office paperwork.

When visiting a farmhouse it was commonplace to see a long wire with scores of bills spiked on to it hanging from the living room or kitchen ceiling. This was the filing cabinet and accounting system for most farmers. Certainly they were all in order as far as their dates were concerned, although it was probably a little difficult when one was required from the middle of the wire.

The hook or nail from which the bills were suspended was what had been used to hang the rolls of bacon and hams to dry and store until required for the kitchen table. The oak beams themselves could be many hundreds of years old. These had been chopped from felled oak trees not by the modern type circular bandsaw, but by hand with a special curved type axe called a foot axe. This left a special chip type surface when the chopping was complete.

Any other softwood on these beams had always been attacked by woodworm and was rather like a pincushion with hundreds of wormholes visible. It was a different story altogether with the centre of the old oak beam. This was so hard the worm could never penetrate and bore holes into it. In fact, it was almost impossible to hammer any type of nail into it. Today these beams are sought after where restoration of old property is being carried out. Unfortunately, there will be no replacements for these irregular shaped old oak beams.

The landgirl had also to get used to the different type of sanitation that was standard on most outlying farms. There was no inside toilet, as she may have been used to back at home, just a communal one at the bottom of the garden. This was, in our case, a long drop type, which was a deep hole dug in the ground and then bricked up on all sides to the correct size with a large flat timber board on top and a large hole cut in the middle. In some cases two or three holes would be cut in the same board to form a two or three seater toilet without partitions. The toilet room was almost always built in local stone with a grey or blue slate roof. The inside was flagged with sandstone flags which were always kept scrubbed regularly. The interior walls were whitewashed with a lime wash. This helped brighten it up, and keep out flies.

It was not long after these landgirls had arrived in the villages that the locals had assessed their characters. There was the straight-laced girl who did everything correctly, went to church on a Sunday, didn't drink or smoke. She would go to the pictures occasionally in town and help the farmer's wife with household chores and become literally one of the family.

Then there were other types of landgirl that would set the locals talking about their behaviour. One type would be out almost every night at the local, smoke and drink and entertain the local, broadminded, country lads. It was not long before they had been christened with their new slang names. I remember two such names; there was Easy Edith and Bonking Betty, both notorious with the local lads. They obviously enjoyed the freedom of the countryside and the limited entertainment which was always inexpensive. To all of these girls, working and living on a farm, was very different from the town life. Not many fully understood the skills and requirements of a livestock farmer and the happenings on such farms.

Many only thought a bull was to chase you out of the field and were not aware of its true use. They were more than surprised when he was introduced to the cow that was in season, and, seeing for the first time, the bull's large weapon a good 2 feet long, they tended to turn the opposite way and turn a bright crimson. After a few months this was no longer an embarrassment. All these activities they had never seen, and possibly never even thought happened on farms. There would be the sheep lambing in spring, a great time of the year with all the young lambs racing and prancing in the fresh spring grass.

It was also a time of death when new arrivals were expected. This, many landgirls could not understand. They thought everything would live and when there was a death of a lamb, sheep or calf they would become very upset. They would get attached to that pet lamb which had been reared on the bottle since its mother died, not realising that soon it would have to go for slaughter to help swell the farmers income, needed to pay for everyday requirements on the farm, such as rent, cattle and sheep food, plus all the food for the farmer's growing family.

There were many varieties of jobs that the landgirl was expected to do on farms during the war. On our farm we were expected to grow various grain crops. The most important of these was oats. This, once harvested, would be ground and rolled for animal feed for all the animals. Harvesting in Bowland could be a very difficult period as the weather was very unpredictable. The village lay in the Pennine range of hills, where drought was never heard of, but rainfall was well above average for the rest of the country. Therefore, harvesting of grain was difficult, and required a lot of extra work, trying to get all the sheaves of corn dry, before transporting to the barns, an ideal job for the landgirls.

There was, also, the weeding and thinning of root crops such as turnips and marigolds, also the cabbage and sprout. All these crops were difficult to grow on our farm, and others locally, because there were scores of rabbits and hares. These ate many of the young plants when they were in early stages of growth. Rabbit pie or stewed rabbit was a regular dish during, and after the war, and was always very tasty, with a few onions and carrots and an Oxo cube to add a bit of colour and flavour.

Today there are landgirls who married local farmers in and around the local villages and who have made perfect farmers' wives. There are also all those who left these scenic villages, never to be heard of again. Some probably returned with husband and family, and were proud to point out that lovely farmstead where they spent a couple of years helping in the war.

Farmers Story:
This buxom, blonde, landgirl arrived on this Bowland farm. She immediately got changed into bib and brace overalls and went

out onto the farm to meet the farmer. The farmer asked, "What can you do lass!" and the landgirl replied, "I don't know the difference between the front and back end of a cow".

The farmer asked many questions about the landgirls' farming skills. Finally he asked, "Is there anything at all you can do?" The landgirl replied, "I can play the violin". The farmer then instructed her to go into the cowshed and play her violin to the cows. The theory being that playing music to the cows made them give more milk, and after approximately 15 minutes the landgirl returned with a smile on her face. The farmer asked, "How did you get on lass?" and the landgirl replied, "Very well indeed, they all clapped!"

The Tramp

Ribblesdale was a sleepy valley with the River Ribble winding its way on the same course it had taken for countless centuries. Over every hill there were breathtaking views. There were stone walls rising from valley to hilltops, painstakingly built many years ago. These were built using local stone from the riverbed and local quarries, having been transported by horse and cart and manually loaded by countless hands. There are many villages, small farming hamlets, and houses with particular character. Whatever the season you travelled through these valleys, there were always different scenes.

During these seasons many different travellers would visit Bowland. There were many hikers who would arrive at the local railway station, or on the local bus. There would be people of all shapes and sizes, short and fat, long and thin, and all would be equipped for a day's rambling in Bowland. They would have plotted the most scenic walks, rambling through fields and woodlands, stopping off at the local pub or coffee house to replenish their expended energy.

There were cyclists from clubs in towns that skirted the countryside of Bowland. Single cycles and tandems, some had sidecars with the youngsters tucked inside. A large yellow oilskin cape would be rolled up and strapped to the crossbar just in case an unwelcome shower occurred.

There were also many motor cycles of different makes, including the large Norton machines, B.S.A., Matchless and Velocet. Some would be connected to a huge sidecar, capable of holding two or three youngsters, plus the wife. These would come from further afield, from cotton towns and urban communities.

Boy Scouts could be seen dragging their two wheeler cart, well over-laden with tent, bedding, ground sheets and billycans, all piled high, heading for that green plateau on the banks of the River Ribble. There were Brownies and Girl Guides, all racing to explore and soak up the fresh air and scenery of Ribblesdale, probably remembering their holiday experience in the Ribble Valley many years afterwards.

Regular visitors, never too welcome in the village, were the tramps. They would appear, unannounced, regularly in the summer months. There would be young and old, just how old was very difficult to tell. Most would be from towns within 20 miles of the village of Bowland. They probably found peace and solitude in the countryside, a complete change from the noise and bustle, smoke and grime of the towns in Lancashire.

They were a very hardy species of the human race, withstanding the worst of accommodation and weather in all seasons, also dirt of the lowest order. They would carry very little with them, what they did carry was, most likely, all they owned. You would see them ambling along with that short stick over their shoulder. Attached to the end would be a large bag or cloth containing all their personal effects. There would be an enamelled brew can, well chipped and definitely requiring a good wash or scour with bleach, tied at the end of the stick.

Most tramps would have long hair, they would rarely have it cut for a few reasons; one would be to keep out the cold, another so they were not easily recognised. It would also act as a thatch keeping out wind and rain. Their hair was usually well entangled with grass, and foreign bodies, very greasy and capable of repelling the heavy showers in Bowland.

They always had large beards, again, they were less recognisable and it kept out the cold. They probably never had any shaving equipment with them anyway, not even a comb, to make them look a little more respectable. I never went too close to one, but I bet the smell was quite revolting in summer.

Their travelling attire would consist of very little on their head. Normally, they would all have trilbys, well worn and saturated with grime and grease, most certainly 100% water proof and as shiny as your Sunday shoes. They seemed to wear many coats, two or three at the same time. This, I believe, was the way they kept their wardrobe, the theory being what kept the heat in, kept the cold out, so it never varied summer or winter.

The tramp's footwear was always well worn. It was common to see his toes sticking out through the toe of the boots. He would use string or wire for the laces, he probably never undid the laces, once tied, as washing his feet would seldom take place. How he kept his feet dry, I never knew. Boots were, most likely, the most difficult items for the tramp to obtain, as most farmers would use them until they were absolutely useless. We, on our farm, would have dry weather boots. These were the well worn ones, not capable of repelling the wet grass or heavy dew in the morning, then we had wet weather boots for winter, or a good pair of clogs made locally in the village of Bowland.

While travelling, the tramp never moved fast, he always had two speeds, dead slow and stop. I suppose this was a mental attitude, in so far as the faster he walked the more energy he used, or, 'What's the use? I am going nowhere in particular anyway, nobody wants to know me, nobody cares about me, nobody needs me or tells me what to do'. He probably never knew which day it was, and only knew the time when passing the village church with the clock high on the steeple for the benefit of villagers or passers-by to see.

He had no communication with anybody, so he never knew what was going on in the countryside and villages around him. Every day was the same for him, the sun would rise in the same place and go down at the same time and place.

We would taunt the tramp if we met him or saw him on our way to school, by shouting, "Sam, Sam the dirty man, washed his face in a frying pan, combed his hair with a donkey's tail, and scratched his belly with his big toe nail." This we got away with most times, as we could always run faster than the tramp, or so we thought. There was one occasion when we were wrong. The tramp must have been much younger than average and he had no difficulty in outrunning and catching us. He gave us a damned good belting, which we deserved. We never told our parents about what had happened, in future, we respected the tramp a little more and gave him a wide berth.

Tramps would never go to church but often could be found sheltering in the porch of the church, especially in bad weather. He would always look to the church for support, and most likely the vicar would fall soft and spare him a few bob from the Sunday collection plate, or the offering box inside the church. In most cases the tramp would have to be content with handouts from anybody.

When travelling, be it in the villages or the countryside, he would always have his grubby brew can handy, to scrounge a brew of tea or coffee. At the same time he would ask for a slice of bread and butter, knowing full well that he would rarely just get bread and butter, but a sandwich of cheese or even beef. If he did well at one house, it did not mean he had to stop begging for more. Often he could be seen getting a brew and sandwiches from a few houses on the same row. Many villagers would give him tea and a sandwich just to get him off their doorstep.

The tramp knew full well that the farms were few and far between in the countryside. Most farmers didn't believe in giving something for nothing. They would expect a little work for food, this was something the tramp was not prepared to do. He would not even work for a few bob either in the villages or on the farms, he probably knew that farmers were notoriously bad payers and if he decided to work for a few bob, he would only get the dirty jobs. He was also not so capable of doing any heavy work, as the diet he was eating was only just enough to keep him alive.

The tramp was also more of a thief than most country visitors. He didn't have any regular income, he was not prepared to work to earn a few shilling on the farms or in the villages. The items he would steal would be milk; this he knew was available at the end of the farm lane in churns or milks kits awaiting collection by the milkwaggon in early morning. He would wait out of sight, when the farmer brought the milk in from the farm, leaving the full kits on the stand and collecting the empty ones for the next days milk. Once the farmer was heading back to the farm, the tramp would fill the billy, or brewcan, with fresh milk and also have a good drink at the same time. The next day the farmer would get notification from the dairy of short measures with the milk he registered.

He would also visit the farmer's poultry cabin when he knew the farmer was at the cattle market, in the hayfield, or well out of sight, and collect the fresh laid eggs from the nest. The farmer would know the culprit, but could do little about it. The only consolation was that he knew the tramp never stopped in the same area for long. Milk and eggs were available to the tramp in most seasons.

In the spring, the tramp would have a more varied diet. He would look out for wild bird nests, these were fairly plentiful in Bowland. There were wild duck, pheasant, curlew and lapwing, whose nests he could find quite easily by just watching the birds, to pinpoint the exact spot of the nesting site. Time was not of any consequence to the tramp. Wild bird eggs were sought after by many people and were regarded as a delicacy in many of the large gentlemen's residences. In most cases, the tramp would cook these eggs on his open earth fire, but sometimes, he would simply suck them down in one gulp when still raw or uncooked. The rabbit was also in demand at that time of the year, the young rabbits were easy prey for the tramp. Regularly the young rabbits could be seen bobbing in and out of the nest, exploring their new surroundings before fleeing their birthplace to that large burrow in embankment or woodland.

These small burrows, where the young rabbits were born, were easily recognisable, with dead grass and fir deposits outside the burrow, a sure sign that young rabbits were present. The tramp had no difficulty in collecting his dinner, or evening meal, as these nests were only short and shallow burrows. These rabbits he would skin and gut before cooking over his open fire.

The tramp always kept his eyes open for a fruit laden tree or orchard, plotting just which tree the best apples or pears were growing on. He also had to plot how easy the fruit was to get at, later in the day when darkness fell, and the owner was asleep or out of sight in the back room of the house. He would not just collect what he required that day, but collect a few and store them in his coat pockets or pack slung on the stick over his shoulder.

The site selected by the tramp for his resting place and fire was usually in a deep ditch alongside a small stream. The sides would be well covered with dead grass and sticks, just right for making a small fire to do his cooking and provide a little heat to help keep him warm and dry.

There was also stone available for him to make a stone surround for his fire. He would also build himself a stone stool on which to sit, not particularly warm, but he had enough coats on to act as a cushion and padding. On the small earth fire he would cook his meal for the day, boiled eggs, barbecued rabbit, or just boil his brew can full of tea.

His toilet was never far from his fire and resting site; it would only be feet away, just about arm's length. It would be noticeable by the discarded handful of fresh pulled grass or leaves he had used as toilet paper. There were no expensive toiletries, or soap, for the tramp.

Sleeping accommodation could vary a lot, it might be in open ground, or under a tree in midsummer when the weather was dry and warm, the sky literally being the roof. I doubt if he ever discarded any of his clothes, however warm it was. In bad weather the tramp had to be more careful where he camped for the night; the favourite place was under a bridge fully protected from the elements.

The only tell tale sign that a tramp was present was smoke billowing from under the bridge from his small earth fire. When the tramp moved on he always left evidence of what he had been eating, eggshell, bones, etc. There were never apple cores, as he always ate the lot.

The tramp would also sleep in the villagers' garden sheds in the bad weather. It was quite a shock for a villager to find a tramp resting there when he was going for his bicycle in the morning, or going for his lawn mower. He could also be found resting in poultry cabins or implement sheds.

In winter it was a different situation; many tramps would return to city or town where they were a little more secure than in the country. They would get accommodation in doss houses, council run homes, Salvation Army, or assisted accommodation. Odd ones would choose to stop over in the countryside and villages, even though they were never welcomed by any of the country dwellers.

Accommodation in the country was plentiful and cheap. It could be in a farmer's barn; where livestock was present it was always nice and warm from the heat created by the presence of cows or pigs.

The inner barn was a popular place for the tramp to sleep. He could climb the ladder and select a section of the stacked hay that was being used. It was always warm from the heat generated when the hay was stacked and compressed together. He would simply remove some of the sweet smelling hay then cover himself completely to help keep out the cold. You can imagine what a hell of a shock it was to the farmer, or staff, when they trod on him or nearly stabbed him with the hay-fork. He would usually leave hastily, with a good cursing from the farmer, the language would be extremely blue, not printable in the English dictionary.

Even after a good cursing the tramp would leave the farmstead at a snail gallop speed, heading out into the countryside along the narrow winding lanes. He would have all the time in the world to observe the scenery and wildlife; he would disappear in thin air never to be seen again. It was not a life to be envied, but for the tramp it probably gave him freedom, independence and very little pleasure.

Farmers Story:
There was the story of a tramp visiting a very tight farmer's farm, were the tramp decided he would definitely get a sandwich and brew from this miserable farmer. He was about fifty yards from the farmstead when he decided to get on his hands and knees and pretend to eat cow dung. It was an extremely cold mid afternoon with a very cold crisp northerly wind. The farmer was looking out of the cowshed door and saw the tramp on his knees, supposedly eating cow dung. The farmer shouted in a loud voice, "Come they sel' up here lad, tha's no need to eat it cold. Tha can have some warm out at cowshed."

Country Travellers

In Bowland, during the summer months, there were countless visitors who came to camp, both on foot and bicycle. I suppose, all they were in search of was a peaceful place to rest, away from the smoke and noise of the mills and rattle and clatter of the looms. They certainly could find that in Bowland, and there was no better place than down by the river, on a level flood plain which could have been specially made for such a purpose.

The plain was almost certainly a silt deposit evolved over, probably, thousands of years. These hikers and campers were really explorers in a small way. They were more than content to travel only a few miles and soak up the hidden beauty of Bowland, that lay in wait around every corner and behind every hill.

There were also the seasonal travellers that visited the farms and villages every year, not always on the same day or week but once, or maybe twice, during the twelve months. It may have been in spring or winter, there was never a set pattern. These travellers always roamed in families, complete with mobile bedrooms, mobile kitchen and a very basic set of tools with which a living was scratched or scraped. They lived on the various foods available in the country, which was not always apparent to town and country dwellers.

They would never beg for food if it was not readily available from natural sources. I suppose they would steal certain items of food from local farms and smallholdings. The Romanies, or gypsies, were different people, leading a wandering life among the hills and valleys of Bowland and further afield, enjoying the livestock and scenery that was plentiful wherever they went.

One particular family of gypsies I remember well. They were regular visitors, at least twice a year, to our farm to collect and buy whatever we had surplus. They would appear when least expected and without notice. The family had used the same campsite for many years. It was on a side track, or farm lane, just off the main road, where the verges were at least thirty feet wide and well covered with young, succulent grass. This was just what they required for food to maintain their team of horses, which was their only mode of transport.

It was quite a picture to see them on the move with their horses, caravans and carts. Their principal caravans were four wheeled in order to be more stable when used for the sleeping accommodation. These vans were the pride and joy of the gypsy family and they would be kept spotlessly clean inside. On the outside the bright red and yellow decorations were kept in mint condition, with intricate designs on the panels and wheels. The ordinary carts were less well decorated as these were used for everyday business around the farms and villages.

The train of caravans and carts usually consisted of two four-wheeled units and two, two-wheeled carts plus several horses and foals. The lead caravan would contain the mother and children, sitting on a seat looking out of the front of the van, with father sitting on the cart shafts directing the convoy, and driving the horse. At the back of the caravan buckets and utensils would be hung. Also tied to the back of the caravan would be a couple of young horses that always knew when to start and stop when the driver in front required them to do so. I suppose it was instinct which these horses had acquired over the years. The second caravan would carry the senior family. The old man and his wife and belongings, plus a couple of lurchers or whippets, slumped out in the back. Behind this van more utensils and a couple of young horses, or maybe one of the old faithful horses, which had supported the family for many years.

One thing I can say about the gypsy was that you never ever saw his horses underfed or cruelly handled. They were far too important for anything like that to happen to them. I think it was a matter of friendship and trust between horse and man, vitally important when you were together all day and every day, year in year out. Gypsy horses were seldom chestnut, bays or strawberry roans, they were nearly always either piebald, which was black and white or skewbald, which was brown and white. They were never very big, always short and stocky, with broad shoulders, and capable of drawing the carts and caravans with ease over long distances.

The gypsy always appeared out of nowhere and arrived at his camp site un-obtrusively. Sometimes, the only tell tale signal that the gypsy had arrived was a smoke signal, produced from their only source of heat, the campfire. The campfire served as a simple cooking stove, where that much used stew pot was always to hand. There would be a couple of wood posts on either side of the stone hearth, supporting a long metal rod from which the stew pot and kettle were suspended over the fire. The pot could also be moved from the centre of the fire to the side by sliding along the metal rod. Also, the pan could be raised or lowered using notches in the timber posts, to increase and decrease the rate of cooking, a simple, but efficient, way of controlling the heat.

The fuel for the fire was always readily available from wood and hedgerow, where annually, trees were blown down or died of old age. Sometimes, the gypsy would remove a few posts from the farmer's fence to start the campfire. When the farmer enquired about his missing posts there was no evidence left, but he knew full well how they had disappeared.

It was always interesting, if you were passing the campsite at night, to see the whole family sitting around the campfire on makeshift seating, watching the well-used stewpot filled with the next nourishing meal. What concoction was in the pot you never knew, the only thing for certain was that it would be inexpensive and local.

The gypsies always made sure that, adjacent to the campsite, there were wide verges where they could tether and graze their horses. They had no rented land, or land they owned, so there was no expense in keeping the sizeable team of horses and foals. Sometimes in a very dry season, the grass on the verges and hedgerows was sparse and quite incapable of supporting a team of horses. This is where the gypsies did a nightshift. They waited until past midnight, when the farmers where hard and fast asleep. They would then open the adjacent farmer's gate, and take the horses into his field, and let them graze for a couple of hours, then remove them to their tethered position on the grass verge, before the farmer rose to collect his dairy cows for milking, from the same field the next morning. The farmer never caught the culprit red handed, but always found out after the event. The usual clue was the horse muck, which the horses had deposited during the dead of night visit, which was much more of a solid deposit than the sloppy cow dung left by his dairy cows. The gypsy, in most cases, was just one step ahead of anybody that tried to catch or reprimand him.

Living in these caravans during summer must have been an idyllic experience, but during bad weather no fun, and during winter months, bloody awful, when the weather was really wet. How they kept everything dry God only knows, or how they actually dried their sodden clothes. The only way I ever saw them drying during bad weather was under their caravans and in the roof of the van in which they slept. How they all slept in the two vans was a miracle.

Sanitation of these campsites was none existent. A toilet tent would never have been heard of. In most cases, an out of sight area would be used for such necessities. It could be behind the adjacent hedgerows away from the caravan where there was always an abundance of fresh hand pulled grass that they used as toilet paper, and a good hand full was all that was required. They would always use the nearest ditch or beck for their washing water and drinking water. They were not too concerned about where it came from, as long as it looked clean in the pool from which they collected it. In many cases upstream the farmer's liquid manure tank would be overflowing into the river, or his cows would be drinking and contaminating it with dung. Personal washing, I suppose, was the last thing on their minds. They always looked as though they needed a good wash. I think they thought and believed washing opened up the pores in their skin letting in cold and disease, also removing protective natural oils.

The gypsies main source of income was from products discarded by villagers or farmers. They always knew where the local village tips were and could be seen raking out the newly tipped loads of rubbish. These always contained something useful for the gypsy, to re-use, or just for scrap. There would be cast-off clothing, a copper kettle, copper wire, cast iron, or a re-usable kitchen utensil or maybe shoes, all useful to the gypsy.

They always visited the villages to collect items no longer required. They would not knock on the cottage doors to warn of their presence but shout at the top of their voice, "Any rag bone, any rag bone", and it seemed to work. Occupants of the cottages would come out with their redundant or useless items. The gypsy would pay no money for such items, but offer pumice stones or clothes pegs to the giver. When visiting the rural or outlandish farm the gypsy would be seeking other items, such as horsehair. This was readily available on most farms where horses did all the work, and hair from their manes or tails soon accumulated into a sizeable bag full, once or twice a year. They would also buy used corn sacks, worn horse shoes, lead, copper or semi precious metals. The horsehair would be used for upholstery making, brushes and many other uses.

Another item they were interested in was sheep wool, not the main fleece, which we sheared off in July, but the goldings. This was wool from around the rear end of the ewe or lamb that had become contaminated with the loose droppings or sheep muck. This usually only became a problem when sheep entered rich pastures in spring or autumn causing them to become a bit loose, or in farming terms, scouring.

The gypsy would pay so much per bag full for this wool, and so much each for grain sacks. The removal of this wool from the sheep was more from necessity than choice. If it was not removed, it was a prime target for blowfly to lay their eggs, and, if not attended to, soon developed into a dirty, stinky problem, not only for the farmer, but also for the sheep. There could soon be hundreds of maggots, feeding away on live flesh, absolutely terrible for the sheep, because it wasn't in a position to do anything about it, and, if not attended to, it could soon result in the death of the sheep. Also it was not so pleasant for the young lambs when suckling, having to find the teat through wool and muck, and in some cases the lambs weaned themselves from suckling.

The farmer also got side effects from this situation. He didn't have surgical gloves or any protection against the stain and stink he had to remove. After a few days of golding, your hands were a distinctive green, and they didn't smell of Eau De Cologne. The gypsy would take this wool, submerge it in a nearby stream to soak, then wash all the offending dung from it, then let it dry before selling it to a wool merchant.

Other items they collected, such as overcoats and woollen goods, they may have used themselves, or even knit new garments out of old, or remake them into kiddies' clothing. They certainly didn't waste anything from their hard-earned spoils.

Another source of income for the gypsy was clothes pegs. These, they would make from hazel sticks cut from local hedgerows. Once cut into lengths they would be split and shaped, bound with a thin strip of tin, and secured with a small nail to form a good sturdy clothes peg.

Other items produced by the gypsies hands, were flowers. They crafted these from fresh cut willow, from boggy ground where it had grown, probably for scores of years. These artificial flowers resembled an incurved chrysanthemum. They would cut the willow into approximately 6 inch lengths and, with a sharp knife, split thin sections about 4 inch long. Then, somehow, they either boiled or steamed the willow that then caused the split willow to curve, to form the flower. Once curved into shape, they would dye them with a secret potion that only the gypsy knew. One thing is certain it would not be purchased from outside sources, it was more likely a single mix of local grass or herb.

The senior gypsy woman was talented at telling fortunes. This she would do while her husband was bargaining with the farmer for his surplus goods. I remember one day, some 40 years ago. This particular day I returned for dinner to the farmhouse, and, sitting on the oak longsettle was the senior gypsy lady, well into her 60's, or so she looked. Well weather worn, tousled hair, with deep wrinkles across her brow, clothes shiny bright with grease. She also had a grey, mousy beard, and brown twisted teeth that had probably acquired their colour through her chewing tobacco twist, or smoking that old clay pipe. There was a brisk kitchen fire stacked high with well-dried oak logs, the heat from which, by now, had activated the strong smell of dried urine which exuded from the old girl's body and clothing. She was almost certainly well overdue for a good soak and bath, but let's remember, the washing and bathing facilities for a senior lady on a gypsy caravan site were non existent.

After a good sales patter, the old lass had convinced me that two bob would be well spent on having my fortune told. I probably thought it was the easiest way of getting rid of her, as she didn't seem to have any intention of moving from in front of the kitchen fire. This particular woman had searching eyes and had probably assessed my personality and character in the few minutes I had been in her company. I sat in front of her, on a four legged wooden stool, in front of the kitchen fire, breathing through my mouth, so as to not get the full smell of dried urine and body odour that by now had been even more aggravated by the heat from the kitchen fire.

She took my hand and looked at my palm, looked in my eyes with deep interest, and, in no time at all was ravelling off with great accuracy, details that I thought were known only to myself. The year I was born, the month and star, I would have good health, I would be successful in business, I would have three children, 2 boys and 1 girl and I would shortly be leaving home. She then looked more closely into my eyes and said, "You will be married, and have a son within 12 months". I went a funny shade of red, and my parents laughed, thinking it was one big joke. I paid the 2-shillings that she had earned in about 10 minutes, she pushed the coin into her apron pocket and left the kitchen to join her husband. By this time, her husband had bargained with my father for any surplus items we did not require on the farm, and probably had done fairly well out of the deal.

It took quite a while for the air in the kitchen to clear of her exuded body odours. The old lady had an exceptional talent. All she told me came true, and are absolutely true to this day some forty years on. I had left the family farm, I had a young son and got married within the specified time, I was in good health, but I hadn't proved myself in business, as that was a far-flung prophecy. Full marks for the old gypsy fortune-teller.

I also remember a particular day in mid January that was very, very cold. There was a North East wind with a flurry of snowflakes settling onto the hard frozen ground. The best place to be on such a day was keeping the fire company in the farmhouse kitchen, or in the barn, with livestock present, helping to take the chill out of that sub zero temperature, which penetrates from foot to finger tips, and almost every other part of your body. It sure wasn't a day to be outdoors.

There was a clippety clop of the horse, and grinding of iron rimmed wheels from the gypsy cart on the hard frozen farm road. They soon appeared in the farm yard and there was the father sitting on the side of this flat cart, well wrapped up in an ex-army overcoat, trilby and scarf, and a couple of pairs of breeches on, just to make sure he kept out the cold. On the seat of the cart, encased in yet another large overcoat were two of his children. I guessed they would be 5 to 7 years old. They were both wearing helmets which were just peeping out from under that tent like coat. They had thick woollen socks, on their hands, that they used for gloves. Obviously, there were no fingers or thumbs on these gloves, but they kept out the intense cold. These were exceptionally hardy kids, both had dark complexions with windburnt features, and both had runny noses, that they had wiped on the sleeves of that oversized overcoat, and there were holes in their helmets from which billowed locks of hair.

The father asked the usual question, what had we to sell. Taking pity on them, we searched for all the surplus items we did not require on the farm which may be useful to the gypsy. He paid a few shillings for his purchases. Just at that particular time, I was mixing the daily mix of hen food. In winter I always mixed this with warm water. This contained all freshly harvested items such as thirds, which is a very fine bran, also India meal, which is ground maize. There was barley meal, fish meal and pea meal, all mixed up and mixed with warm water. This made a very appetising meal for my Rhode Island reds and brown Leghorn pullets. Watching me mix with interest, the father said, "I have a few bantams at home, can you spare a good handful for me". I replied, "No problem", and promptly rolled a couple of pounds of this appetising smelling hen food into a ball. He pulled a soiled rag out of his pocket and wrapped it around the hen food, thanked me and went back to his horse and cart, where the 2 youths still remained under this huge coat, hopefully keeping out the cold. In no time at all he had turned the horse and cart around in the farmyard and was heading for the open road. They had travelled not 50 yards before the dirty rag appeared, and soon both father and sons were tucking into that hot mix of fresh cereals, which originally was destined for his bantams. I often wondered if it was just a story, to obtain that farm fresh meal for him and his sons. He certainly convinced me.

The gypsies also knew just where and when a meal was available in the countryside, where most people least thought it existed. They knew that in every season there was a crop to be harvested. They had probably acquired this knowledge over the years, handed down from father to son. They knew what type of weather it took to grow certain mushrooms or fungi. They knew the woods where truffles and hazelnuts grew, where to find the best blackberry and raspberry beds, or the unattended orchard. They would take the odd brown trout or eel from the local stream, also the plover's eggs from the ploughfield in the spring. These all added up to that extra variety in their diet when out for the day, collecting and buying items from village or farm. There was always the whippet or lurcher dog basking in wait on top of the gypsy's cart, ever ready to be released to outrun that rabbit or hare spotted from their vantage point. Once captured, the hare would be stored under the scrap on the cart, well out of sight of farmer or gamekeeper. These would finish up in the stewpot above the earth fire, as jugged hare or stew.

They were always capable of taking the occasional pheasant, which they would carefully watch, and if necessary, follow to the tree where they roosted for the night. In most cases, they would have knowledge of just which trees they had roosted in over the years, and would go prepared to collect their bird. The trees would always be in a sheltered, warm place, by a stream, or beck, with embankments on either side and well off the main road. They would, in most cases, check beforehand to see if the graceful pheasant was using these particular trees for night accommodation. It was a simple check, if fresh droppings were under the tree the pheasant had been roosting there the previous night. At dead of night, long after the gamekeeper had retired to bed, they would visit the area and, with a long hazel stick with snare attached to one end, they would carefully guide the snare over the pheasant's head, and pull. There was no bang to alert the gamekeeper of their presence, the only clue the gamekeeper had that they had visited was a few feathers on the ground where the pheasant had unsuccessfully tried to avoid death. Also, the gamekeeper would have one or two pheasants less to count in the morning, when feeding took place. The gypsy would have a tasty meal that he probably deserved.

Many farmers were always worried when the gypsies were camping near their farms, because items disappeared or a bit of petty thieving would take place. A typical example was a marked reduction in milk from single cows when gypsies were present. Normally, the cow would produce around 2 to 3 gallons of milk at a morning milking. On some days this cow may only produce 2 or 3 pints, a sure sign that the gypsy had been up early and milked the cow before the farmer had risen to collect his dairy herd.

Most of the semi-illegal activities occurred at night, under cover of darkness. I suppose they could see better in the dark than most country dwellers, being used to long, dark nights with very little, or no, artificial light. Food in the countryside, to the gypsy, could be an item least imagined by ordinary country folk and probably revolting to most town folk. I have in mind the hedgehog, plentiful around country lanes and farmsteads. The hedgehog would be collected, on sight, by the gypsies. This was supposed to be a delicacy, but I could never fancy eating one, no matter how it was marinated or cooked. The method of cooking the hedgehog was to roll or encase it in clay, then bake it on the open hearth until cooked, then remove the ball of clay containing all the prickles, leaving the carcass accessible, clean and ready for consumption.

Once a year, there was a gathering of gypsies from the length and breadth of the country. Some would travel for weeks to gather for the annual fair at Appleby in Cumbria. There would be from the really wealthy gypsy to the poorest, both having something to sell or display. There would be the most exotic and expensive caravans on show, decorated with the best of everything, Royal Doulton pottery and solid silver dinner services. Only the best of everything was good enough, with fantastic dresses for the gypsy ladies, accompanied by their best jewellery. The best horse harness, and antique porcelain figures, of the gypsy caravans and people, would be on display.

Dancing and celebrating would carry on late into the night. Young gypsy boys would meet their future wives, old families would be united, new acquaintances and friendships formed, there may even be a wedding. Horses that had been born and bred by the gypsies would be brought to Appleby for sale or barter. The monies obtained for these horses would help the gypsy to survive over the next 12 months. Townspeople and villagers would travel scores of miles to see this gathering and their displays. Stalls would be set up alongside the road and adjacent fields, selling harnesses, clothes and pottery. Also, many artists would be displaying their works of art. The pictures would be typical gypsy scenes, some a bit bloody, with lurchers making a kill, also wild animal scenes and drawings. There were paintings to suit everybody's' preference and pocket, and the fortune-tellers were plentiful.

The fair would start with the washing and swimming of the horses in the River Eden. Both banks would be lined with spectators, and on the bridge, which was an excellent vantage point, where people stood shoulder to shoulder. The horses seemed to enjoy a good wash and soon their grubby coats became bright and clean, so much so, that they didn't look like the same horses. Their grooms, or minders, also looked much better after their episode with horse and soap in the river. All worked up to the waist in the clean, fresh water that was never very warm, even in midsummer. The water below the bridge acquired that extra additive of horse grease, personal odour and soap.

After the washing, the horses would be taken back to where the caravan was sited, to be prepared for the running and sale. Once back at the van intensive grooming would take place, tails would be plucked and combed, manes would be combed and plaited with great pride and skill, and hooves would be greased, to complete the washing and manicure. The horse was now ready for the showing and running, which could be in two or three different ways. One could be in a flat cart or a trap, or maybe, ridden bare back by a young gypsy lad. Whichever way, this was the main spectacle at Appleby fair.

The horses would assemble at the top of the road which, on the running days, was blocked with spectators on both sides of the road, and frequently in the centre. The horse and driver would then be directed down the hill, the faster the better, at horrendous speed, with no apparent way through the crowd. Miraculously, the crowd parted only just in time to allow horse and navigator through. It always seemed there was a major accident just waiting to happen, but I never heard of any.

Once the running was over, vendors and buyers would assemble in bunches of ten to twenty, mostly weather beaten males, all with ears cocked, trying to hear the price being asked, or obtained, for horse or pony. There was plenty of bargaining taking place and the vendor would be telling all the good points about the horse he was trying to sell. Most would be true, but many points would be little white lies, or, sometimes, big ones. There were no better storytellers than horse dealers. The purchaser would be pointing out all the visible faults, hoping to bring the final price down a pound or two. After a lot of bickering and bartering, a final price would be agreed and confirmed by a good slap of hands. There was never any paperwork, order number, or written contracts, and the word of mouth and slapping of hands was the contract. Anybody who did not honour such an agreement was never trusted again.

Cheques were never paid for horses or goods, because gypsies would seldom have bank accounts; as they were always on the move, they always dealt in cash. After all the washing, running, bartering, selling and festival activities all good happenings had to come to an end for another year. New purchases would be harnessed or tethered behind the gypsy caravans. Valuable items were packed carefully away, probably not to be seen again for another year. Best clothes would be cast and replaced by the more tatty workday attire. Horses would be harnessed for the homeward journey. This could be scores, even hundreds, of miles away. Soon the individual family caravan train would be leaving the Appleby fair, with some heading north and some heading south. All, I believe would be richer in some shape or form, maybe monetarily, or with a fresh horse, maybe a girl or boyfriend, maybe a wife, or a reunion of relations or friends. All had smiles on their faces, and most would return to the area from where they had trekked, happy to scrape a living, all-be-it sparse, from the villagers, farmers and that ever fruitful countryside. I bet none would exchange for a town dweller life, with all the harassment of modern living and transportation, taxes, rates and mortgages. All they had, they treasured and carried in that caravan, and probably never owed a penny to anyone.

Old Pat

Haytime was when the lush grass, which had been growing for around 6 weeks, became ready for mowing. It had to be dried naturally by passing through various stages.

Mechanisation was more or less unheard of, so most processes had to be done by hand and, obviously, extra staff was required. This was available from a few sources. The main one in those days was the Irishman, or 'paddy', as they were commonly called. They would arrive in the first week of July, when the meadows were ripe and ready for cutting.

Old Pat was the name of our Irishman who had been coming to Bowland to work on our family farm for many years, and was now in his late forties. Over the years we had built up a picture of the type of croft, or homestead, Pat came from. We knew he was married to a hard working country lass, who had to look after the family without any help from Pat, while he was over in England, earning money to support his large family of 6 boys and 2 girls. She would have no help with the washing, cooking or management of the small farm unit. The farm consisted of some 12 acres in County Mayo, and was very poor land. It was just enough to keep the family cow and followers, Ned the donkey for transportation purposes, a few hens for a regular supply of fresh eggs, and a single pig to keep them supplied with bacon and lard the year round. The pig would live on any household waste, which would be minimal, with a family of that size, and on a small budget. Surplus eggs would be pickled to cover winter months, when fresh eggs were not available.

Before leaving his small farm Pat would have made sure his potato crop, or Murphy's, were planted. His vegetables and winter crop of hay would be growing well, peat from the local peat bog cut and stacked for winter fuel, and all the work that was required to be done was completed before he left for England. Once he left there was no chance of returning until he had earned the family coppers in the autumn.

He would leave home with that big portmanteau, or case, containing all the clothes required for the period he was away. He would have a pair of very strong boots, 2 pairs of thick, woolly working socks, which his wife had painstakingly knitted for him, and 2 thick, woolly vests, striped union shirts with removable collars, in order to avoid extra washing, a few spotted handkerchiefs for head protection or necktie, and heavy working pants which must have got unbearably hot in mid July. He would only have two of each item of clothing to allow for my mother to do his washing. He also had a very thick and wide leather belt, which was probably part of the donkey harness, a hefty overcoat and a well-worn trilby and cap. His handkerchiefs were good big squares of Irish linen, not even hemmed, just raw ragged edges.

Pat would travel in his best clothes and boots. His suit was a fairly bright blue that shone on the surface with the years of service it had given him. It was, most likely, his wedding suit. He would have brown, auction type boots that shone from the polishing, probably done by his faithful and hard working wife. These, he only used on special occasions. His shirt was a well-washed white that was probably quite difficult to maintain, with the washing equipment his wife had at hand. His tie never matched his suit and was a bright red, but it suited Pat. All his work clothes were stuffed firmly into that well-worn portmanteau and firmly fastened with a piece of rope, to avoid any loss of his personal belongings. It was also, well labelled to avoid any chance of loss.

Leaving wife and family was probably an emotional time for Pat, as he knew it would be many months before his return to County Mayo. His little croft with its livestock was his personal fortune and could only have been very small. It was home to Pat, not much wealth, but a wealth of happiness, and that's all that counted with Pat.

He described leaving his homestead for the nearest town with eldest son, donkey and cart, with case stacked on top, and waving goodbye to his wife and family. He was on his way to earn that extra money to support them. He was heading for Dublin to catch the boat for Holyhead on the mainland. This was not a passenger boat, but one that also carried cattle, a major export from Ireland to the U.K. There would be many hundreds of Irishmen on this boat, destined for farms throughout the NorthWest, to help out with haytime. Some farmers would hire 3 or 4 men, depending on how many acres of meadow they had to harvest. From Holyhead, it would be a train journey to the nearest station to the farm where they would work. In most cases they were hired by the same farm year after year, if they liked the farmer, and the farmer was satisfied with their ability to work.

Hiring day in the villages was always the same in the Bowland area, but varied in other parts of the country, where crops matured much earlier. That day was usually in late June, early July, and the gathering place was the Coach & Horses pub in Bowland. They would arrive on the local 10:45am bus. This was the busiest day of the year for the bus company. The bus would be crammed tight with men and cases, and were carrying twice as many passengers and weight as would be legal today.

The pubs would have to hire extra staff to cope with the influx of customers, and extra beer would have been ordered to cope with extra demand. By this time of day most would have worked up a thirst, and the barman would be working overtime trying to keep up with demand. There were plates of thick, sliced bread spread with local farm butter, and filled with thick slices of cheese, just what Pat and his mates required. Many had travelled a long way, and by this time they were ready for a substantial snack.

Outside the pub, village life had changed from that sleepy, noiseless atmosphere to a bustling village centre. Farmers, with their horses and carts, were arriving in large numbers to select and bargain with their future temporary staff. I had to stop off school to hold the horse from straying, whilst my father went in to the pub to find old Pat and re-negotiate his wage for the next month. You could only hire Pat for a month, because there was work down in Lincolnshire waiting for him which he had done for years previously. This was first, grain harvesting, then root crops, potatoes, etc. If, however, haytime was finished within the month, Pat would be paid up and released for the next job. Then it was back home for Pat, to wife and family. Some of the single men would stay back and work on roads, buildings and civil engineering projects, and spend all their hard-earned income on drink, lodgings and women of ill repute.

There would be plenty of bartering going on back in the pub. I thought my father was never going to emerge from the bargaining session. Inflation had to be taken into consideration, and, 12 months on, Pat had acquired more family, so he needed extra money, or so he said, to support the new arrival. Pat had always come up with the story of more kids every year, and, by my father's reckoning, he now had between 15 and 20. He probably didn't think my father had such a good memory. The going rate for the month was £60, just £15 a week and that was a lot of money in those days. You also had to feed Pat, do his washing, and provide a roof over his head.

Accommodation varied on many farms, some would scrub out the loose box in which the calves had made their winter home, then whitewash it with a mixture of lime and water. The bed would be an old iron one, with straw mattress. Maybe, a sheet and blanket and a chest of drawers would be included in the temporary accommodation. In most cases, it was a 4 inch nail driven into surrounding timbers from which they could hang their clothes and belongings. If no loose box was available a redundant poultry cabin would be used, after being thoroughly scrubbed and disinfected. There was seldom any complaint about accommodation. I suppose many lived in cramped and, maybe, less deluxe accommodation at home. These Irishmen were definitely a tough race, seldom having time off work through illness.

After a long wait in blistering heat, holding onto Betty, our faithful farm horse, my father appeared at the pub door, slightly the worse for drink. As he was normally teetotal, a couple of pints had taken its toll. Pat followed, having drunk a few more pints, but it apparently had no effect. Pat went to collect his case from under the old Oak tree, which was many hundreds of years old, and was saturated with nails on the street facing side, where public notices had been fixed for many years.

My father staggered into the cart, followed by Pat, looking quite smart in his best clothes. My father said, "Tha might as well drive home lad", as he was in no fit condition to keep Betty in the centre of the road. The gateposts were very close together and a wheel could easily be lost if a navigational error was made. Just $1^1/2$ miles to go, and we would be back at the farmstead that was going to be Pat's home for the next month. Pat remembered every member of our family and was always very polite with all of us.

My mother went upstairs and showed Pat his bedroom. This was a room of considerable size, which spanned the full width of the house and contained 3 beds, 1 for Pat and 2 for part of our family. My father's motto was, "If you want them to work like you, treat them like yourself". This always happened on our farm but was not always the case on others, where they were treated like second class citizens. It was not long before Pat appeared, changed from his Sunday best into his working attire. I had, by this time, unharnessed Betty from the cart and returned her to the stable where it was nice and cool. I then returned to the farmhouse where a hot dinner was being served. My father was tucking into it, pretending that he was no worse for the drink. It was potato pie with rice pudding to follow, which I was ready for, after spending most of the morning looking after Betty and the cart.

My father had previously made sure all the haytime equipment was ready for use. He had put new peg wood teeth, where required, in the rakes, the hayforks had been sharpened, and all the machinery had been oiled and new parts fitted. New teeth had been fitted to the mowing machine blades and every blade sharpened. A sharp knife on the mowing machine made it much easier for the horses when mowing and also left less grass on the meadow. This was important, as that little extra was always needed in winter for cattle feed.

Father also made sure old Pat's scythe was sharp. This was achieved by using the old sandstone-grinding wheel that was a good 3 foot in diameter and approximately 4 inches wide, and was lubricated by water. This wheel was powered by anybody who would offer to do the winding. That was very hard work, especially on a hot day. Pat had now got all his working clothes on, his vest and union shirt, minus collar; thick trousers with a tuck in below his knee that gave a plus fours effect to his trousers. He had on a pair of very hefty boots, which looked as though they would never wear out, and a well-worn neb cap. He asked, "What have I to do, boss?". My father said, "Get your scythe and I will show you where to go". Pat said, "Where is my sharpening stone?". This was a stone which Pat held in his hand to give the final touches to his scythe before commencing to mow. With long, smooth strokes Pat sharpened both sides of the blade. The finished blade was as sharp as a razor and Pat was soon mowing a wide path with long graceful stokes on the scythe. He made it look so easy; it was a highly skilled job that could only be achieved after years of practice. He carried on mowing effortlessly for many hours before returning to the farm for tea, not seeming to be the least bit tired after such strenuous work.

Tea usually took about half an hour and would consist of a couple of boiled eggs, fresh from the farm's free-range hens. These eggs had exceptionally rich yolks and tasted delicious. There were also piles of newly baked bread, fresh from the oven, and fresh farm butter, plus a stone jam jar full of home made blackberry jam. Tea was soon over, and there was a pile of dirty pots, plates and forks from the teatime sitting which had served 12 hungry mouths. Father would find Pat work until about 7pm, but, if there was hay to cart back to the barn, work would continue until maybe 9:30pm, or even later. If Pat finished work early he would make a beeline down to the local pub in the village, where there was a gathering of the newly arrived Irishmen. No doubt they would be comparing their new living quarters, the wage they had negotiated, the crops, and, most important, the weather. After a couple of pints Pat would make his way back to the farm, not the long way home, but by the shortest route. This route Pat knew well, as he had walked it scores of times over many years.

Back at the farm, my mother was still up, waiting for Pat to return, and a cup of tea would be brewed, accompanied by a big slice of jam pasty. After a short talk, a candle would be lit and Pat would retire to bed. Pat had no night attire, only his thick, long lapped working shirt that came down just below his knees. When asked, "Why do you have your shirt with such long laps?" Pat replied, "I need them so long to keep my arse warm in winter".

Pat had no trouble in sleeping, as we soon found out. The bedroom soon took on a different note, we could have been in the pigsty, Pat was snoring so loud and long. In fact, I don't believe I had heard the old large white pigs snore so loud. The one consolation was that Pat was only to stay for 1 month. There was more to follow as we were soon to find out. All at once there was a horrific stink, and we wondered if Pat had had an accident in bed. That turned out not to be the case. Had Pat accidentally stepped in some dog dirt while returning home from the pub? It certainly smelt the same, and it also smelt much worse being in a confined area and on a warm summer night. It was obviously dark at the time, so there was no chance of tracking down the offending culprit. At sunrise, Pat was soon out of bed and ready for work on the farm. It was the ideal opportunity to find the source of the horrific stink. We searched the bedroom from end to end, looked around and under Pat's bed, but no real trace of the culprit. We had our suspicions, could it be his stockings and feet? This was most probable, as the smell had gone and so had Pat.

The following night we were ready, when Pat came in and took off his boots. The evidence was there, he had a terrible problem. So much so that he left his boots outside under the stone slab by the back door where they had time to cool down and ventilate the horrific stink before the next day. His socks were another problem. The thick hand knit pair had really absorbed the foot odour so much that we made him hang them outside the bedroom window to freshen up. I think they acted as a fly repellent as well. Looking at Pat's feet, which were whiter than white, I believe this was caused by the heat produced by the thick heavy boots and woolly stockings. They looked as though they had been scalded by boiling water.

There were yet more problems with Pat that we soon discovered early that night. This turned out to be little black 'jumpers', with teeth like needles, that must have stowed away in Pat's thick vests and decided to migrate into my bed. You soon knew you had an extra occupant in your bed when the little black flea decided to have its supper. These bites soon turned into lumps half the size of an egg. There was then no alternative but to track the little blighter down, very difficult in the middle of the pitch dark night. We lit a candle, which was not the best of lights, it was a case of 'any port in a storm'. By this time 3 or 4 large lumps had appeared on my legs, so we knew the flea was towards the bottom of the bed. It couldn't be in my nightwear because I didn't wear any. My other brother had not been attacked at this stage, the flea must have decided I was the most succulent meat. From now on our plan was to confine the flea, or fleas, to the inside of the bed so a tent had to be formed under the bed sheets. My brother held the sheet up to form the tent whilst I scanned by candle light for the offending flea. I soon spotted this small black flea and made a grab for it, but missed it by a mile.

I soon found that these were Olympic fleas, and jumped at great speed. After 2 or 3 attempts, the flea was captured. When I squashed it between my nails it made a significant crack. So much for that single flea which caused so much of a problem and discomfort to myself. When doing Pat's washing, my mother found the root problem and where the fleas had made their home. This was in Pat's thick woolly vests, under the armpits, where the wool was matted and shrunk.

The weather was perfect for making hay, sun from morning till night. Father was rising from his bed around 5:30am to catch the 2 horses that would do the mowing. An early rise was necessary in order to avoid working 2 horses in the midday heat. The mower was a Deering twin horse mower, a pretty sight when being pulled by the 2 Clydesdale horses. Betty, the black one, and Captain, the bay, with father sitting on the back, giving instructions and driving the horses around the area that had to be mown. Father always discarded his old neb cap in haytime for a wide brimmed straw hat that was much cooler in the sun. During this time Pat was scything round the perimeter of the field cutting almost every blade of surplus grass, all to be dried and preserved for winter-feed.

Two hours soon passed and breakfast was coming into the field. This was a large straw basket solely used for haytime because of its size. Breakfast would be porridge, bacon and egg and a large can of tea. The horses would be tucking into a pile of fresh mown grass. Breakfast was also the time for sharpening the mower blade. This my father did on his knee with a brand new file he had purchased for the season's haytime from a stall in the village on hiring day.

After mowing, the next task was to start to turn the grass that had been mown the previous day. All this was done by hand. The idea was to turn the swathe of grass over so as to expose the underside to the sun. This was another task that Pat had perfected to a fine art. The wooden rake he used was the same that he had used over the years which he had engraved with the letter 'P', so only Pat used that rake. Pat's actions were like clockwork when turning the swathe of grass. The speed at which he worked never allowed the grass to fall flat. The muscles on his arms were obviously well used, and strong. The sun, by now, was overhead and it was extremely warm. It didn't bother Pat, he still had his vest and shirt on, heavy boots and thick pants, plus his spotted hankie tied to form protective headwear.

It was a great sight, seeing five or six men swathe turning, all following within a yard of each other, and all pulling the rake at the same time with military precision. This sorted the men from the lads, when stamina and strength was required. There was no chance of slacking when five or six worked in a team. This hardwork ensured that no freshly mown grass lay unturned, vital when making hay. Only one process a day was done to the new mown grass. If the weather was exceptional it took three days to make hay, but crops varied. If it was a heavy crop four days would be required, providing it didn't rain.

If it rained, father had plenty of jobs lined up for Pat. Most urgent was the spring cleaning of the shippons or cowsheds. These had become caked with cow muck on the walls and the woodwork had become soiled with milk and grease after the cows had inhabited it for the last six months. The cobwebs all had to be brushed down from the roof of the cowshed. The walls and timberwork had to be well soaked to make cleaning easier. Once well cleaned, the walls had to be whitewashed with a lime and water mixture. This helped to keep the flies out of the cowshed when milking during summer months.

Another job Pat had to do, on days when haymaking could not

take place, was thistle mowing. There was a good crop of thistles every year, in almost all of the pastures where the young stock, milk cows and sheep grazed during summer months. Pat would also mow rushes that would be gathered, and used as bedding for the young calves during the winter months. Other jobs, when there was no weather for haymaking, would be weeding the garden, paths and cobbled stones in front of the farmhouse and the cobbled farmyard and paths leading to the shippons or cattle sheds.

Pat would also clip the hedges around the farm or clean out the clogged up ditches to allow the water to drain from the fields. During bad weather, Pat had only the bare necessities of rain wear. It consisted of a good thick provender sack, draped over his shoulders, which was fastened with a horse-shoe nail. This allowed the arms to be used freely. Most of Pat's work was manual hard work. He was more used to this than technical, light precision work. Most Irishmen were incapable of working farm horses, or so they pretended. They acted quite 'thick' sometimes when asked if they could do a particular job. I often wondered who was the 'thickest' when we were left to do that particular job ourselves.

One certain thing was that Pat would never work on a Sunday. It was the day for God bothering. Pat would get up early, clean his shoes, and use the iron to press his pants and tie and make sure his shirt was clean. He would get washed and shaved but, as there was no bathroom, Pat would take towel and soap to the farm trough, where that deep down wash could take place. The water was always stone cold from the ever-flowing farm spring.

Shaving would always take place at the stone kitchen sink, with a pot of warm water from the cast iron side boiler, that in most cases was fairly rusty. Pat would use a cutlass razor that he sharpened on the broad belt used to hold up his Sunday and workday breeches. There was no automated method available which could sharpen a razor half as sharp as Pat could. He also had a well-worn shaving brush that he probably got as a wedding or Christmas present. The shaving stick was well-worn too and was only about an inch long and would have been discarded, by more affluent people, many shaves ago, but Pat's motto was 'waste not, want not'. Pat would lather his face and chin until he resembled Father Christmas. This always fascinated us when Pat was shaving. He would then take his cutlass in between finger and thumb and with a few long gentle strokes Pat's dark growth of beard had completely disappeared. There was no after-shave lotion, all he used was a few handfuls of cold spring water.

He had no toothbrush or paste, I doubt if he had ever used any, but he had a set of really strong, healthy teeth, but they weren't very straight or white, as Pat used to chew the twist tobacco.

Soon, Pat was ready for town and mass at the nearest Catholic Church. Most Irishmen were Catholic, so Sunday was a day of prayer and reunion with his fellow Irishmen who had all gone to town on the local bus for mass. I don't think Pat would have to ask Father for forgiveness, as he was an honest, clean living, Irishman. He probably would have had to do if a few pints of beer were a sin. Pat would not return to the farmstead until after the last bus left town, normally at 10.45pm. Where he went, and what he did, was always a mystery, and how he passed away so many hours, we never found out. They most likely visited the same pub that they had gathered in together for many years, and caught up with all the latest news from back home, discussed the farms and families they had been hired at for the season's haytime.

Pat would always be ready for work on Monday morning, no matter what had taken place on Sunday or how much beer he had consumed, it never seemed to affect him. If the weather was good it was more or less the same pattern of work every day. It would be scything round the outskirts of the meadow first, before the sun got too strong and the heavy dew had not evaporated. Father would never allow any major movement of mown grass until the dew was off. He did not believe in turning a wet outside of the swathe of grass into a roll and locking in the dew. Pat would then have to rake the grass from the outskirts of the meadow and shake it out by hand on a more accessible part of the meadow. This all helped when the hay was dry and ready to cart to the barn for winter-feed. Pat would then be asked to shake out any large heaps of grass to ensure all parts were being exposed to the sun.

By mid morning the mowing for that day was finished, and the two horses would be taken back to the farmstead and stable for the first real meal of the day. This consisted of a large bucket of bran and rolled oats, dampened with water, to make it more palatable and less wasteful. This smelt very appetising, especially when you were the wrong side of your morning teabreak. After about half an hours rest the horses would be ready for work again. The next job for the horses would be strawing the hay. This machine was a Lister Blackstone with sharp spiked impellers, that picked up the semi dry grass and tossed it high in the air to allow the sun to dry almost every part of it. While all this was going on, Pat, without a grumble, was still hard at work raking and strawing the drying grass which was, by now, smelling beautiful, and was getting crisper by the minute.

Dinner could be anytime from 12.30 to 2.00 p.m. This was because you had to finish the particular task you were doing in a short time, so the crops of hay were ready to cart at the same time of day. Dinner would be potato hash or hotpot that was always ready and piping hot, whether you were early or late for lunch. The rice pudding was also ideal when flexible dinner times occurred. Pat had a huge appetite and Pat said half a pan of spuds was nothing to a working man.

After a few inspections by my father he decided it was dried enough to get ready for rowing up, prior to carting to the barn. The rowing up took place with a machine called a side delivery. This machine separated and rolled the hay into large rows ready to be forked and loaded onto the cart and delivered to the barn. This Pat did to perfection. The secret was to get the fork into the rows of hay and push the hay until a standard forkful had emerged. Too small a forkful was a nuisance when the loader had to make a level and straight-sided load. Too large a forkfull had the opposite effect, and in most cases was bad to handle by the loader. If too many bad forkfulls were presented to the loader they would be pushed off the side of the cart back to the ground, only to be gathered again by the forker for re-presentation to the loader. The forker soon learnt the correct size of forkfull the loader required. The fork had also to be turned with the prongs facing inwards not upwards, this was less dangerous to the loader who had much less chance of being stabbed by the fork. The forker would also have to leave little or no hay on the ground during this operation. Pat's skill left only a few straws of hay for the next process of raking up.

After loading, the load had to be tied down by ropes to secure it until it arrived at the barn. There was nothing more annoying than having to re-fork and reload a cart. Once under the barn, the hay had to be forked from the cart and shaken level and even, so preservation for winter was best attained. Pat was a professional in this job, he made sure the forkfull of hay was forked to the correct area of the stack so the least extra work was necessary. When levelling, my job was trampling the newly stacked hay round wall sides and corners of the barn. This was important, to consolidate the newly harvested hay, to avoid waste over the next six months.

On very fine, warm days the carting of the hay would continue late into the night. After a late night carting hay you were always covered in sweat, pollen and dust and, as there were no bathroom facilities, the river Ribble came in very useful. It was only about

600yds from the farm along a meadow, and down a steep embankment, planted with large oak and ash trees, that we had to negotiate in semi darkness. There were two good pools for swimming, a small one where the not so good swimmers swam and the big pool where the competent would swim. This big pool was called Denholmes wheel, because of the whirlpool that was caused by water rushing over the large weir of grey limestone. Nobody had swimming costumes at that time of night or even underpants to use as a costume. The big laugh was Pat, with that extra long shirt and laps that hung about a foot from the ground. After about 15 minutes in the river with a nice big bar of carbolic soap there was no sign of body odour. We were perfectly clean from head to toe. By this time it was total darkness and a difficult path lay ahead from the river to the meadow, at the top of the very steep wooded embankment, which must have been a 3 to 1 incline.

Soon we were back at the farmhouse where the second supper was waiting. Some nights would be scrambled egg on toast or just toast and home made jam or maybe soup. After such a long, hard day's work in the heat you looked forward to a sound nights sleep hopefully before Pat started to snore like the old large white sow.

If the weather was good you would complete the gathering of the hay within the month, so Pat was really pleased. My father never counted haytime as being finished until all the implements were washed, oiled and stored away under the shed. The outside edge of the stacks would have to be plucked by hand, leaving a perfectly straight edge and airtight seal to avoid waste of the valuable hay.

Once all these jobs were completed Pat would be free to go to the next job, which was harvesting down in Lincolnshire. My father would go upstairs to the secret hide, where a bundle of large white five pound notes were hidden. He would then count out twelve for Pat's wage for the month, then return to the kitchen with them and tuck them into my mother's top apron pocket. My father, in the meantime, had harnessed Betty into the trap and arrived at the back gate. Pat had done his packing and donned his light blue suit and red tie. His case had that length of rope securely tied around for security. My brothers and sisters were all outside in the yard waiting to wave old Pat on his way.

My mother called Pat to the kitchen table where she counted the twelve five pound notes carefully before Pat's eyes. It certainly was a lot of money for three weeks work. Pat had worked hard, all the hay was top quality, and there was enough to feed all our sheep and cows for the winter months. Pat gathered his case and loaded it on the trap and joined my father on the seat.

Soon, horse, trap and Pat were on their way. Pat gave a wave and a smile as he left the farmstead. Hopefully, he would return another year to help with the hay. This we would never know until the next summer.

Old Pat had been coming to England to work on the same farm for nye on forty years. It was time to leave for the very last time. He was very upset and almost broken hearted at the thought of never returning.

Farmers Story:
The farmer went into the large barn and found Pat with a strong cart rope fastened to the large oak beam supporting the barn roof. At the loose end of the rope, Pat had made a slip knot, and tied it tightly round his waist. The farmer rushed over to Pat and asked, "What on earth are you doing?" Pat replied, "Boss, I am trying to commit suicide". The farmer said to Pat, "You don't fasten the rope round you waist when you try to commit suicide, you fasten it around your neck!"

Pat replied, "I did boss, but I started to choke!"

Old Joe

Joe was a victim of the 1st World War and had received serious head wounds. Part of his forehead was blown away by shrapnel leaving the brain almost visible, only protected by a thin layer of skin. I know this gave Joe continuous pain as you could often find him protecting that area with a woolly cap in winter and a light handkerchief in summer.

I suppose Joe was one of the lucky ones that only just survived that bitter conflict. Joe was in his late forties when he came to work on our farm in Bowland. This was after the land girls had returned home after the war effort to their town surrounds. Joe had been in an institution for the mentally ill, at a centre many miles away in Yorkshire where my father located him. He was like many in those particular institutions, they were permanently stuck there, until people like my father got them released for work, which they were more than capable of doing.

When Joe arrived on the farm via the local railway station some 3 1/2 miles away which he had walked on the cold winter's day, the whole of his personal belongings were very scant. What he owned he was wearing except for his old leather tobacco pouch and an old briar pipe, plus an ounce of Bruno smoking tobacco, which was in a well decorated tin. I suppose he was over the world with joy, thinking that he was once again a free citizen and able to lead a normal life away from the institution, which was like a prison where you weren't allowed beyond the high brick walls and guarded gates.

Joe soon got used to living on the farm and all the different jobs he was required to do. I believe Joe had worked on a farm prior to his injury in the army, but he never revealed much about his past. Maybe with the brain and skull damage he suffered, he couldn't remember. He was a good stockman knowing what to look for when livestock were sick and unwell. He was also good with the farm dogs, old Tim and Laddy. These dogs would work better for Joe than for my father, who had a much shorter temper with the dogs, if they didn't do what was required of them. Joe would never physically hit a dog but could often be heard cursing them at the top of his voice, many fields away. Joe had a very strong voice, but I don't think he was ever a Sergeant Major.

His vocabulary when cursing or swearing was complete, and when in a bad mood with the farm dogs, it was bluer than blue. Luckily he was miles away from the village and farmhouse. Joe had only one other major fault and that was beer. Every penny he earned he spent on beer, there was nothing set aside for clothes or footwear so my mother ran a type of club where she purchased his pants, shirts or boots and knocked a little off each week from his wage. For this she kept a small book to log down every deduction, as Joe always doubted how long it took to clear his debt. Joe was lucky in so far as he was about the same size as my father so many of my fathers cast-offs fitted Joe perfectly. Joe would always sell his clothing coupons in the pub to the landlord's daughters for beer money. This was never too much of a problem, as having a large family there was plenty of clothing coupons spare, should Joe require anything.

Beer in those days was only pence a pint, so Joe could consume teens of pints a night on only a small wage. He had no lodging expenses or other outgoings and therefore his entire wage went on beer. Joe told the story that he knew someone that could drink 12 pints of beer while the local town clock chimed and struck twelve o'clock. It was sometime later we found out who this person was, none other than Joe. He had no need to swallow he just poured it down. Carrying so many pints of beer never affected Joe, seldom did you see him totally drunk. There was a saying that once you drank so many pints you then drank yourself sober.

Maybe this was the case, the room in which Joe slept was the largest room in the farmhouse and in winter the coldest. Most mornings you would have to scrape the ice off the window to see out, so keeping warm in bed meant plenty of blankets. These were not the nice white woolly type but the thick black ex-army type. Joe had a single bed just in at the door, there was another single bed, plus a large double bed in which my brothers and I slept. There was no electric light, so it was always to bed by candle.

Joe was always last to bed returning after the local had closed the doors to his thirst. He would then walk the 1 1/2 miles home or maybe use his old Raleigh bicycle. I remember his old bicycle well because he had made it himself. The handlebars and brakeblocks were made out of hazlewood cut from the hedgerow. This was standard on most cycles during the war because of the shortage of rubber. Returning home Joe would quietly ascend the stairs to the long bedroom where he slept, seldom did anyone hear him arrive home, or go to bed. Once in bed Joe had one problem to overcome. This was the large amount of beer he had transported and stored that evening. However Joe overcame this quite easily by insisting on two chamber pots, jerry's or poes, or whatever you care to call them, under his bed. The idea was that when one was full he changed over to the second. Joe never spilt or overfilled the chamber pots. He used a unique method and probably only used by himself. This was the thumb test. It worked quite simply by placing his thumb on the inside of the chamber pot and when the level rose, and his thumb sensed the warm liquid, he transferred to the second pot. He never spilt any on the patterned oilcloth that was used for floor covering in the bedroom.

Joe worked for my father on the family farm for about three years. During that time he had become very short tempered with the livestock. He would use a stick on both the cattle and horses at the least provocation. This made them difficult to handle and with the horses difficult to catch. Even though they were only animals they soon found out who were their friends. During Joe's later days on the farm he would always have spent his wage by the weekend and for the rest of the week would want a sub for his beer. He always had an excuse to go down to the village for something each night.

My father would hide in the cowshed when Joe was after a sub, leaving Joe to go round every place on the farm in search. After every shed, Joe's language would get worse until he got a sub. It was only, in most cases, a matter of two and sixpence, or a maximum of five bob, and Joe was happy.

Joe left our farm and found work in the village on the farm adjacent to the pub and run by the landlord's son. So I don't suppose Joe ever received another wage. It would be a case of drink for work. I was told Joe's language didn't improve and with living in the village, it was not acceptable, so he lost his job.

He spent his final days in the hospital type workhouse on the outskirts of the local town. Not a good ending to his varied life but probably far better than a lot of his pals in the first world war.

The Country Fling

Nearly all villages in Ribblesdale had a school and hall. The schools attended by the villagers' and farmers' children. These school halls varied in size, depending on how many pupils were expected to attend from the villages and local farms. Many of these village school halls were too small for a reasonably sized country-dance.

One room, I remember, was up a flight of stairs and would hold a maximum of approximately 100 people. It was a total fire hazard, with only the single door as entrance and exit. There was no bandstand or stage and no electricity, just a couple of paraffin mantle lamps in the middle of the room.

The floors on all of these types of dance halls were scrubbed clean every week, so they had little or no slip when attempting to dance. It was my job, most times, at Bowland school hall, to go round and sprinkle the beeswax, ballroom floor polish when a country-dance was being held. The country lads and lasses would travel from to 10 and 15 miles to attend. In my early days the mode of transport was mainly the bicycle, and that wasn't ideal, because of the many hills in our area of Ribblesdale. Distance, in our teens, didn't seem to put us off attending the many dances held over the late summer and winter months.

Most dances would be held to make money for a village cause, such as the Young Farmers' Club, the Church fund, village hall, the war memorial, Womens' Institute or maybe June sports day. I can say for certain the dances in Bowland were always well attended, and many times over attended, leaving little room to actually dance.

Somehow, no matter what cause the dance was for, my father always seemed to get the doorman's job. I suppose this was because he would insist that everybody paid the two and sixpence admission charge. He had many arguments with the late arrivals, who had spent all their evening drinking in the local pub. They always argued that it was late and they had missed the dancing, and there was only one and a half-hours of dancing left.

I always had to spend the whole night at the dance, mainly because I daren't visit the local pub. If I had, I would certainly have had to sleep in the barn with the cattle close to hand. The other reason was that I had no money to spend on drink or cigarettes, because I was never paid a wage all the time I worked on the family farm. The only money I had was from catching rabbits, spreading farmyard muck, or haymaking for a neighbouring farmer. Getting money out of some of these farmers, was like getting blood out of a stone.

Most of the lads that went to the pub either worked on the farms or had a job in the nearest town, Clitheroe, that gave them a regular income. With this regular income they could afford the many 'bad habits' as my father called them. It was at one dance when I was offered a cigarette by a farmer's pal and when I refused his offer he said, "Why don't you smoke?". So I asked him the question, "Why do you smoke?". He replied, "I feel a silly bugger stood at a dance wi' nowt in my hand". I promptly replied, "When somebody tells me I look a silly bugger for not smoking, I will start smoking". Nobody ever did.

Even though I never was paid a penny at home while I worked from 15 years to 23 years old, when I got married and left home, my father carefully calculated how much per week I was worth, less my food and lodgings. The amount was one thousand pounds for four hundred and sixteen weeks work, or two thousand nine hundred and twenty days, a total of two pounds ninety two per week, inclusive of overtime. The big advantage over my farmer pals, and lads that worked in the town, was that at 23 years old, I had one thousand pounds to get married, set up house, and start up in partnership with my father in law, whereas my pals had smoked and drunk their wages, and had next to nowt left.

In the village of Bowland the school hall was, I believe, the best dance hall in that area for miles around. There were many more at outlandish villages that were only small, but very popular, when a dance was held there. One, I remember, in particular was a disused or redundant ex army hut at a village a good six miles from Bowland. This small village consisted of a pub, a few cottages and adjacent farms. Whenever a dance was held at the village of Tosside there was never a specific cause, unlike Bowland, and was always run by the local farmers who organised the date, band and refreshments. The refreshments were always made by the same bunch of farmers' wives and help from the villagers.

The band was mostly a four-piece band consisting of a piano, drum, violin and an accordion to increase the sound of the music. Many times the band wasn't in tune and they sounded like someone was torturing the next door neighbour's cat. Whenever I attended this village dance there was always the same management and M.C (Master of Ceremonies). This was a tight old farmer called Ellis Wilson who mostly collected the money and announced the next dance. Over the many years nobody ever found out where the proceeds of their successful dances went. The best and most probable answer was into Ellis' back pocket and the other committee, or organisers' pockets.

The first time I cycled to a dance at Tosside was mid November, on a dark, but dry, windy night. It was mainly uphill so it took quite a while to cover the six miles from our farm. The only consolation we cyclists had when cycling to Tosside was that we knew, after the dance, it was all down hill back to Bowland.

The floor at this dance hall was pine timber boarding which, unfortunately, had developed rot in the centre section, allowing the dancefloor to drop a good 3 inches. This was no major problem to the organising committee of farmers who simply got a fencing rail 3 inches wide x 1inch thick and nailed it to the side of the sunken floor leaving a drop of 3 inches right in the centre of the dance floor, a hazard to dancers if you didn't know where the step was.

At this particular dance hall, in my early years, there was no electricity, just paraffin tilley lamps that gave off a reasonable light in the dance hall. There were no outside lights or toilets, well, if there were, I never found them. On the first occasion when I visited the Tosside dance hall I decided at, maybe, 11pm that I would visit the outside loo. On leaving the subdued lighting of the dancehall, I hit total darkness. Not even a single star or a ray of moonlight brightened the area outside the dancehall. There wasn't even a ray of light from the small windows in the dancehall, so I decided to feel my way up the side of the timber building until I thought it was a safe distance to relieve myself. I had only just finished and buttoned up my flies when the dancehall door opened, and two lasses stepped out into the pitch-black night and shut the door behind them. Their first words were, "Christ, I can't see a bloody thing", and their second words were, "It doesn't matter a bugger, I am going to have to go somewhere". What they then decided to do was exactly what I had done, and started to edge their way alongside the timber building, towards me, just a few feet away. These two lasses edged nearer to me and I stood perfectly still, not uttering a murmur. They got within 3 feet of me when they decided to relieve themselves. Their conversation was short at this particular stage. One lass said, "It doesn't matter a bugger, Mary, I am going to have to piss here". So they both went up with their frocks and down with their knickers within a couple of feet of me. In fact I could have touched their bottoms with my shoe toe, I was so near. They certainly didn't take too long to relieve themselves, exerting the maximum pressure on their bladder for a few seconds. They soon uprighted themselves, rearranged their clothes, and edged back towards the dance hall door. On opening the door, and with the light reflecting outside the door, I noticed two piles of froth similar to the head on a pint of beer. I never did find out who those two lasses were.

The lasses at most of these outlandish country-dances were from the local farms. These were easily identified with their wind swept complexion, rough hands, and welly marks around their legs. Unlike the lasses from the town or villages who worked in the towns with petite hands, white complexion, and legs they had daubed with a product called leg tan. This was meant to look like they were wearing stockings and they also put a thin pencil line mark down the back of the leg to imitate the stocking seam. This was, most likely, a difficult job and many lines were far from straight.

The refreshment at all village dances was always the same, a pot of tea. There was never any coffee or mineral water. A slice of bread with potted meat spread, or bought-in fish paste, and a rock bun or piece of gingerbread. The women committee members always made the sandwiches as they were required, and did the washing up. If, at the end of the dance, there was plenty of bread and cakes left over they would organise a bargain butty time, where everything was sold at a give-away price. This was when the big, strapping farm lads devoured the remaining left overs. This made a little more for the organising committees' good cause and nothing was wasted.

There was also a local bus service that allowed the town lads and lasses to visit the country-dances. The trouble with the country-dances was, they were a bit territorial, in that the country lads didn't like the town lads dancing and dating their local lasses. Many times this could lead to conflict on a mini scale, resulting with the town lads getting a stern warning to keep away from the girls or, if not, a good hammering from the strong, lean farm lads who could throw a punch like a horse had kicked you. Seldom did these youths return to Bowland for a second dose of the farm lads' hospitality.

At most village dances, the parents would attend either as helpers or spectators, and also have the occasional dance. Often, they sat on the wooden forms or benches that were placed around the outside of the dancehall floor. These parents were professional lip readers, or so I thought. It was almost always the case, if you agreed to take a girl to the pictures on a night out, that they knew first, and then, once they knew, so did the whole village.

Most dances in our school in Bowland were held on Friday nights. For most functions these were best for the revellers, because they always went on into the early hours of Saturday morning. In most cases, it wasn't the time of morning, it was how much longer will the band play. With a little bribery of a few pounds they would go on that extra hour. The noise didn't offend anyone, as the school hall was at the top of the village green, a good 300 yards from the village centre.

If the dances were organised to raise money for the Church funds, be it for the organ repairs, or Church roof, these were always held on a Saturday night. This was because the school was a Church school and no dances continued until early morning, but ended usually just before the stroke of midnight. On one occasion, I remember, we had a small, awkward vicar called Mr Smithies who was less co-operative than the normal village vicar. I always found, in the village of Bowland, the short, stubby gents more awkward to deal with than the more robust, large gents. This particular dance was in aid of Church funds and was just getting into the swing when our short stubby vicar decided to call a halt at 11:30pm. Normally, there would have been another 25 minutes left to dance. This went down like a ton of bricks with the young farmers and friends. We instantly pointed out to the vicar that there was still nearly 30 minutes left to dance and that some hadn't been dancing long, and had paid two and sixpence admission, and hadn't had any supper. There was no way Mr Smithies was going to alter his mind and extend the short remaining period of dancing. He got called many names we know he wouldn't be repeating from his pulpit the next morning at Church.

Also, he was in for an unpleasant surprise; something I can certainly say no other vicar in Bowland had experienced. What a couple of farmer pals and I did was leave the school hall that few minutes early, and climb over the iron railings alongside the road leading to the rectory and bottom end of the village.

We then started to dig an arsenal of sods of turf to bombard our awkward little vicar as he proceeded home after the dance. We had probably dug 20 sods each before our prey came into range, walking on the footpath alongside the school green. This footpath was lined by large chestnut trees and was a beautiful sight in the spring when in full flower. It was quite dark, as there was no lighting in the village at that time, so the vicar couldn't see my sod-throwing pals and me. It was also just as hard for us to see the vicar, so he had a reasonable chance of survival.

We let go with the first salvo of sods. I don't think we scored a direct hit, but for-warned the vicar of what to expect. He immediately retreated behind the large chestnut trees, moving from one tree to another, when he thought it safe to do so, at great speed, cursing us in his polite manner. We probably scored three or four direct hits before he was out of range and back inside the wall and gate of the large vicarage fortress.

The vicar did mention, during his sermon the next morning, about his late night bombardment from persons unknown. From then on Mr Smithies always let the dances carry on to within a few minutes of twelve, after that unheard of experience.

As the years passed by a few farmers obtained mechanical transport. One, in particular, bought a green Ford ex-army van. This van was ideal for carrying sheep, calves and pigs to the local markets. It was also very useful as a taxi for local dances, holding quite a number of revellers when packed in tight. The name we gave this van was 'Prof's passion wagon', Prof' being short for the Professor. Prof's van was quite large and held about 10 fat lambs or 6 adults plus driver and navigator.

Prof's van was far from perfect, and low so you always had to sit flat on the floor or kneel up. It always smelt of livestock such as lamb manure, pig muck, or worst of all calf muck. When full to capacity it was always well overloaded. The van floor in the back he could have covered with sawdust, but instead, he had obtained a large pegged rug, more or less made to measure, most likely from a jumble sale or from someone who had experienced the discomfort of riding in the back of this van. Prof's saying was that a second class ride was better than a first class walk. I always found that saying to be true, especially on a wild and windy night around Bowland.

The outward journey in Prof's van was a reasonably organised and well-behaved journey. On the return trip you could expect anything. Many times the van driver would have gathered a few girls and decided to visit another dance, leaving his regular passengers standing at a far-flung country-dance. Other times you had to get in the back as best you could. There was no sitting room as most of the passengers were in horizontal position with a number of legs and feet in all directions. There were various conversations while travelling at a low speed home. It varied from, "Give up", "Keep your hands off", "Stop it", "Give up until we get home". The male passengers in Prof's van were christened the 'Bowland bulls'.

On our farm, to help raise money for the village hall fund, we would organise a huge barn dance. This was always in early June, because it was the time all hay, straw and livestock was out of the farm buildings. Once the entire barn was empty it was given a good scrub down in all departments. The barn roof had to be brushed down to remove all the cobwebs that had been suspended between the old oak timbers for many years. The cowsheds, or shippons, had to be soaked and scrubbed clean. This was where the suppers would be prepared and served. There had to be steps made onto the hayloft so that there was extra dancing room for the barn dance revellers. A bandstand had to be made in the barn porch, at the back of the building, for the 5-piece band that had never played in the Bowland area let alone in a barn. Extra lights were to be fixed which I did myself, by a series of extensions and, I hoped, wouldn't overload and fuse on the barn dance night.

Ladies toilets had to be sorted out. These we made in the redundant pigsty as our 2 pigs had long since been killed for the farmhouse pantry and the next years young pigs had not arrived. The layout of these toilets was very crude. They were more of a perch than a toilet seat with a splashboard at the front to stop the occupants weeing down their legs.

The barn dance was advertised in the paper shop and Co-op shop windows plus the local weekly papers that most people bought in Bowland and local villages. We had expected a possible 100 to 150 revellers on a good night. We had a shock. At about 10:00pm there were only a few early arrivals, but as the night proceeded more and more people came until there was in excess of 200, all paying three and sixpence towards the purchase of a new village hall.

The refreshments on that night were extra. The demand for pots of tea, potted meat butties and cakes far exceeded supply, so my father had no need to organise a left over give-away sale. The band was the best-heard in Bowland and the music could be heard halfway up the first meadow, a good 200 yards away. The singer, a big lad, had a magnificent voice and was far too good for our humble surrounds and barn dance.

My father once again was the money collector gathering the cash for the village's major project. At about 11:30pm there was such a crowd that, for safety reasons, the main large door to the barn had to be opened. This was my father's decision as he had decided that all the admission money had been collected for that night. The dance went on into the early hours of the next day, without any interruption from the vicar or complaints from the villagers. There were no scuffles or fighting, probably because there was no beer available. My father also insisted he could organise a successful dance without a bar. He was right in this instance. Many farm lads stayed late and reported they only just arrived back at the farms where they worked in time for morning milking around 6:00am.

It was through the village dances that many farming families were united, continuing the many family traditions going back in time. Their children continued to attend the Church and school, contributing to the thrifty and thriving village of Bowland, one of the best communities in Ribblesdale.

The River Rich

There are many rivers in the British Isles, all varying in length and feature. Some are quite long and slow moving. These rivers normally drain the vast areas of arable land that is mostly flat and close to the estuary and sea. There are also many rivers that pass through towns and villages after emerging from a mere trickle at the source, that is normally a spring, rising directly out of the ground. These springs can rise either at the base of a hill, half way up, or at the top of a hill. A good spring never varies its output of water during flood or drought. This is because the supply of water to the spring can rise from hundreds of feet below the ground.

The river that flowed past our farm in Bowland, where I was born, was the River Ribble, hence the named area of Ribblesdale and the Ribble Valley. There were many streets and public houses named after Ribblesdale and also businesses using that name.

The River Ribble, from its source to the sea, had many uses, and was not just a waterway winding its way down wooded valleys, flood meadows, marshes and tidal estuaries, all rich in wildbird population. The Ribble Valley, from the onset, was an interesting historical place to study and visit. You could see the various places where cheap energy had been made available, through the use of the plentiful water that drained into the river from hills and valleys in Ribblesdale.

Mention can be made here of a few historical sites in the Bowland area adjacent to the river. The nearest one to our farm was Sawley Abbey, where monks farmed, and most likely fished the river, many hundreds of years ago. Another Abbey in Ribblesdale is Whalley Abbey, just a few miles further down stream. Both these Abbeys were built on the fertile, rich land adjacent to the rivers. This, I believe, was a shrewd move, because the monks knew that land on mid to lower reaches of the river was more fertile and much easier to grow and cultivate crops. There was also a better climate for their livestock to live and breed. I have never seen an Abbey high on the Pennine range, where the winters are long, and the growing season weeks later than on the lowland farms.

Whalley Abbey

Sawley Abbey

Adjacent to most of the estates along the river, manmade weirs had been built, to divert water through waterwheels to drive sawmills and corn grinders for flour and cattle food. The river, from its source, was a cheap supply of power to farms and villages. It was vital for the watering of livestock during the summer months, when many small tributaries had totally dried up.

The River Ribble was, I suppose, a kind of a mongrel river as far as rivers go, as it wasn't just a true River Ribble. It was the River Ribble at its source and at the estuary, but in the middle of the river, I would guess twenty miles upstream, it was joined by two other major rivers, one on the left-hand side and another on the right hand side. The one on the right, if you were facing downstream, was the River Hodder. That was a sizeable river of quality water and exceptionally well stocked with both trout and salmon. This river was probably not as good a river for fishing as it had been at the turn of the century, before the huge Stocks reservoir was built. With the building of the reservoir there wasn't the high and low waters as were previously experienced before the dam, and, obviously, there was much less water in the river. The water from this huge dam was piped across land some 35 miles to Blackpool, where more and more was required, especially when the holiday makers from the large towns and cities visited Blackpool for their summer break. When the Stocks reservoir was built, I believe there was discontent and outcry among the many farmers and villagers of the valley where the reservoir was to be built and flooded.

The huge dam wall towered above the small Dale Head village and church and a few farms, plus hundreds of acres of farmland. Today, the village of Dale Head is many feet below the water, except for the occasional few weeks when there is a major drought and the water level is very low. The village remains and Church appears to rise from the still waters. Farmers and visitors would visit the remains and point out which house they lived in, and reminisce about the history of their old country village. Although I never visited the Hodder valley much during my youth, I did see many of the historical landmarks, bridges, villages, etc which probably have many fascinating farming stories to tell, if I only knew them.

The River Calder, flows into the river Ribble at the village of Mitton at the same position as the River Hodder. At this point there is a local saying or statement, that is 'Hodder, Calder, Ribble and Rain all meet together at Mitton De Main'. Below that junction the Hodder and Calder disappear and become the much-enlarged River Ribble. The Calder River, in my early days, was a much-polluted river mainly because it wound its way from Mitton up through the heavily industrialised valleys where the many cotton mills, dyeing factories and every other industrial process took place. The River Calder was the least expensive place to dispose of their chemicals and industrial waste.

Wier at Whalley

I remember the weir at Whalley where the Calder was easily seen. Where the water swirls and plunges many feet this caused a massive froth, or foam build up, from the pollution caused upstream. There definitely were very few fish caught in the Calder in those years until local authorities and government disallowed the depositing of factory waste and possibly sewage into the River Calder and its many small tributaries.

The river Ribble, I suppose, was very lucky because it didn't pass through any major towns where widespread manufacturing took place. Probably the local council controlled the pollution situation better. There would be the occasional farmer who would release his sheep dip when the water level in the river was low, killing hundreds of fish and, most likely, got hauled before the local magistrates and fined a few pounds. In general, the River Ribble and the many tributaries were pollution free.

There were a few major tributaries in the area around Bowland. These were never called rivers, even though they were sizeable. The name in Bowland for these was 'becks', the largest being Skirden beck. A major house on Skirden beck was called Skirden Hall and a small farm dwelling Forest Beck.

The beck that passed through Bowland village was called Kirkbeck. Why it was called Kirkbeck I never found out. I don't think there were any farm dwellings called after this beck. Kirkbeck flowed on the topside of Bowland village and during my early years always seemed to overflow its banks at least once a year.

During summer months, when thunderstorms were prevalent, most villagers had slide-in flood boards at their front doors which they slotted in when the flash flood occurred. This saved major damage to their properties. A normal flood could be up to 2 feet deep in the houses in Bowland village. It was hard luck if they were out when a flood occurred, although if any household was unlucky, the rest of the villagers would give a helping hand at mopping up.

I remember one sizable flood when I was about 12 years old and my farmer playmates bet me I couldn't ride the old Raleigh bike through the 2 foot deep water. Being young and a little big headed I took up the challenge. The villagers were looking on, none too happy at me making a medium sized wave as I stood hard on the peddles, trying to propel myself and bicycle through the deep water. I had got a good half way through the floodwater when, for no reason at all, the chain slipped and came off. I went straight over the handlebars, heading into the murky, but warm, floodwater, totally submerged for a few seconds, but getting absolutely wet through to the skin. There were many not so pleasant remarks, probably the worst from the more refined lady residents of Bowland. It was none too pleasant pushing my bike the one and a half miles back home, bedraggled and wet. I definitely didn't get offered a change of clothes or clogs.

No matter how large or small the village becks were, they usually had a name. The names could be called after the farms in many cases, or the small hamlet. The village of Bowland was divided by Kirkbeck. The school, village green, police station and church at the top of the village and the pub, Co-op shop, butcher shop and post office at the bottom. There were two bridges, one the main road bridge and the second a wood, single person bridge with wood side rails. This wood bridge, I remember, was on its last legs and unsafe to use, so the solution was to get a replacement. The problem was that the bridge was going to cost a few hundred pounds, and the money had to be raised by the villagers, not the Parish Council or the landlord. This caused conflict, as the bottom side of the village never, or seldom, used the bridge, and was not prepared to pay. The top end of the village wasn't prepared to raise all the money for the bottom end of the village to use the bridge, so stalemate existed.

Kirkbeck Bridge 1956

Kirkbeck Bridge 1956

My father was chairman of the Parish Council at that particular time so he suggested he would help build the bridge with his farm staff, and assistance from the willing villagers. The cost of girders, stone and cement was only about £40. The villagers were highly delighted at the cost and an agreement to proceed was reached. My father bought the girders, sand and cement and the Estate donated the stones for the base and sides of the bridge. The date was arranged for the project to commence. This was early evening, when the villagers had finished work, and my father and farmstaff had finished milking. The day and evening soon arrived, and as we approached the site we found only the odd villager. The villager, I remember, was one that seldom worked, except as a linesman or road-sweeper, and his nickname was 'Lazy Bill never worked and never will'. At least he was prepared to work on the footbridge project. Bill was very handy helping mix by hand the concrete for the bridge structure, and didn't live up to his nickname slogan at all.

My father made the observation and relevant remark I have always remembered about the villagers. This is as relevant today as it was in 1956, the year we built the footbridge. The saying was that, 'A lazy man has time for nowt, a busy man has time for owt'. This saying weighed up the villagers of Bowland. The bridge is still in use today, and if one looked carefully at the wall facing downstream you can see the date 1956 in sandstone slate.

As a young lad the becks of Bowland were a particular attraction for me even at junior school, when I was just nine or ten years old. I spent many hours during summer months learning to tickle the brown trout that was plentiful in the beck just below the school. On many days I would be late home, but not particularly wet, as I used to remove my clogs and stockings before I commenced fishing. I was not always successful, so I explained how large the trout was and how it got away. However, it was rewarding if I caught a fish and had it fried in fresh farm butter for my tea.

As I got older the large becks and river became more attractive for both leisure and sporting activities. We probably got the most pleasure during summer months when the river was in low ebb and reasonably warm and clean. The clarity of the river could vary within hours, especially in summer months when thunderstorms were about. The thunder rain was never cold; in fact the river was much warmer, after thunder rain, than the clean normal farm drains and springs water. Many times we would go to the river, unprepared for swimming, only to find the water reasonably warm and clean, and decide to have a swim. We would first have a quick look around to check if there were any pic-nickers or hikers in the area. Seldom would there be anybody, because it was in a fairly isolated area of the river. If it was all clear, we would take off our clogs and clothes and swim in the nuddy, or wi' nowt on. I remember one such occasion, when we thought all was clear, and a party of girl guides appeared on the riverbank and decided to set out for a picnic, unaware that the five or six farm lads were swimming nude.

We were in a bit of a predicament as our clogs and clothes were hidden in bracken just behind the picnic site. The water was far from warm so we hadn't intended to remain in the river for so long. However, we had to put up with the cold. Most of us were getting colder by the minute and our hands turning blue. Also, our vital parts were going blue and shrinking to a less embarrassing size, as the teenage girl guides were now set up for the enjoyable picnic outing. I think the guides knew we had nowt on, so they sat the situation out, without letting on to their leader for that afternoon.

Something had to happen; either, we had to take the hard line, which was to emerge from the water in full frontal to collect our clothes, or go home with nowt on and return later for our clogs and clothes. Luckily, one of the lads uprooted a large mass of weed, which was fairly prevalent in the river at that time, and covered his by now dishevelled private parts. He then went up to the slightly embarrassed girl guides and requested they moved away until the rest gathered their clothes. We learnt our lesson.

The beck that ran adjacent to our farmyard was called Fooden Beck and was only a small beck, probably only a mile long in total. This beck was, most likely, the most unusual beck on the Ribble because of a sulphur spring that emerged out of the blue limestone rock face just below our farm. The sulphur spring was gin clear and very cold, and obviously rose many hundreds of feet below the rock face. The sulphur water smelt strongly of rotten eggs, a smell that was much worse than its taste. Occasionally we used to drink a glass or cupful of this water, supposedly able to cure boils and carbuncles, rashes, spots and almost any other complaint. I never knew whether it did us any good. All I know is that it didn't do us any harm. My father told a true story of a horse he owned for many years that always went down to the sulphur well to drink. The same horse had a good healthy foal for a total of 15 years. The sulphur water definitely didn't do that horse any harm.

Sulphur Well

The River Ribble in and around Bowland had a few features or landmarks not found anywhere else on the river. The most unusual and spectacular was Pudsey Leap. This was a sheer rock face rising, I would guess, a hundred and fifty feet from the river below. This was most likely a natural fault in the blue limestone rock and not caused by erosion over the millions of years by the water from the Ribble. The name for this rock cliff was derived from a gentleman who lived in the Bowland village, called Pudsey. He, allegedly, was minting counterfeit silver coins and, when the king's men came to arrest him, he mounted his horse and galloped past Bolton Hall across the meadow and jumped over the rock face landing safely on the opposite bank, and escaped arrest, hence the name Pudsey Leap. To commemorate Pudsey there is a separate chapel called after him in the Bowland Church, where he was buried with his three wives and children.

Pudseys Leap

A few hundred yards upstream from Pudsey Leap is a natural weir that rises just above the surface of the water. This weir, once again, was formed out of the natural blue limestone rock formation over many centuries. The weir was an ideal place to cross from one side of the river to the other, without removing stockings and clogs when the water was low in mid summer. The weir had, also, I believe, very unique features, again formed over hundreds of years by water erosion. These were scores of perfectly round holes in the rock surface approximately 4 to 6 inches deep. The name known locally for this weir was the 'piss-pots'. I do know that the Lord of the Manor always called it the Piss-Pots; what I can't say for sure was whether that was its official name!

Upstream a half-mile was another, different, medium sized pool where sometimes the fresh run salmon would rest. This was called the flag shop (shop being a slang name for place). This pool was a large flag, or rock formation, with literally no small or large boulders as in the rest of the river. On the left hand bank, that was now rising steeply from the river, were large elm and oak trees, hazel trees, wild sloe and limestone outcrop, or rock face. At this point was the otter's cave, that was, most likely, the most secure place on the river for the otters to breed and rear their young. Most times when I visited the otters cave, there would be an abundance of otter paw marks in the sand on the cave floor, also large fish bones totally devoid of any fishmeat. You could also see where the young otters had been sharpening their claws on the large limestone boulders that were present in the entrance to the cave.

'Piss Pots'

'Piss Pots'

Piss Pots Wier

Otters Cave

Upstream from the otter's cave was one of the best salmon pools on the river for many miles. This was a large deep pool formed over many years below a multi tier of blue limestone outcrop. The water falling may be 6 feet in total. This salmon pool was called Denholmes Wheel. The wheel name, I believe, was derived from the fact that there was a whirlpool which was always evident if you looked carefully at the centre of the pool. Denholmes Wheel was an excellent pool for swimming, providing you could swim, but extremely dangerous if you couldn't. The problem was that the blue limestone fell away from being shallow adjacent to the weir to a drop into a deep pool of maybe 12 to 14 feet, a more than ideal place for the trout and large salmon. The pool was a favourite place for the many anglers that fished the River Ribble.

The pool also had many happy memories for me and my family, but also a few sad memories. It was most likely in the early fifties, when scouts, cubs and brownies used to visit our farm for their summer holidays. Also, camp-school boys came from a small village near Nelson. On this particular day in midsummer there was a party of six or seven lads of up to sixteen years old from this campschool, with their teachers, who decided to swim in Denholmes Wheel. Unfortunately, one of these lads couldn't swim, but he decided to walk into the water below the weir.

What he didn't know was that the weir was a deathtrap for anybody who couldn't swim. He simply walked down the weir, then dropped off into the deep water and drowned, also nearly drowning the brave lads and teacher who attempted to save his life.

My cousin and I arrived on the riverbank, totally unaware of the tragedy that had just taken place, only to be told by the schoolteacher and the lads who were totally exhausted after trying to save this unfortunate boy. We immediately went back to the farm and raised the alarm, and about half an hour later the local Bobby arrived, who, luckily, was a good swimmer. It was obviously too late to save his life, because he had been in the water for too long. I remember going back to the farm and gathering half a dozen draining rods and a large hook which we used for lifting sacks of grain, plus many yards of rope and string. I returned to the river as quickly as possible. Since living close to the river, we always used the quick descent route, which was straight down a near vertical section of woodland, taking only a few minutes instead of the normal footpath of at least a quarter of a mile.

The local PC Dean was waiting in his underpants and the teacher and lads had now more or less recovered from exhaustion. The next problem was to assemble the rescue equipment. First we decided that our gallant local Bobby would require a safety line to the riverbank, so enough lightweight rope had to be attached to his body. This was simply a secure piece of rope around his waist attached to the long rope on the bank. The next problem was to make the rescue equipment from the drain rods and sack hook. This we managed to do by screwing the four rods together making an extended rod 12' long. Then, with the hook and string we soon had made a reasonably efficient grappling hook to recover the poor lad from the depths of Denholmes Wheel. The next major problem was to locate the body in the deep dark water, by no means an easy task in a fairly vast area of deep water. The teacher and the lads all had their own ideas of where the body was lying on the riverbed, but were totally wrong. This was probably because they had had such a horrendous struggle, both trying to save the lad and escaping from his extremely strong grip during his last minutes of life. The teacher was literally black and blue from the horrendous struggle he had had, trying to escape from the struggling, drowning youth. It was a good ten minutes before the local Bobby located the body lying in the deepest part of the pool 12 to 14 feet deep. The next major problem was to engage the body onto our makeshift rescue equipment that was far from ideal.

Luckily, or unluckily, the poor lad had gone into the water with his long jeans on so there was a much better chance of our grappling hook rescue equipment working. After a few attempts the hook engaged into his jeans and then it was up to us on the riverbank to gently haul out the body which, by this time, had been dead about an hour. It was shortly afterwards that the ambulance arrived in the field at the top of the wood, a good three hundred yards from the pool. I remember it was a hot day and one hell of a task carrying the stretcher up the near vertical wooded bank, to the awaiting ambulance in the field.

Years before there was also another drowning at Denholmes Wheel which my father spoke about many times. This was a local farmer who committed suicide. The farmer was, most likely, in a depressed or mental condition and went to bury a dead sheep one day in mid winter. The farmer had actually dug the hole for the sheep then backfilled the soil and clay he had excavated but omitted burying the corpse. He left the spade at the burial site then totally disappeared without trace. There was a police investigation and local searches by farmers and villagers but no trace of a body. It was midsummer the following year when a fisherman was wading in Denholmes Wheel, when he stood on the by now decomposed body still fully clothed. This unfortunate fisherman then arrived at our farm to report the find. My father told of the recovery procedure. This was by way of a large cowshed door and a spiked muckdrag that was used for raking cow manure out of the cart into heaps in the fields. This seemed the ideal tool for recovering a body that had been in the river six months, and was by now well-decomposed and stinking heavens high. They simply raked the remaining clothes and bones onto the cowshed door with the muckdrag. The body was only identified by the farmer's large leather belt that had remained intact in the watery grave for six months. My father always remembered the horrendous smell when they carried the body up to the farm on the cowshed door. Even with a regular wash the door was many weeks before it lost its smell.

The River Rich

The Wier at Denholmes Wheel

Denholmes Wheel

In any major pool on the river there were many ideal trout and graying pools, plus pools which were deep enough to swim in safely and also where the salmon was less secure. In these pools we would spend endless hours tickling trout for our own use, an exceptionally good meal when food was scarce during, and after, the war, and was on ration. These shallower pools were also ideal for the large seatrout, or small salmon, that we used to catch on a regular basis when the river was low and the water was warm and clear.

The trouble with farming was that when the water was warm, low and clear we were always making hay, so we seldom got down to the river, because it was work from light until dark.

About half a mile upstream was yet another special pool about 4 feet deep and was called the Sheep Wash. This was used by local farmers who would wash the sheep before shearing them. Two men would wade waist deep in the pool fully clothed, and one on a suspended door slung from the branch of a large sycamore tree. Another one or two men would catch and lift the sheep onto the door that would be held to the last second by the man on the door, then dunked into the water when the door had reached the farthest point from the bank. The idea was that if the wool was washed, they received an extra few pence more for the sheep's fleece.

For myself and farmer pals, the river was a very pleasurable, inexpensive way of passing time in a picturesque background, pollution free, and graced with the birdsong of the many species that lived and nested in Bowland.

New Arrivals

Every year, as a young lad, I always enjoyed the fun of the winter months when we could sledge down the many hills in and around Bowland village.

Normally, winters were not too long and cold, so, when there was a moderate snowfall, the whole family would be out sledging, with neighbours and children from the village. If it was really frosty the small ponds used to freeze over to form an instant ice rink.

Once winter ended and spring began, it was the time for new arrivals for most of the animals and fowl we kept on our family farm.

Even though, as young children, we should have been used to all the new arrivals, we never were. From a small, fluffy, newly hatched chicken, young gosling, new born lambs and piglets, baby calf, kittens from Milly, our farm cat, or puppies from Bess the farm sheepdog, we excitedly welcomed them all. They helped to maintain the variety of livestock on our family farm.

With all farm animals, there was skill and husbandry required in the breeding and rearing of livestock, be they bird or beast. It was not as simple as just putting male with female. It was the improvement of the herd or flock that farmers aimed for, e.g. cows to give more milk; hens to lay larger and more eggs per year; turkeys and pigs to convert the food into meat at a better rate than before, beef cattle to produce more lean meat and less fat, also, less bone and better steaks.

Simply hatching your own chickens to maintain an egg supply had to be planned. You tried to obtain the best stock cockerels, to cross with your existing hens. All this took time. Before setting eggs you had to select the best shaped eggs of a standard size, also the best brown eggs. This was important when selling your eggs on a market stall. The eggs were no different from the white eggs, but the public always selected them.

Once you had selected 12 of the best quality eggs, you had to find a broody hen. A broody hen was a hen that had decided to discontinue laying eggs, but still sat on the same nest for maybe three to four weeks without moving, only to eat and drink maybe once a day at the most.

When you had both broody hen and twelve quality eggs, you then set the eggs in a secure brooding box. The best boxes had no bottom and therefore the eggs had slight contact with the ground through the small nest which had been formed by the farmer. The idea of direct contact with the ground was to keep the eggs at a certain moisture level. This helped the chicken to hatch when the due date arrived, which was twenty one days after setting. Even though you had painstakingly selected the best cockerel, it was no guarantee that all the eggs would bear a chicken. So, after 10 days, you would have to candle the eggs to check there was actually a chicken in the egg. This we did by removing all the eggs from the nest and placing them above a naked candle flame, or torch. With the light from the candle you could observe the air cavity and the dark area where the chick had started to grow within the shell. If there was no chicken in the shell the candle light would pass straight through the egg. The name always for these eggs was 'clears'.

The clear eggs were saved for feeding to the new baby chicks when hard boiled and mixed with oatmeal. The high protein mix was never offered until 2 days after the chick had hatched. This was because all new born chicks lived off the yolk of the egg within themselves, immediately after being hatched. Not every chick had a long life expectancy; this was because you could, hopefully, expect fifty per cent male and fifty per cent female. As soon as the young males or cockerels were of a suitable size, they finished up plucked and dressed ready for a casserole or chicken pie.

Normally, when a large commercial hatchery hatched chickens, all the cockerels finished up in an early watery grave as soon as they had been sexed and confirmed as males.

The farmyard goose and gander did not require as much attention as the broody hen, they tended to look after themselves, from pairing to hatching. The large gander, or male goose, was always very protective of his female partner, especially when the nesting place had been selected and the nest built. The nest was a simple arrangement of rush, dead grass and feathers which the goose plucked from its breast for camouflage and insulation in cold weather.

Once an egg had been laid it was as much as your life was worth to approach the nest and remove an egg. The gander would certainly attack you and bite or beat you with its extra large, strong wings. The goose incubated or sat on the nest for twenty eight days, one week longer then the broody hen. Once the young gosling had been hatched there was no requirement to feed and protect it. The mother goose and gander attended to that. The young goslings started to pluck the fresh grass shoots within hours of leaving the nest, so supplementary feed was not required. They grew at a fantastic rate, simply by consuming large amounts of fresh grass.

Every evening the young geese would gorge themselves with grass and then settle down to sleep in a confined area all night.

The next morning there were huge piles of digested grass where the geese had spent the night. It was my job, every morning, to sweep up all the goose turds, as we always called them.

There was no early killing of the young geese because of the various sexes as with chickens; they all finished up on the Christmas dinner plate of some large local family.

It was usually late March or April before the lambs were born, this was because better weather was expected at that time of the year. Also there was more fresh grass from which the mother ewe would produce the milk to feed the new offspring. I would go round the fields with my father, many times a day, to check for new births, and difficult births, learning all the tricks of the trade, even at my early age.

Normally, at lambing time, you could experience extreme variation in climate from very mild, reasonably warm days, to very wild, windy, wet days, to snow and below zero frosty days.

All these different climates could cause problems at lambing time.

When the weather was warm and dry the ewes would not lamb and seemed to hold on until the wild, wet and windy weather arrived. Then, we would have what we called a 'shutter', which was ten or a dozen sheep lambing all at once. This was a major problem if the ewes were lambing indoors.

We would visit the maternity shed, where all the expectant ewes were indoors for the night, perhaps once every hour, checking for imminent births and new arrivals. At twelve o'clock there might be nothing, only one or two ewes showing symptoms of imminent birth.

At two o'clock, you could have, maybe, three or four ewes with twin lambs or triplets all mixed up, with little or no way you could tell which lamb belonged to which mother, a major problem.

What you had to do then was stand and watch which mother was licking which lamb and if the mother, or ewe, would allow the new arrival to suckle for milk. If the mother did not allow the new born lamb to suckle, you knew it did not belong to her. Once the ewe had licked the lamb dry, and allowed it to suckle, you then removed them out into another shed, or a run within the main lambing shed. If you had a total mix-up, it could take days to get the lambs correctly mothered.

In lambing time you also had to experience the extreme cold, not every time, but maybe, once every two or three years.

This normally happened when you were lambing outdoors. You could have heavy snowfalls or extremely cold winds or frost. On these occasions you had to have twenty four hour supervision.

My father would stop up all night, visiting the small meadow, where we were lambing the ewes continuously until dawn, checking that the new born lambs were on their feet, or standing up and sucking the ewe for that extra rich cholesterol milk, vital for all new born lambs.

My father would also take the new born lambs from the exposed part of the meadow to a place behind a wall or fence, which gave protection from the icy cold winds. Most healthy lambs would be on their feet and sucking the ewe within five to ten minutes, if not, they could soon be in serious trouble from cold and wet, and would soon starve to death, when not attended. Most times we would carry a dry, used, hessian cattle feed bag with us when conditions were so cold. This always came in handy to convey the starving, cold lambs back to the farmhouse kitchen fire where you, hopefully, warmed the lamb up to normal blood temperature before returning it to the ewe.

Many times during my early youth when lambing sheep, the lambs were born with a defect. My father always knew, within a minute of birth, if the lamb was either perfect, or affected by this ailment. The symptoms of the defect were a very poor, weak bleat, or call for the ewe, shivering and shaking, plus difficulty in standing and normal, common mothering and feeding sense.

My father remarked as soon as he observed the telltale signs, "That's another silly bugger". He knew, and I soon learned, that trying to rear these lambs was a waste of time, so he gave me the job of killing the new born lamb. This was one of the more unpleasant jobs during lambing time for a young lad of 10 years of age, but one I had soon to get used to. Once I had killed the lamb I had then to remove the skin from the dead lamb, so a new spare, or kade, lamb could be mothered onto the ewe with little trouble as its own lamb.

If the defective lamb had been allowed to live, it had little chance of survival as it grew older. The problem with this particular disease or, maybe, defect, was that the lamb lost control of its back half or rear end, so it was almost paralysed. The name of this defect was called swayback, and it was exactly that. My father would remark, "That's another with my heads coming and my arse is following".

The total cure for this deficiency was found out in later years to be a simple, single injection of liquid copper under the skin, which absorbed into the ewe's bloodstream slowly. This simple cure saved thousands of lambs and also made lambing time a far less stressful time for the farmer and shepherd.
Often my father would assist the ewe with minor or major difficulties in the birth of the lamb. Mostly, the lamb would be born alive, but on odd occasions he would not be successful. Many times I would have liked to assist the ewe, but I did not get the chance while my father was present.

Most births which required help, ranged from the lamb having a single leg, or both legs back, the more difficult birth with the head back. Normal births are when both legs and head present themselves at the same time. When the lamb is being born with one or two legs back the normal procedure was to push the lamb's head back into the ewe and bring forward the feet and legs into the correct position. The lamb would then be born more or less immediately. The lamb being born with the head back was more difficult, first the legs had to be pushed back into the ewe and the head, hopefully, brought forward. The method we used was to make a slipknot on a piece of strong string and lasso the bottom jaw of the lamb, then draw the head forward to the correct delivery position.

By the age of around nine to ten years I had seen my father deliver many lambs in this manner, but I had never had the chance to test my own untried skills. One day my father was away at the cattle market when a young ewe suffered from the latter, the lamb was not being born because the head was back. It was up to me with my visual knowledge to now put it into practice. First I had to find a piece of suitable string, then catch the ewe, which was very difficult, single handed. Once caught, I had to secure two legs together so the ewe could not stand-up and escape. I then proceeded with my untried skills in midwifery. I soon found I had one major advantage over my father, that my hands were much smaller. This was always critical, as there was little room to manoeuvre inside the ewe.

After a few unsuccessful attempts I got my noose of string round the lamb's bottom jaw and, with gentle pressure on the string, I brought the head forward. Soon the large, single lamb was born. I was well proud of my achievement that day, as a young shepherd boy of 10 years.

When a lamb was born dead, or died after birth, there was a major problem; you had to sort out a replacement for the dead lamb. In the area of Bowland these were always called spare lambs, or kade lambs. A spare lamb was mostly a triplet, or a lamb from a sheep with only one teat or nipple, so when a spare lamb was required it was a matter of getting on your bike and cycling round the local farms until you found one. A spare lamb was normally fifteen shillings to a pound, with a little deducted for luck, which was a tradition when farmers bought livestock. Once you located a lamb you had to transport it home. We did this by putting it inside a used cattle feed bag and tying the top, then carrying it over our shoulders. This was ok until the lamb decided to relieve itself down your back.

Once at home, the next hurdle to overcome was how to convince the ewe or mother sheep that the spare lamb was hers. Normally, you would have to skin the dead lamb and secure it on top of the spare lamb by a series of string ties. The difficulty with this method was how big was the spare lamb, or how small the dead one, many times it was like fitting a quart in a pint pot, or vice versa. There was always a difficult problem when the fox had taken the new born lamb. This happened many times on Bowland farms, until the culprits were eliminated by the farmers, or hunt. With no lamb to skin, the only method was to hand milk the ewe onto the lamb until it was totally saturated with milk. Also, whenever possible, to cover the lamb with the ewe's urine, which was the only other way to, hopefully, get the ewe to adopt the lamb. Adoption could take a few days with the latter method. In some cases we would bring our sheepdog into the pen where the sheep and lamb were and let the dog mark the ewe, and try to move it from protecting the lamb, this worked well many times with an obstinate adoption.

On our farm we seldom kept a breeding sow or female pig and it was probably when I was in my early teens that we bred a litter of pigs. Pigs normally did not require assistance when giving birth, unlike sheep and cows which normally had only a single offspring. Pigs usually had multiple births, from six to twelve, or even more. It was a master stroke of nature when you found twelve squealing piglets being born and feeding from the sow. Twenty four ears and eyes, forty eight legs, twelve curly tails.

The sow would also have twelve teats or nipples to feed her rich, plentiful milk supply to the new arrivals. From day one, each young piglet commandeered its own teat and sucked the same teat for the first eight weeks. The young piglets would fight violently with each other over itsown teat. The top and bottom jaw would be torn and bleeding with the damage done by their sharp needle like fangs or teeth. It was the farmer's first job to clip off these four sharp fangs within hours of birth to avoid damage to the sow and piglets. We also clipped off the end of each young piglet's tail. This was no gimmick. The reason was, when a litter of young pigs are together over many weeks they get bored, so maybe a single pig will resort to tail biting and if this single pig gets into the habit of tail biting, much damage will be done to its fellow piglets. In fact many would eventually die or simply not grow and become stunted, or only small.

The reason we only clipped off the end of the tail was because the pig's tail at the end, has no nerves, so the cannibal piglet could bite and draw blood without the attacked piglet knowing. So, once the tail end had been removed as far as the sensitive section, when the cannibal piglet bit the pig's tail, it immediately jumped out of the way.

When the young piglets were four weeks old, all the males had to be castrated. This, we did ourselves, without assistance from the vet, or any local anaesthetic. All that was required was a Dettol type antiseptic and a sharp pocket knife. When undergoing this short, minor operation the piglets screamed and squealed, something you soon got used to on a farm. Normally, within a few day's time, newly castrated pigs would be one hundred per cent fit. The only signs of castration were two little incision marks below the tail.

The cows on our farm seldom gave birth in early Spring. This was because we relied on the extra income from the milk produced from the early growth of the grass in meadow pasture or field. When eating this early growth of grass we reduced the cows' intake of bought-in cereals or food, so there was maximum profit for our farming enterprise.

Our cows normally calved in August/September, approximately nine months after being mated, or put to the bull. The cows would be put dry, or not milked, for the last two to three months before calving or giving birth. This was because the female cow required a rest from giving milk all the time while preparing to give birth to her next calf. Many townspeople did not realise that before a cow gave milk it had to produce a calf. The normal age of a cow giving birth to her first calf was three years, a lot of time and work for the milk, butter, cheese and cream that most families just take for granted.

On our farm we reared only a few of the calves that were born each year. We kept only the best quality from the best cows. The remainder we took to the local cattle market at Gisburn or Clitheroe, to sell. These calves were christened Bobbys, whether male or female. The reason they were called Bobbys was that they only made a few shillings, or bobs, when sold.

These calves normally finished-up in meat pies or steak and kidney pies, to help feed the many mouths in the cotton towns of Lancashire. The skins from these calves, which were very fine and thin, were used for purses, handbags and lightweight shoes.

As a lad of ten or eleven years old, I used to go with my father to look at his expectant cattle, both when they were outside in the fields or tied up in the cowshed, during winter months. Normally, there was little difficulty when a cow gave birth; mostly it was a simple pull with a piece of rope or strong string fastened to the front legs of the calf.

Over the years I had gained a lot of experience on what to do when a cow was giving birth. Unfortunately, I was only visually experienced as my father always assisted the birth and never let me have a go.

I was probably twelve years old, at the most, when my father was away at a horse sale, I was the stockman for that day. There was a cow about to give birth and I thought, "This is my chance to deliver my first calf".

Normally cows give birth within one to two hours, but this cow was different, after four hours there was no calf. All I could see were two feet presenting themselves to the youthful, inexperienced, veterinary surgeon standing at least four feet tall.

I went to the farm dairy and got a cob of soap and lathered my arms and hands like a true professional vet. Once back in the cowshed I followed father's instructions, as best I could remember. I gently forced my hand into the cow, I was always told not to rush procedures, but first assess the position of the calf's legs and head. I soon realised that this birth was going to be different, I found two feet well forward in the breach and a head with two mouths and two noses but only one forehead plus four ears. In fact, what I had to calve was a twin-headed calf.

I had never heard of or seen a twin-headed calf being born on our farm, so I had a problem. I decided to get 3 lengths of strong string, attaching two lengths to the front legs of the calf and one round the jaw. After, maybe, thirty minutes I did, in fact, deliver the calf, but on arrival it was dead. Luckily for me, the calf was probably four weeks premature, so it wasn't too big, or too difficult, to deliver. It was also a black and white female.

When my father came home I was waiting with the news of the two-headed calf. He was very surprised and remarked that in all his farming years he had never delivered a two-headed calf. In fact, many vets, during their life as a vet, had never seen a two-headed calf. I later found out that my grandma had a stuffed two-headed calf that was born in 1917 on their family farm. This calf was a Red Shorthorn breed. It was a few years later, when my grandma died, that the calf came to our family and hung for many years over the house part door. When visitors came they were amazed at this, probably, million-to-one, marvel. Since my parents died, being the eldest son, I got this calf's head with the instructions to look after it during my life and then hand it down. No matter how modern a farmhouse may be, there is always room for the twin-headed calf.

The female horse was called a mare, and on most farms, when I was young, they were used each year to produce a foal. They were always referred to as breeding mares, be they the Clydesdale or Shire, or any of the many breeds of horses and ponies which were called after the counties in England.

The horse's period of gestation was 11 months, so the female horse didn't have much rest between one foal and the next. Foals were born in mid April. Most mares had to work while carrying a foal, and we didn't want them born later, because of all the hard work that had to be done in late June/July gathering and making hay for the oncoming winter.

All our family looked forward to the birth of the baby foal each year, not such a baby in most cases, they were quite large when born with exceptionally long, gangly legs. The legs of foals born to large horses had to be long, so they could reach up to the underside of the mare to obtain milk.

The mare was totally different from the cow when it came to dispensing milk. Firstly, it had only two teats instead of four like a cow. It also only had a small udder, or bag where the milk was stored, unlike the cow. The milk was also much richer in content than the cows'.

Most of the foals, that we bred, were Clydesdales. These foals always had a white blaze covering the front of the head from ears to mouth. They also had large feet which, most of the time, were entombed in a mass of white hair. The foal's tail, when newly born, was covered in short curly hair, unlike the mature horse or pony which, if uncut, would soon drag on the ground. All our foals would be kept for two years, before any serious training took place. This was because you always wanted the horse to be fully grown before pulling the farm carts or implements, so that it would not damage it for future years.

When we had surplus, trained horses, we either sold them privately or took them to the annual horse fayre at Clitheroe.

Spring was also the time when the farm cats gave birth. We kept only one farm cat, a female called Milly. She was a white and black tabby. It was quite remarkable, when the cat came into season, where all the tom cats came from.

Our farm was a good mile from the nearest farm that kept a cat, but somehow the male cats knew the precise time to visit. They always seemed to fight and squabble for the favours of Milly, normally during the night, on the wall immediately under my bedroom window. My cousin, who was an exceptional shot with a catapult, used to delight in knocking the tom cats from the wall, rather like coconut shies at the fair.

It was only a few weeks after mating that kittens would be born. Milly used to hide these in the barn or outbuilding on the farm. Most times there would be six or seven kittens, but unfortunately we would allow only one to be saved, so once we located where the kittens were, it was drowning time. This should have been an emotional time for myself and my younger brothers and sisters, but we got used to new arrivals and deaths on the farm.

Almost every year we would have a litter of puppies from our farm sheepdogs. Mostly, these new arrivals were never planned, as was the case with most of the animals on the farm. It was almost impossible, keeping male from female when our dogs, most of the time, roamed around the farmyard freely.

Often during the period when the bitch was on heat, there would be stray dogs arriving at the farm. They were nearly always the collie type farm dog from neighbouring farms. Occasionally we would get the mongrel type dog, which was always a persistent waiter and would hang around the farm for days.

With these dogs we had a special way of dissuading them to stay around the farm. What we did was, catch the dog, get a medium sized tin, drill or punch a hole in the bottom, fasten a piece of strong string through the hole, then securely attach the loose end of the string to the dog's tail. Once secure, we would then release the dog, followed by the tin. The faster the dog ran the more noise the tin made. This terrified the stray dogs, so they never returned to our farm.

When the puppies were new born, seldom did we keep more than one. The rest, I would be told to drown and bury.

Departures

Through time all over the world, man, beast, fish and insects are continuously being born, incubated or hatched to guarantee life for these particular species.

Many species live longer than others, some die early through predators, many through accidents and all eventually through old age. There has not been any bird, beast or man spared from the final act.

On our family farm with all the various livestock, death was something we always had to accept. Normally my father would sell all of his livestock before they got old. This was a shrewd policy because, as with humans, the older you get the more ailments you suffer and the more likely you are to die.

The trouble with farming was that there were so many death traps before the animals or fowls reached a ripe old age

When we hatched chickens, predators were the main cause of death; the carrion crow and magpie were real villains. They would take any small chicks that were not protected in a wire netting pen.

The rat, also, would gnaw through the small wooden chicken huts and remove and kill every chicken during darkness, when the broody hen was asleep.

The farm cats would try to take chickens during the day, especially when the chicks were only a few days old. Once the chicken became a hen, after sixteen weeks, there were major problems with the fox, he would kill every hen in the poultry cabin just for the sake of killing.

The farm terrier, which was kept for foxing, would also kill similarly to the fox, leaving your entire poultry flock dead. If this occurred the terrier would be immediately shot, the reason for such drastic action was that once a dog had tasted hot blood it would always worry again at the first opportunity.

When, if it was lucky, the hen lived to a normal age of two years, it would then be killed for a boiling fowl, which we would eat warm with white sauce and onions, a good meal.

The farmhouse goose always had its days numbered and only the breeding geese would be left alive after Christmas, therefore, the normal age of the goose, before death, was seven to nine months.

Lambs were different again, obviously only a few select lambs were kept for breeding replacements, so most had only a short life, normally five to six months, before being taken to market and then being sent to slaughter. This would upset many townspeople when those lambs had been carefully brought into the world, nurtured until sufficiently large, then sent from the farm for killing. This never affected me as a young farmer, seeing them leave, knowing they would never return to our farm.

Normally, however good a farmer you were, you would always have deaths in your flock of sheep, and the longer you kept your sheep the more likely you were to have a death. Normally, when a sheep died you would have to dig a deep hole and bury it. On our farm we had a small paddock or field that was fairly sandy, with little clay and stones and this made digging easy when burying the corpse.

When I was only 10 or 11, we had another way of burying a sheep, unknown to my father. Our farm skirted the River Ribble, and when the river was in full spate, or in flood conditions, we would drag the corpse to the side of the river then roll it down the bank into the raging water. It was only minutes before the body was out of sight, travelling at a great speed on the white water torrent.

My farmer pals had another unique method of burial above ground, which was a little bit naughty. My pal's father's farm was split in two by the main railway line which was probably used more for freight than passengers. At the juncture where the railway line passed through their land, it was quite a steep rise, so the trains only proceeded very slowly, ideal for depositing the dead sheep from the railway bridge into the empty goods truck heading north.

I never heard that anybody found out whose dead sheep they were, but one thing is for sure, after a few days, they would stink heavens high!

Sheep didn't always get old before we had to sell them for killing, this was because an old sheep, or on few occasions, a young sheep, would loose its teeth. Sheep only have one set of bottom teeth, so when tooth loss occurs, this restricts the ability to graze properly on short grass, so these had to have an early departure from our farm.

Cattle, as with sheep, always died one way or another, obviously the loss of a cow to many farmers was a serious financial blow, compared with losing a smaller farm animal, like a pig or sheep.

No matter how many prizes or championships were won at a local or national show, none of these prime examples of livestock were forever, which many flock and cattle herd owners believed.

It was a major problem, when a large cow, or bull died, getting rid of the carcass. The dead cows on our family farm mostly went to the local hunt, whose kennels were only two miles down the road. If the kennels couldn't take the cow, the knackerman would come and collect. No matter how good the carcass was this knackerman never paid a penny for it, he always had an excuse that the carcass was totally useless. We were always glad that someone came and removed the carcass, because I can assure you, that, even in sandy ground, you have to dig a hell of a large hole to bury a cow.

Horses we seldom lost, or let die, on our farm. I believe this was because horses are a hardy strain of animal, with a much longer life expectancy. The horses on our farm were mostly home bred, so that you knew exactly how old your working horse was and my father's policy was never keep stock until they get very old, their lives are much more at risk.

My father was born on the family farm and lived there during his youth and all his working life, which was right up to his death at sixty eight years old. He always told us of his wish to be cremated and his ashes spread on the paddock among all the dead livestock he had buried during his life, which could only be counted in hundreds.

He also remarked that his ashes would be good fertiliser and make the grass grow for a new generation of farm stock.

I actually spread his ashes on the paddock, as he requested, but I didn't see any significant extra growth of grass over that area.

Farmers Story:
This farmer died, leaving his wife and family to make the funeral arrangements. The undertaker arrived and sorted everything out for the report in the local newspapers. The report started by saying, 'On the 10th of November 1996, Nathan Robinson died, aged 76 years, leaving a dear wife Mabel, a son James and two daughters Jane and Mary'.

The undertaker asked, "Is that all you require printing in the paper?" His wife was very cost conscious and replied, "Yes". The undertaker said, "You can have up to sixty words free in a bereavement report!" Mabel thought for a minute and then replied, "Put this in as well then. For Sale, Fordson tractor, complete with muck loader and muckspreader. In good working order £250.00".

The Birds Of Bowland

The River Ribble, from its source to the sea, was very rich in fish. With so many different types, from the common eel to the large fresh run salmon. These came up stream when spring and summer rain raised the water level in the river, allowing the fish to proceed to the various salmon pools.

The Ribble Valley was also rich with the many types of birds and wild animals. There were some areas of the Ribble valley more suited than others for bird population, where many more different species could be spotted and observed.

Bowland, I believe, was one of these areas which was probably the most suited for such a varied bird population and was well sited as a farming community on probably some of the richest farm land. In the mid section of the River Ribble, with various tributaries, or becks, flowing through the village. These becks wound their way through a rich deposit of sandy soil and gravel which was once a lakebed, many thousands of years ago. These sandy soil deposits, up to six feet deep in many areas, formed an ideal place for sand martins to bore their hole into the bank and build their nests to rear young.

The becks never took the straightest route before joining the River Ribble, and when winter flooding, or even spring floods occurred, erosion took place. This, over the years, has left many acres of gravel and sand on both sides of the beck, an ideal place for that unusual bird to build its nest.

It was quite interesting on a midsummer evening, to stand and listen to the varied bird songs. The sandpipers, which only nested on sand and gravel, found Bowland to be ideal. The oystercatcher was also another water bird that visited Bowland, just to nest and produce the next generation. The oystercatcher was a colourful bird with a very pronounced call, which could be heard from quite a distance. The golden plover, and lapwing, would also nest on this gravel and sand outcrop, which made excellent camouflage for all the wader or waterfowl species.

The kingfisher, also quite common, but never nested on such areas. It always nested on a riverbank, above flood level either in a rock crevice, tree root or crack. The kingfisher would frequent the same nesting site year after year, probably until death.

Lakebed in Bowland

The dipper, or water ousel, was another such bird using a similar type of nesting place. The dipper was black, with a white throat, unlike the kingfisher, which was a bright blue with an orange breast.

The water hen or moorhen, always nested on the low branches of a willow tree, or similar, that overhung the small becks. Many times these nests would be destroyed if a flash flood occurred, simply because the water hen had built its nest too close to the water.

In Bowland, the heron had rich picking on the many small streams and river. The heron was quite rare, I suppose because the water bailiffs and gamekeepers were ordered to keep the population to a reasonable level, protecting the fish for the many fishermen that visited Bowland. The heronries were miles from the river, in most cases always on top of the tallest scotch pine tree that had just a few branches. This made it impossible for egg collectors to collect their eggs. On many occasions, when visiting a heronry you could find the ground below the trees totally covered with dead fish that the young herons had dropped from the nest.

The wild duck, or mallard, also plentiful in the Bowland area, nested alone in almost any area of the river where there would be ample food for the young and reasonable protection against predators. The baby ducklings would follow their mother on the river within hours of being hatched, requiring constant observation and training.

If, by chance, you came across a clatch of wild young ducks and they felt in danger, the whole clatch would dive for cover. This, they could do, when they were literally only days old. They would swim underwater, for up to 20 yards, before resurfacing for air and hopefully by that time, unobserved.

The wild duck population could be drastically reduced, if there was heavy rain and high water levels on the river at hatching time. A normal clutch of young ducks could be up to 12, which would mostly survive if the weather conditions were perfect.

Wild mink was a major threat to young ducks, and would completely wipe out a clutch of young ducks, just for the sake of killing. The mink mostly killed any kind of waterfowl that lived on the riverbanks, or around ponds. I also believe that mink was quite good at catching fish, both large and small.

Adjacent to the village of Bowland, and belonging to the Bowland Estate, was Wybersey Hill, or mound. This was a small limestone hill that could well have been a strategic site for Bowland castle, simply because when you got to the top of this small hill, you could see for miles in all directions. But, instead of it being the site of a castle, during the early forties and fifties, it was the nesting and roosting place for hundreds of rooks. The rooks nested in the various trees that grew on the mound. The trees the rooks selected to build their nest in, was always the tallest oak or ash tree which had the least branches, making climbing almost impossible by the many youthful egg collectors that resided in Bowland. The rook mostly built its nest on the longest branch and as far away from the main trunk as possible. During nesting season there was a continuous cawing, from dawn till dark, by the many scores of pairs of nesting rooks.

In the spring the undergrowth, below the trees, was mainly wild garlic. But, instead of being a rich green, it was always completely white, with a dense splattering of crow droppings, which stank heavens high, if you dared to venture under the trees in the nesting zone area. One thing for certain, it was not advisable to look up!

Wibersey Hill

The only other bird that nested in that area was the jackdaw. This bird only built its nest in holes in the mature trees. Mostly, these holes were where a branch had fallen from the tree many years ago and then rotted back into the tree to form a perfect nesting place. The jackdaw was smaller than the rook and instead of making a cawing sound like the rook, the jackdaws' call was more of a chattering sound.

There was also another place in Bowland where the Jackdaw always built their nests, that was in the belltower on steeple of Bowland church. A fairly safe place to build their nest well out of the reach or range of most preditors including the human type. It was on a few occasions that the local vicar would take a couple of village lads to the clock tower where he would rewind the clock. It was on one of these visits with the two youths that an unusual incident occured.

The church tower to the south overlooked the main road some thirty yards away and a considerable distance below. It was mid afternoon on this particular day when this refined looking twenty two year old redhead was walking towards the centre of the village. She was actually staying at my Aunt's cottage at the time, so I was well informed of the afternoons event. She had spent a good half hour arranging her hair into raised bird nest type of bow and looked really attractive before deciding to walk to the village centre of Bowland, where she would have been surveyed and assesed by the very observant villagers of Bowland.

When she set out from the blue slate porched cottage some fifty yards from the church, she was described by my aunt as a real bobby dazzler, not seen so often in Bowland. The next few minutes were soon to alter her afternoons planned walk down Bowland village. She was walking past the church when from out of thin air a Jackdaw egg landed right in the middle of her fancy bird nest hairdo. She was totally shocked when she found out it was an egg.

Returning back to my aunts cottage she could not believe that a fast flying Jackdaw had laid an egg so accurately as to land right in the centre of her head. On a close inspection near truth was revealed. The egg was partly incubated and contained a chicken. What a mess in that well groomed red hair. My aunt soon put two and two together and decided that the missile egg had been thrown from the church tower. They also soon guessed who were the culprits, which was confirmed by the vicar. What an aim, which I doubt could never be repeated. It was a talking point for a few days. I don't think the young lady visited Bowland again after that incident.

Both the jackdaw and the rook were classed as minor scavengers. These lived mainly on worms and grubs they unearthed from the dry cow pats, and grain that was available from the many farms that kept free range hens.

The worst crow in Bowland was the carrion crow. These crows were much larger than the rook or jackdaw, and more of a menace to both farmers and the wild bird population. The carrion crows mostly operated in pairs consisting of male and female. You would never see scores together in one flock, as with rooks or jackdaws.

The carrion crow always built its nest in fairly isolated trees, or hedgerows, or in the centre of a field. The nest was mostly in the fork, or centre of the tree, unlike the rook that built its nest on the branches.

When feeding young, or during a cold spell of weather in spring, the carrion crow was a real villain. Many times, on our farm, we would find a newborn lamb minus a single eye, or both eyes. The carrion crow would peck out the lamb's eyes before they had become mobile, or as farmers mostly said, "got on its feet". They would also peck at the newborn lamb's backside and pull out the intestines, which obviously meant an early death. This caused the farmer both expenses and hard work, obtaining and mothering a spare lamb onto the sheep.

Many times the farmers would hold a 'carrion crow shoot'. This was always on an evening before nightfall, when the carrion crow was preparing to roost for the night. The shoot was organised so that every farmer or local villager with a gun went to the many woods in Bowland and waited for the carrion crow to arrive. Once the crows arrived, which was just before darkness fell, the farmers would shoot and hopefully kill the roosting crow. If he missed, or disturbed the crow, it would then fly on to the next wood to roost for the night where it got the same reception from the waiting farmer, or villager, with his gun.

The carrion crow problem mainly occurred through the lack of gamekeepers working on the large estates. The gamekeepers made sure the carrion population was small to safeguard young pheasant, wild duck, partridge, and many other wild bird species nesting in the Ribble and Bowland area. This was commonly called 'a good wildlife balance', where all species had a chance to hatch their eggs and rear their young, for future continuation of the many species.

The magpie, very much like the carrion crow, was more colourful with its black and white head and extra long tail. The magpie was capable of doing damage to livestock similar to the carrion crow, but was much more of a villain with the small bird population. This bird would pillage the nests of various birds like the song thrush, blackbird, hedge sparrow, wild duck, pheasant, curlew, lapwing and almost every bird that dared to nest in the open area.

The magpie always nested fairly close to the ground in a dense thorn hedge or holly bush, which was almost impossible to spot before the young had fledged the nest. Whilst feeding their young, the magpie would take the young birds from the nests of smaller birds. This was quite distressing if you had watched a song thrush painstakingly build its nest, lay its pale blue speckled eggs, hatch the eggs, almost rear its four or five young chicks then have them stolen and killed by the magpie to feed its growing off springs.

The gamekeepers, once again, helped keep the magpie population to a minimum, so that the small bird population had a fair chance of laying its eggs and rearing its young. Sadly, gamekeepers are becoming a fast dwindling species and this, in turn, will lead to a loss of bird population in the rural areas like Bowland, and in the future may even lead to the total loss of certain species.

The wood pigeon, another bird reasonably well established on the many estates in Ribblesdale, was never a particular nuisance, as very little grain was grown in the Bowland area. The wood pigeon would seldom be seen in the large flocks of up to five hundred birds, as was common at certain times of the year in the larger grain growing areas of Yorkshire and Lincolnshire.

Normally, the pigeon flocks in Bowland, would be a maximum of a dozen birds. This was because there were vast areas of woodland where the birds lived and bred. The pigeon would mostly nest in the conifer trees, which were plentiful in the Bowland area. The pigeon made a very simple nest with probably only a score of flimsy twigs laid into a circular nest on a conifer tree branch. This, I believe, was the simplest of bird nests to be built by any bird, except the cuckoo that didn't build a nest.

The pigeons in Bowland mainly lived on the young shoots of the new sown crops, such as, clover, oilseed rape and corn when available. The wood pigeon would, for its size, literally gorge itself with hundreds of the newly emerged shoots of these plants, causing extensive damage in the arable growing areas.

Most woods on the Bolton Hall Estate were mixed hardwood, oak, beech, ash, elm and sycamore with smaller intermingling trees such as silver birch, crab apple, hazel, yew and thorn. In many woods, rhododendrons at ground level, and wild raspberry and blackberry bramble, which had seeded and grown on the many fallen and decomposed trees. This all added up to a very environmentally friendly area for the many birds that lived permanently in that area, also the seasonal visitors, which migrated and returned to the same tree or shed, year after year, until death. It was absolutely amazing how these migratory birds travelled literally thousands of miles, returning to their same breeding destination each year, within a few days. We humans have a lot of catching up to do with navigational technology.

On our farm there were many birds that nearly became domesticated, or part of the family. One particular blackbird I remember well was a hen, or female, blackbird. It was easy to identify a male or female blackbird by the dark brown colouring of the female, and the rich black sheen of the male bird. This bird literally lived on our back door step and the kitchen windowsill. When she became hungry, she would look straight through the kitchen window and peck the glass until food was forthcoming. Once food or breakfast had been served, normally toast or bread crusts, she would then fly away to join her partner until more food or nourishment was required.

Blackbirds mainly lived in pairs and most likely stayed together as a breeding pair for life. This blackbird, even though she appeared to be unafraid of our family, never disclosed the whereabouts of her nest. The same bird frequented our kitchen window for years until one day when she never returned. She either died of old age, or Molly, our farm cat, may have had her for lunch. We never knew how long a blackbird could live, maybe five or ten years.

We also had a pet, or tame, robin that always nested in the same place every year, for many years, and always reared five or six young each year. This bird frequented our back yard bird table every day, without fail, and when any digging or cultivating took place in the garden, she almost sat on the garden spade, waiting for the large garden worms to be unearthed.

She would only be inches away when grabbing the worm and flying off to feed the ever-hungry nest of fledglings. Around the farmhouse, there was maybe a dozen different species of birds that nested annually in the same tree, barn or cart shed. Swallows always nested in the cart shed and was a migratory bird that always arrived early to mid May, after migrating to North Africa for the cold winter months.

This bird built its nest using mouthfuls of liquid mud. This she collected from the mud puddles on the farm track, where the cows passed over twice daily, to and from the cowshed after milking. They simply blew the mouthful of semi-liquid soil into a circular nest shape, and, when dry lined it out with feathers collected from outside the poultry cabin in the farmyard. How many hundreds of miles these superb birds flew with their mouthfuls of soil, forming a labour intensive nest, one could never guess. The swallow and house martin, once fully grown would prepare for the long migratory flight, around late August, early September.

A sign that migration was imminent was the young and parent birds perching in long rows on overhead wires, clothes drying lines and on the farm wire fences. This may last up to a week, then until one day, they would all disappear and not be seen for the next seven to eight months.

Out in the pastures and meadows on our farm, there were many more large and small species of wild birds, which, over the years, left for the winter months and returned in the spring. These birds left our farming area but didn't totally migrate, they simply left for the warmer climate on the seacoast where food would be more readily available and it was far less cold. Swampy tidal marsh and shingle beaches provided rich pickings for large and small bird alike.

The most popular birds in our pastures and meadows were the curlew, lapwing, snipe, skylarks, pheasant, partridge and many various wagtails. All these birds, or most of them, would nest in rough grass or rushes around ponds and poor pastures. Sometimes they nested in the hay meadows grown to feed cattle during the winter months, or simply in a woodland area amongst the brambles and small bushes or vegetation.

Birds like pheasant, partridge, curlew and lapwing that nested on land used for hay and crops were more vulnerable to loss and death by mechanisation on the farms. The use of modern fertiliser to make the meadows grow and the crops ready for harvesting two weeks earlier than normal was bad news for the birds nesting on meadowland. The skylark was probably one of the first casualties of modern farming, as they mostly nested in the uncut meadow grass. Therefore when the grass was ripe two weeks sooner, the nest and young would be destroyed when mowing took place, whereas normally they had time to hatch and fledge their nests.

The partridge and pheasant would sometimes nest in the meadow grass and would normally have nested, and be able to fly, within a few weeks of hatching. Once again, the early mowing would take place before the eggs had hatched. The hen bird, which had been sitting for two to three weeks, would not be prepared to leave her eggs. So, it was bad news when the horse drawn mowing machine arrived in the meadow to mow the grass. Many times I have seen the partridge and hen pheasant with both legs amputated by the mowing machine, ending up with a dead bird and no young for future generations.

These birds nesting on ground sites were always at a disadvantage compared with the ones that nested off the ground, simply because there were more predators prepared to kill. The fox was a major cause of early death to many wild birds; the farm cat also took young game and birds to feed her litter of young kittens. The stoat, weasel, ferret or polecat, which had escaped when being used to ferret for the wild rabbit in winter, the carrion crow, magpie and sparrow hawk, all took their toll on the many species in Bowland. As the gamekeepers disappeared, so vermin soon started to increase. This would lead inevitably to the disappearance of many of the rarer species in Bowland and nation-wide.

The abolition of the various traps farmers used on these farms to catch rats and mice, were replaced by new poisons. This was bad for the barn owls and the kestrels, that would either catch the poisoned rat or mouse or take the dead corpses. Once they had feasted on these, it would result in death, and so the barn owl population almost died out.

The common starling was a particular nuisance in Bowland, not because it nested in that area during spring and early summer, but because when they came to Bowland, there would be thousands leaving the town and coming to roost in the village conifer woods. There were so many flying together they almost blacked out the sun. They would also foul the conifer woods where they roosted, killing many of the young trees.

The starling was also blamed during the early fifties for carrying the foot and mouth virus. This was a deadly virus, and once the cattle herd was infected it was instant death by ministry vets. A bad outbreak could lead to the slaughter of tens of thousands of cattle sheep and pigs. The foot and mouth virus only affected the cloven-footed animals, so ponies, horses, dogs, cats and even rats were immune from the virus.

One annual bird visitor we all looked forward to hearing was the cuckoo. The bird always visited our area every year to breed and lay its eggs. There were always plenty of egg collectors scouring the hedgerows looking for that elusive cuckoo egg. The cuckoo never built a nest, but always laid its egg in the nest of the small bird like the hedge sparrow, thrush, blackbird or skylark. The cuckoo was a much larger bird and when the young cuckoo was hatched it always outgrew the other young birds in the nest. It also took all the food from the foster mother, causing all the other young birds to perish from starvation. The exact number of eggs laid by the cuckoo was never known; a guess was in the region of ten or twelve. The trouble with trying to find a cuckoo egg was that most times the colour of the cuckoo egg often matched those of the foster parents.

The cuckoo was a very shy bird so you never ever got close enough to have a good look at it. I suppose the closest look-a-like to this bird was the fieldfare, which was much more common in certain areas. There was always the occasional very rare bird that visited our area of Ribblesdale and Bowland. The one I remember quite well was the osprey. This extra large fish eating bird visited our area in approximately 1948, and had never been seen on the River Ribble before. It stopped on the river just below our farm for at least a couple of weeks before flying off, never to be seen again. There were many bird watchers that travelled many miles to see this unusual visitor. The wingspan of the osprey was at least six feet and was a rare spectacle in flight, when being chased by many of our resident birds that obviously didn't like the rare visitor.

There was just so many different species that were either resident or seasonal visitors, in Bowland. These greeted the many town visitors and country people with their varied birdsong. It must have been an absolute treat to hear these birds for the townspeople that visited Bowland, after spending every day working with the clattering looms in the Lancashire cotton mills. The birdsong was totally free and always will be. I only hope that the many various species will survive and prosper for future generations to enjoy their song.